C. G. Jung's
Psychology of Religion
and Synchronicity

28

SUNY Series in Transpersonal
and Humanistic Psychology

Richard D. Mann and Jean B. Mann, Editors

C. G. Jung's Psychology of Religion and Synchronicity

Robert Aziz

STATE UNIVERSITY OF NEW YORK PRESS

Published by
State University of New York Press, Albany

© *1990 State University of New York*

All rights reserved

Printed in the United States of America

No part of this book may be used or reproduced in any manner whatsoever without written permission except in the case of brief quotations embodied in critical articles and reviews.

For information, address State University of New York Press, State University Plaza, Albany, N.Y., 12246

Library of Congress Cataloging-in-Publication Data

Aziz, Robert, E. 1954–
    C. G. Jung's Psychology of Religion and Synchronicity / Robert Aziz.
        p.   cm.—(SUNY Series in Transpersonal and Humanistic Psychology)
    Bibliography: p.
    Includes index.
    ISBN 0–7914–0166–9.—ISBN 0–7914–0167–7 (pbk.)
    1. Coincidence.   2. Psychology, Religious.   3. Jung, C. G. (Carl Gustav), 1875–1961.   I. Title.   II. Series.
BF175.5.C65A97   1990
150.19′54—dc19   89–30039
                                                                    CIP

10   9

For my wife, Marguerite,
and our sons,
Nicholas and Jonathan

Contents

Acknowledgments

This book is the product of approximately eight years of work on the subject of synchronicity. Over the years, many individuals have participated in this project, and through their presence the work has been furthered. Some of these individuals I have known for many years; with others it was the case of a brief but nonetheless meaningful encounter. I would like to take this opportunity to thank these people and also my family, especially my wife, Marguerite, for their support. I would particularly like to acknowledge the following individuals: Volney Gay, John Dourley, Adrian Cunningham, Ross and Marion Woodman, and my editors, Richard and Jean Mann.

Introduction

The synchronicity concept is, arguably, the single theory with the most far-reaching implications for Jung's psychology as a whole, particularly for his psychology of religion, yet both within and outside the Jungian circle it remains perhaps the least understood of Jung's theories. To date, no comprehensive study of the synchronicity theory in relationship to the individuation process has been undertaken and, consequently, the great import of this theory for Jung's psychology of religion has been overlooked. The purpose of this work, therefore, is to examine the synchronicity theory in relationship to the psychological and indeed spiritual journey Jung has termed the individuation process so as to reveal the specific import of this seminal concept for Jung's psychology of religion.

Synchronicity, it will suffice to say at this early stage, describes the meaningful paralleling of inner and outer events. These events, which by definition are not causally related to each other, are understood to be manifestations of a type of orderedness in nature itself—an acausal orderedness, to be sure, that transcends space and time. As a simple example of a synchronistic experience we could take the following. An individual dreams that a friend, someone whom he has not seen or heard from for many years, comes to his house to visit with him. The next day, having received no previous notice of his friend's planned trip with the exception of the dream, that same individual finds his friend at his front door. This is what Jung described as a synchronistic experience, for there is a meaningful paralleling of two causally unrelated events—the inner event being the dream image, the corresponding external event being the arrival of the friend.

The synchronicity concept was first introduced by Jung to a private group of his followers in a seminar given in November of 1928.[1] Two years later, in an address delivered in Munich in memory of the German sinologist Richard Wilhelm, Jung for the first time spoke publicly of the synchronicity theory.[2] From this time onward, the synchronicity concept was to become very much part of

the Jungian vocabulary and worldview, appearing in Jung's lectures, letters, interviews, and scientific writings, and most, significant, it came to play an important role in the actual practice of
Jungian analysis. Still, not until the early 1950s was Jung led to
write his principal essay on the subject: "Synchronicity: An Acausal
Connecting Principle."[3] Writing in his foreword to that essay, Jung
reflects: "In writing this paper I have, so to speak, made good a
promise which for many years I lacked the courage to fulfil. . . . I
have been alluding to the existence of this phenomenon on and off
in my writings for twenty years without discussing it any further. I
would like to put a temporary end to this unsatisfactory state of
affairs by trying to give a consistent account of everything I have to
say on this subject."[4]

Unfortunately, it was the case, however, that the principal essay fell far short of its above-stated goal. The principal essay clearly
did not "give a consistent account of everything" that Jung had to
say on the subject of synchronicity. Specifically, and this is a most
crucial point, it failed to give a thorough account of the case material upon which the theory itself was based. The reader, accordingly, was given little sense of the great import of this concept for
the individuation process itself. As Michael Fordham rightly points
out with reference to Jung's work on the synchronicity concept,
"The main bulk of his investigation and indeed the basis for formu-
lating the concept [was] derived from clinical observation of individual patients."[5] Yet as Ira Progoff notes on the other hand, the great
shortcoming of the principal essay was that it focused away from
the "human element," that is to say, the clinical material that
formed the actual basis of Jung's concept was not developed.
"Jung," Progoff writes, " . . . placed himself in the position of un-
deremphasizing the human base of Synchronicity. It seems that he
became so fascinated by the larger possibility of connecting depth
psychology with theoretical physics and with the natural sciences as
a whole that he let his attention be drawn away from the human
elements that needed to be studied."[6] By placing too great an emphasis on peripheral material such as the parapsychological research conducted by J. B. Rhine, Jung's own highly controversial
"Astrological Experiment,"[7] and analogous concepts in modern
physics, Jung failed to convey to his reader what he himself then
understood to be the great significance of the synchronicity concept
for his psychological model in general and, by extension of this, for
his psychology of religion.

Although the literature on synchronicity that has followed Jung's principal essay is quite broad in its scope, a comprehensive study of the synchronicity concept in relationship to the individuation process has yet to be undertaken. Before I outline specifically how this work attempts to fill that particular gap in the literature, giving special consideration to the import of this concept for Jung's psychology of religion, I would like to indicate just how wideranging the literature on the synchronicity theory actually is.

Robert McCully has used the synchronicity concept "to venture further in speculating about how strange, complex images arise in the Rorschach" test.[8] Carl Meier has drawn attention to "the connection between the cure of somatic illness by means of psychological processes and the phenomenon of synchronicity."[9] The relationship of the synchronicity theory to analogous concepts in physics has been investigated in detail by Mary Gammon,[10] Marie-Louise von Franz,[11] and Carolin Keutzer.[12] Much along this same line, L. Zinkin has examined ways in which the holographic paradigm may provide insights into the workings of synchronicity.[13] The synchronicity theory, quite rightly, has also found its way into the parapsychological literature. Some very insightful contributions have been made by Hans Bender,[14] Lila Gatlin,[15] and K. Ramakrishna Rao,[16] who evaluate the importance of Jung's concept as an explanatory principle of parapsychological phenomena grouped under the general term PSI, that is, extrasensorimotor communication with the environment. Gustav Jahoda has similarly given consideration to synchronicity as an explanatory principle of parapsychological phenomena, but has been markedly less impressed with its value in this regard.[17] Finally, Aniela Jaffé's contribution to this theme of synchronicity and parapsychology should not be overlooked.[18] Moving to yet another area, the relationship of synchronicity, number, and divination has been investigated thoroughly by von Franz.[19] Number, which plays a central role in divinatory methods, "should not be understood solely as a construction of consciousness," von Franz writes, "but also as an archetype and thus as a constituent of nature, both without and within."[20] J. F. Zavala has similarly looked into the question of synchronicity and divination, specifically the problem of the synchronistic aspects of Mexican calendar-systems.[21] An examination of the synchronicity principle in relationship to the more general problem of human destiny has been carried out by Progoff.[22] In that his treatment of the subject tends to be philosophical in character, he does not focus on specific case material. Jean Shinoda Bolen, by contrast, presents some very good synchronistic case material.[23] What she fails to do, however, is give this material a solid theoretical basis. Other contributions to the clinical side of the synchronicity literature have been made in papers by Mary Williams,[24] Fordham,[25] and Keutzer.[26]

As wide-ranging as the literature on synchronicity is in its scope, one of its serious shortcomings has been its failure to ground the synchronicity theory in relationship to Jung's model of the psyche, particularly his notion of psychic compensation. Accordingly, one of the objectives of this work will be to address that very problem. In doing this, I will introduce a framework that identifies the key components of the synchronistic experience. One of the problems with the literature on synchronicity is that in the absence of such a framework the key problems of the synchronicity theory tend to be avoided, either unintentionally or perhaps intentionally, by individuals writing on this subject. When one's examination of the synchronicity theory is pinned down by such a framework, however, one is forced to come to terms with Jung's often very problematic discussions of key issues, such as his discussion of the "time factor" or his discussion of the "meaning" associated with these experiences, in a manner that one otherwise would not be forced to do. Certainly the absence of such a framework has led to considerable discrepancies with respect to both the quality and quantity of information that is to be found in the synchronistic case histories that appear in journals and books. Developing a framework, then, in which the key aspects of the synchronistic experience can be explored in relationship to Jung's model of the psyche is a central objective of this work.

A second objective is to demonstrate the pervasiveness of synchronistic phenomena in both Jung's personal life and his work, and to study the way in which these events were interpreted by Jung. Jung, it will be shown, came to live his own life and view the lives of his analysands very much in terms of the synchronistic perspective. This, however, is something that has most certainly been overlooked, partly, I believe, because the references Jung makes to these phenomena are, in the main, scattered far and wide in his scientific writings, interviews, correspondence, and autobiography. Moreover, because they often appear in an obscure and abbreviated form, the reader can easily pass over this material without grasping the full significance of Jung's statements. The synchronistic events of Jung's life and work must be reevaluated, for these events, along with the often subtly concealed interpretations that Jung assigns to them, stand as a genuine testimony to Jung's thinking on this subject that goes well beyond that which is disclosed in Jung's principal essay.

The third and final objective of this work is to reveal systematically the import of the synchronicity concept for Jung's psychology of religion. Clearly the synchronicity theory places Jung's psychology of religion in a completely new light, yet its thorough study in this regard has, understandably, given the above-described problems, not been pursued. Indeed, at best, only passing references to this seminal concept appear in the literature that is concerned with the study of Jung's psychology of religion, such as is the case with James Heisig's *Imago Dei: A Study of C. G. Jung's Psychology of Religion*,[27] and Harold Coward's *Jung and Eastern Thought*.[28] An objective of this work, therefore, will be to redress this problem.

In speaking of Jung's psychology of religion, it should be emphasized that I am not referring simply to Jung's specific writings on that particular subject, but rather also to what might be described as the spiritual or religious aspects of Jung's psychology itself—the religious or spiritual aspects of the individuation process. Actually, it is my own impression that a direct investigation of Jung's psychology yields far more to the study of the psychology of religion as a discipline than do Jung's formal writings on that subject. No doubt it is this particular understanding of what the study of Jung's psychology of religion entails that has served to spark my interest in Ninian Smart's work on worldview analysis. As Smart explains, "It is a result of perhaps an ideological rather than a scientific divide that we put traditional religions in one basket and secular ideologies in another."[29] Along this line, it could be said that it is perhaps equally arbitrary to separate Jung's formal writings on the psychology of religion from what we might characterize as the more "secular" aspects of the Jungian worldview, especially if the vision of the "meaning of life"[30] offered by the latter is equal to, and even exceeds that of the former, much as is also the case with the Freudian system.

The third objective of this work, then, is to disclose the import of the synchronicity concept for Jung's psychology of religion. In pursuing this objective, I utilize as my basic guideline for comparing and contrasting what I refer to as the intrapsychic and synchronistic models of Jung's psychology of religion Smart's six-dimensional framework for the analysis of worldviews.[31] The six dimensions are as follows: the ritual dimension, the doctrinal dimension, the experiential dimension, the social dimension, the ethical dimension, and the mythological dimension. Although a certain degree of overlap in moving from one dimension to the other can never be avoided with such models, I have nevertheless found Smart's framework very valuable for revealing, systematically, the transformation that Jung's psychology of religion undergoes when the synchronicity theory is taken into consideration. It should perhaps be noted here that Smart's six-dimensional model, in a slightly revised form, has previously been put to use in the area of the psychology of religion by Donald Capps, Lewis Rambo, and Paul Ransohoff in their comprehensive survey of the literature in this field.[32] For my own purposes, however, I have found Smart's model as it exists without these revisions to be superior.

The five chapters contained within this book unfold as follows. In chapter 1, what I describe as the intrapsychic model of Jung's psychology of religion is investigated utilizing Smart's six-dimensional framework for the analysis of worldviews. Although I qualify the material under investigation in this chapter as the intrapsychic model of Jung's psychology of religion, it is the case that this same model is regarded by most as Jung's only model; that is to say, it is understood to constitute the full extent of Jung's position on this subject. Accordingly, the charge persistently brought against Jung is the charge that his treatment of religious experience and religious contents is "psychologistic"; that is to say, he views religious experience and religious contents strictly as manifestations of unconscious processes. This problem is a critical one for anyone engaged in the study of Jung's psychology of religion, and in this work it will be dealt with at some length. In chapter 2, the study of the synchronicity theory gets underway. In this chapter, special attention will be given to Jung's description of the archetype as a psychoid factor—a concept that is fundamental to the synchronicity theory. In this chapter, moreover, the above-mentioned framework, which identifies the key components of the synchronistic experience, will be introduced. Here, two specific types of synchronistic experiences will be identified.

Each specific type of synchronistic experience identified in chapter 2 will then be examined in greater detail in chapters 3 and 4, respectively. Without attempting to explain here how the two types differ, I will just say that in each chapter material from outside the Jungian corpus will be introduced that will complement the study of the specific type of synchronistic event under consideration. More specifically, in chapter 3, this will involve tracing the development of Freud's thinking on the subject of telepathy through his correspondence and scientific papers and identifying points of conflict and agreement between Freud and Jung on this subject. In chapter 4, as we move to the second type of synchronistic experience, considerable attention will be given to the study of certain parallel concepts that are to be found in traditional Chinese philosophy.

Finally, in chapter 5, Smart's six-dimensional framework will once again be utilized as we turn to investigate directly what I describe as the synchronistic model of Jung's psychology of religion. Although the emphasis in this chapter is primarily on the specific contribution that the synchronicity theory makes to Jung's psychology of religion—a contribution that is evaluated here both by way of the study of new synchronistic material and through the reexamination of some of the synchronistic material presented in the preceding chapters now viewed in terms of Smart's six dimensions for worldview analysis—it is also the case that relevant points made in chapter 1 about Jung's intrapsychic model are recalled as we progress through the different dimensions. Therefore, in that the final chapter summarizes the essential points of the book as a whole, the model that emerges in chapter 5 actually constitutes a synthesis of both the intrapsychic and synchronistic models of Jung's psychology of religion.

Jung's Psychology of Religion: The Intrapsychic Model ❦

Ritual Dimension

The ritual dimension of religion describes that which serves as the sacred retort for one's religious life. Ritual is that within which and through which one achieves communion with one's desired religious goal. While the ritual dimension of religion is often conceived of in terms of outward forms of worship such as offerings, sacrifices, and petitional group prayer, it certainly also encompasses, as Smart has emphasized, physical and mental methods of self-training, such as exist in the yoga systems, which serve as the means to specific religious experiences.[1] It is into this latter category that the ritual dimension of Jung's psychology of religion falls.

The Terry Lectures, which Jung delivered in 1937 at the invitation of Yale University, stand out as Jung's most cogent and indeed forceful presentation of what we have characterized as the ritual dimension of his psychology of religion. In contrast to the many psychological commentaries on religious experience Jung would write over the following years, such as his "A Psychological Approach to the Dogma of the Trinity," Jung's Terry Lectures deal directly with his understanding that analytical psychology could provide a much-needed alternative or, as would be the case with some, complement to the Judeo-Christian forms of religious ritual, which, Jung had come to see, were losing their efficacy for ever-increasing numbers of people in the West.

The shortcoming of Western religious rituals, Jung told his Yale audience, is in the emphasis that is placed on highly structured, as opposed to spontaneous, religious experience. Following patterns of worship that employ a very small number of approved religious symbols—symbols that give expression to long established creeds and dogmas—Western forms of religion, Jung suggested, leave little room for "immediate religious experience." "What is usually and generally called 'religion,' "³ Jung explained to his audience, "is to such an amazing degree a substitute that I ask myself seriously whether this kind of 'religion,' which I prefer to call a creed, has not an important function in human society. The substitution has the obvious purpose of replacing immediate experience by a choice of suitable symbols invested in a solidly organized dogma and ritual."²

Not everyone, Jung knew, is ready for or even wants, for that matter, the challenge of a direct religious encounter beyond the safety of the "approved" symbols and laws of established religion. Accordingly, highly structured forms of religious ritual have been prudently employed since "the dawn of mankind . . . to delimit the unruly and arbitrary 'supernatural' influence."³ For those, however, for whom these more limiting forms of ritual are bereft of meaning, and Jung's analysands had convinced him that the numbers of people concerned were not small, what is now needed, Jung told his audience at Yale, is a new approach that opens the door to a direct, spontaneous religious encounter with nature, by which Jung meant a direct, spontaneous encounter with the living symbols of the unconscious psyche.

Clearly, the religious attitude that most interested Jung was the quest for a highly personalized experience of wholeness—the quest for a highly personalized experience of truth. For genuine seekers of such individualized revelation, the more collective forms of religious rituals, Western or non-Western, which use a very limited symbolism, invariably prove inadequate. Certainly traditional ritual and creed may surpass "immediate experience" in expressiveness and beauty because the former is a product shaped by many individuals over several centuries and is "purified from all the oddities, shortcomings and flaws of individual experience"; nevertheless, Jung emphasized, for the seeker of personalized truth and wholeness it pales beside the "warm red blood" of "immediate experience."⁴ Reflecting this same sentiment, Victor White writes with direct reference to the analytical process, "Sometimes a deep and successful analysis is more like a religious retreat than most religious retreats, because it makes deeper and more particularized and more exacting demands, because it is less stereotyped, less conventional, more moving, more personal, more imperative."⁵

The distinguishing feature of Jung's concept of religious ritual is, then, what we might describe as the search for a highly personalized experience of wholeness through direct relationship to the spontaneous manifestations of the unconscious. "The religious need," Jung would write in a later work, "longs for wholeness, and therefore lays hold of the images of wholeness offered by the unconscious, which, independently of the conscious mind, rise up from the depths of our psychic nature."[6] Here, in this "laying hold" of the symbols of the unconscious we enter the ritual dimension of Jung's psychology of religion.

I would like now to expand the scope of our understanding of the Jungian notion of religious ritual by way of an examination of certain parallels that exist between the analytical process and shamanism. It should be noted that the parallels that will be drawn here will provide the reader with a type of impressionistic sense of what the analytical ritual entails. A more sharply focused understanding will emerge when these same points are reexamined in greater detail in the sections to follow.

Although the term *shaman* is often alternately used with terms such as *sorcerer, medicine man,* and *magician* to describe persons in "primitive" societies who possess magico-religious powers, the function of the shaman, Mircea Eliade explains in his comprehensive study of this subject, is not subsumed by any one of these designations, for even though the shaman may perform functions identified with each of these figures, sorcerers, medicine men, and magicians, on the other hand, need not necessarily be shamans. The shaman, above all else, is distinguished by two qualities: first, by the intensity of his experiences of spiritual ecstasy and his ability to enter these states at will, and second, for his consummate skill as psychopomp, that is, his ability to escort and direct the soul. "The shaman," Eliade writes, "is the great specialist in the human soul; he alone 'sees' it, for he knows its 'form' and its destiny."[7]

In a way analogous to shamanistic intervention, the analytical process is concerned with the treatment of the soul. Indeed, in that the analytical process engages both the conscious and unconscious aspects of personality in a process of radical psychic transformation, it is no mere metaphor to say that analysis, when undertaken in the fullest spirit of the individuation process, is concerned, like shamanism, with the direction and transformation of the soul.

As with shamanistic intervention, which is resorted to primarily in situations when the soul is endangered,[8] in-depth analysis, that is to say again, analysis that is undertaken in the fullest spirit of the individuation process, is also reserved for comparable situations of self-alienation in which the reorientation needed far exceeds that which will be achievable through less comprehensive spiritual or psychological interventions. In recognition of this, Josef Goldbrunner makes the point that like the country doctor who ac-knowledges "the potentialities of his great colleague, the surgeon," the priest, clergyman, and doctor "should be aware of the methods of big analysis—in order to realize their own limitations."[9] Clearly "big analysis" should be reserved for situations of self-alienation in which the reorientation needed exceeds that which can be achieved through less radical methods such as confession and other tradi-tional religious practices, or through psychological interventions concerned, for instance, solely with the development of relationship skills. It is an interesting fact that Jung would add Freudian analy-sis to this list, as we see in the following. "If, therefore," Jung told his Yale audience,

> a patient should be convinced of the exclusively sexual origin of his neurosis, I would not disturb him in his opinion because I know that such a conviction, particularly if it is deeply rooted, is an excellent defense against an onslaught of the terrible ambiguity of an immediate experience. As long as such a defense works I shall not break it down, since I know there must be powerful reasons why the patient has to think in such a narrow circle. But if his dreams should begin to de-stroy the protective theory, I have to support the wider personality.[10]

As a radical and comprehensive method of psychic interven-tion, in-depth analysis, Jung emphasized repeatedly, is only to be undertaken as a last resort, for like the shamanistic ritual itself it has as its objective the resolution of a spiritual crisis in which the soul, understood as the personality both conscious and unconscious, is endangered, yet remains inaccessible to other interventions. Once, however, indications appear that this comprehensive process of healing must be undertaken and will receive the support of the un-conscious, that is to say, once "dreams begin to destroy the protec-tive theory," it would be equally dangerous not to proceed with the prescribed analytical work. Commenting on the relevance of this type of "call" for those who are to undergo training as shamans, Eliade writes:

> We may remember . . . the premonitory dreams of future sha-mans, dreams that, according to Park, become mortal illnesses if they are not rightly understood and piously obeyed. An old

shaman is called in to interpret them; he orders the patient to follow the injunctions of the spirits that provoked the dreams. "Usually a person is reluctant to become a shaman, and assumes his powers and follows the spirit's bidding only when he is told by other shamans that otherwise death will result."[11]

At the heart of the traditional approaches to the training of shamans and still very much central to the training of analysts today is the emergence of such a spiritual crisis. For both groups, the entanglement of the individual in spiritual crisis and the ensuing struggle for self-healing constitutes the core of one's training as a healer, for it is through such direct and personal experience that one acquires the insight and skills that are needed to heal others. Henri Ellenberger uses the term *creative illness* to describe such struggles at self-healing and suggests that both Freud's and Jung's systems of analysis were very much the result of their respective "creative illnesses." "It is our hypothesis," Ellenberger writes in his major study of dynamic psychiatric systems *The Discovery of the Unconscious,*

> that Freud's and Jung's systems originated mostly from their respective creative illness. . . . In short, it presents the picture of a severe neurosis, sometimes of a psychosis . . . [and] throughout the patient remains obsessed by . . . the pursuit of some difficult aim. He lives in utter spiritual isolation and has the feeling that nobody can help him, hence his attempts at self-healing. . . . The illness may last three or more years. The recovery occurs spontaneously and rapidly. . . . The subject is convinced he has gained access to a new spiritual . . . truth that he will reveal to the world.[12]

For both Freud and Jung, not only did their respective creative illnesses provide them with the insights and methods that would constitute the foundational principles of their analytical schools, but, moreover, as Ellenberger explains, the idea of the creative illness was itself to play, through Jung's influence, a key role in the training of analysts—an emphasis that would become even more greatly pronounced in Jung's own school following his break with Freud. "Jung," Ellenberger writes, "promoted the training analysis, and Freudians accepted it for didactic value, but the Jungian school later came to consider it as being a kind of initiatory malady comparable to that of the shaman."[13]

Like the shamanic initiate who enters the spirit world under the direction of the old master shaman,[14] the modern day analysand is too led into the mysteries of the unconscious by a "knowing advisor" who has himself undergone such a journey. As with the shamanic initiation, the knowing advisor serves as a guide only, with the real burden of the work falling on the initiate himself. "If he [the analyst]," von Franz writes, "tries to get analysands out of the suffering it means he takes away from them what is most valuable; cheap comforting is wrong, for by that you get people away from the heat, the place where the process of individuation takes place."[15]

With individuation there is no vicarious atonement. Accordingly, the visions and dreams that confront both the shamanic initiate and analysand are those of torture and dismemberment, followed by reconstruction and renewal of the body.[16] "The shaman's experience of sickness, torture, death, and regeneration," Jung writes, "implies, at a higher level, the idea of being made whole through sacrifice."[17] Here, the individual must himself walk the path and bear the burden of the suffering that is invariably part of this process of transformation. Here, and this is where the support of one who has himself undergone this process is particularly valuable, the initiate must see his suffering not as punishment, but as a necessary tempering of his new, emerging personality. Commenting on the importance of recognizing this distinction and directly facing up to its demands, Jung writes: "For the neophyte, it would be a real sin if he shrank from the torture of initiation. The torture inflicted on him is *not* a punishment but the indispensable means of leading him towards his destiny."[18] Accordingly, in recognition of the great importance of such initiatory ordeals to the development of the skills and spiritual character of the healer, it is believed in both shamanism and analytical psychology to be the case that one's skill as a healer, one's ability to shamanize, is proportionate to the severity, and length of time, of one's "creative illness."[19]

Doctrinal Dimension

Central to Jung's psychology of religion is his concept of individuation. About the individuation process, Peter Homans writes, it "was the lens through which Jung viewed the Christian faith."[20] To emphasize an important point through extension of this statement, we could say that the individuation process was the lens through

which Jung viewed all religious experience. In this section, in seeking to reveal the essential features of the doctrinal dimension of
Jung's psychology of religion, we shall, therefore, examine the
theoretical formulations associated with Jung's concept of individuation.

One of the distinguishing features of Jung's analytical psychology is that in contrast to the position taken by Freud it moves beyond the mechanistic-causal model in its characterization of the
movement of psychic energy. Freud, Jung explains, was very much
caught in the trap "of the outmoded rationalism and scientific ma-
terialism of the late nineteenth century"[21] and this, coupled with
his "over-valuation of sexuality,"[22] led him into an extreme reductive causalism. The mechanistic-causal orientation to which Jung
here refers is clearly evidenced in Freud's *Totem and Taboo*, in which
Freud found it necessary to create a pseudoprehistorical event—the
killing of the primal father by his sons in order to obtain access to
the women of the clan—as a means of demonstrating "that the beginnings of religion, morals, society and art converge in the Oedipus complex." The Oedipal complex, Freud reasons, which
"constitutes the nucleus of all neuroses" and all developments in
"religion, morals, society and art," must also stem from one specific
cause. This one cause, this great beginning of the vast mechanistic-
causal unfoldment of the whole of psychic life and culture must,
Freud concludes, have been a concrete, single event of prehistory.
Having satisfied this conceptual criterion with his fictional account
of the killing of the father by the primal horde, Freud thus is able to
assert to his reader, in summary, "that 'in the beginning was the
Deed.' "[23]

Quite rightly, Jung describes the basic weakness of the Freudian view as resting "in the one-sidedness to which the mechanistic-
causal standpoint always inclines, that is to say in the all-
simplifying *reductio ad causam.*"[24] In contrast to the position taken by
Freud, Jung maintains that psychic phenomena must be examined
from "a twofold point of view, namely that of *causality* and that of
finality."[25] Finality is a point of view which, as Jung explains, is
"empirically justified by the existence of series of events in which
the causal connection is indeed evident *but the meaning of which only
becomes intelligible in terms of end-products (final effects).*"[26]

Whereas the mechanistic-causal view regards a psychic event,
such as a dream symbol, as solely the product of antecedent psychic
contents, the finalistic view regards the same event as an expression
of the purposive course that psychic energy follows. To use the re-

ligious tendency as an example of how this works for Jung, we could say that even though specific historical psychic contents, for instance, associations with one's actual parents, may arise in connection with the emergence of the religious tendency, those contents are not viewed as the exclusive reason for this religious development, as Freud himself was led to believe,[27] but rather, as the specific contents that the unconscious must necessarily draw on to lead the individual to the higher understanding.[28]

When, accordingly, a symbol is interpreted from the mechanistic-causal point of view, it acquires a fixed meaning. The mechanistic-causal point of view inclines, as Jung relates, "towards uniformity of meaning, that is, towards a fixed significance of symbols." The final point of view, however, "recognizes no fixed meaning of symbols."[29] Jung argues that when symbols are interpreted simply as products of antecedent psychic contents, that is, reductively, they are being treated as mere signs.[30] The finalistic point of view, on the other hand, in regarding the symbol as an expression of the purposive course that psychic energy follows, treats the symbol as a symbol in that it is received as representative of "a definite but not yet recognizable goal."[31] The symbol, in other words, is understood to point beyond itself to a higher synthesis.

For Jung, in summary, the psyche is "characterized by *fines* (aims) as well as by *causae*."[32] Jung maintains that cause in itself does not produce psychic development. Psychic development requires "the attraction of the symbol, whose value quantum exceeds that of the cause." Accordingly, when, counter to the natural movement of psychic energy, the method of *reductio ad causam* is applied exclusively, "the very reverse of development" results.[33] Exclusive application of the reductive method serves to bind the movement of psychic energy and with it the development of the personality. Therefore, although Jung fully acknowledges the historical causal content in evaluating psychic data, it is, however, most important to realize that for Jung "its chief importance lies in the fact that it has a meaning for the actual present and for the future, in their psychological aspects." This being the case, it is clear that Jung is quite justified in describing his methodology as "not only analytical and causal but synthetic and prospective."[34]

Fundamental to the above-described methodological approach is Jung's discovery that the psyche is a self-regulating system, capable not only of maintaining its own equilibrium, but of bringing about its own self-realization. In analytical psychology, the relationship between the conscious and unconscious spheres of the psyche is described as compensatory. In this model, the regulating element is understood to be situated in the unconscious itself. "The unconscious processes that compensate the conscious ego," Jung writes, "contain all those elements that are necessary for the self-regulation of the psyche as a whole."[35]

When the compensatory activity of the unconscious is directed toward a specific conscious attitude, one of three general approaches is usually followed. First, the unconscious, through the symbol, may take a rather neutral position if it is basically satisfied with the conscious one. Second, the unconscious may give expression to a position that is quite the opposite of the conscious one. Third, the unconscious may strongly reinforce the conscious position.[36] It is important to note that psychic compensation is very personalistic and interpretation must be handled accordingly. For example, a person whose view of life is very dark and pessimistic will not necessarily have dreams that are bright and effusively optimistic. This particular compensatory approach will only be used if that person's "nature allows him to be stimulated and encouraged in this way." If, however, the person is of a different nature, the unconscious may take a position that is even darker and more pessimistic than the conscious one. In doing this, the unconscious, Jung explains, follows "the principle of like curing like."[37]

One of Jung's key insights concerning the compensatory process that led him toward his concept of individuation was his observation of the presence, in a series of dreams, of a more comprehensive compensatory pattern. In contrast to the compensatory activities of the unconscious that address the immediate compensatory needs of consciousness, this more comprehensive compensatory pattern, whose existence would be largely undetectable in an isolated dream, acts, Jung came to recognize, as "a kind of developmental process in the personality itself."[38] The compensatory principle is thus understood by Jung to function not only in accordance with the immediate needs of the individual, but also to facilitate the comprehensive development of the personality.

In Jung's autobiography, *Memories, Dreams, Reflections*, we find an account of Jung's personal experience of this more comprehensive compensatory movement of psychic energy. The following passage, which is taken from that text, deserves careful consideration, as it reveals three important characteristics of the individuation process. First, it points to the fact that in the individuation process, as with those compensatory activities that address the immediate needs of the individual, the regulating element originates in the unconscious. The ego, in other words, is not the one that chooses its goal, rather it is the one being led by the unconscious to it. Second, it illustrates how the only productive course of action for the individual is to move with the current of this comprehensive process. One must, to a great degree, simply submit to it. Third, this passage indicates how the comprehensive compensatory movement characteristic of the individuation process has as its goal the conscious realization of that which constitutes the center point of orientation and meaning for the psyche as a total phenomenon. It seeks to facilitate, in other words, the realization of that which Jung has termed the self. The text reads:

> The question arose repeatedly: What is this process leading to? Where is its goal? From my own experience, I knew by now that I could not presume to choose a goal. . . . It had been proved to me that I had to abandon the idea of the superordinate position of the ego. . . . I was being compelled to go through this process of the unconscious. I had to let myself be carried along by the current, without a notion of where it would lead me. When I began drawing the mandalas, however, I saw that . . . all the paths I had been following . . . were leading back to a single point. . . . During those years, between 1918 and 1920, I began to understand that the goal of psychic development is the self.[39]

Jung thus came to understand that the more comprehensive compensatory process seeks to facilitate the conscious realization of the point of orientation and meaning for the psyche as a whole, the self. The personality associated strictly with ego-consciousness represents "only a part of the whole man, and its life does not yet represent his total life."[40] Accordingly, the ego must become connected, through the process of psychic compensation, with those yet unconscious potentials in order to attain the flowering of the full personality. To the extent that the ego is able to integrate this compensatory material, the conscious personality will develop a broader, more stable base. In this way, the comprehensive growth of the personality is realized and the individuation process is furthered. Individuation, therefore, is essentially a comprehensive developmental process wherein the ego consciously integrates those compensatory contents of the unconscious which are necessary for the unfoldment of the complete personality, those compensatory contents which serve to bring about the conscious realization of the self.

As it is perhaps becoming apparent, the ego-self relationship is very much at the heart of the individuation process. Before proceeding, however, to examine the ego-self relationship in greater detail, it is necessary first to give consideration to Jung's model of the psyche. In his model of the psyche Jung distinguishes three psychic levels: ego-consciousness, the personal unconscious, and the collective unconscious.

The field of consciousness is described by Jung as the sum total of all that is known to the subject. At the center of the field of consciousness is the ego, the necessary subjective factor without which the field of consciousness would not itself exist. "The relation of a psychic content to the ego," Jung relates, "forms the criterion of its consciousness, for no content can be conscious unless it is represented to a subject."[41]

On the periphery of the field of consciousness is that which Jung describes as the personal unconscious. "The personal unconscious," Jung writes, "consists firstly of all those contents that became unconscious either because they lost their intensity and were forgotten or because consciousness was withdrawn from them (repression), and secondly of contents, some of them sense-impressions, which never had sufficient intensity to reach consciousness but have somehow entered the psyche."[42] As Jung's description indirectly indicates, the personal unconscious is so named because its contents are acquired in the course of an individual's life and, therefore, are unique to each individual. We shall be looking more closely at the personal unconscious when we come to the section dealing with the ethical dimension of Jung's psychology of religion.

In contrast to the personal unconscious, whose contents are acquired, the contents of the collective unconscious, the archetypes, are indigenous to the psyche. The archetype is essentially an unconscious factor that is never directly perceived by the subject but known only through the archetypal images that enter consciousness. Even though Jung himself greatly contributed to the mix-up, one of Jung's central concerns about the archetype concept was with the failure of others to distinguish the archetype from its image. The following is one of Jung's most precise explanations of this important distinction: "The term 'archetype' is often understood as meaning a certain definite mythological image or motif. But this would be no more than a conscious representation. . . . The archetype is . . . an inherited *tendency* of the human mind to form representations of mythological motifs—representations that vary a great deal without losing their basic pattern."[43]

The "mother archetype," for example, which is the inherited tendency to form representations related to the maternal, takes a variety of forms when it manifests itself on the conscious level. This archetype may be symbolically represented by one's own mother, grandmother, stepmother, or mother-in-law. It may also take the form of a church, university, country, woods, or sea. Jung states that this archetype "is often associated with things and places standing for fertility and fruitfulness." It is important to note that the symbols of the mother archetype may have a positive or negative meaning, the witch being an example of the latter.[44] It should be understood, then, that the archetypal image is not to be confused with the archetype, which, as an unconscious tendency to produce representations related to its ground theme, is never directly perceived by consciousness.

For Jung, the collective or archetypal unconscious is that from which the numerous symbols of the myths and religions of mankind have arisen. "One could almost say," Jung writes, expressing his conviction of the psychic immediacy of this vast collection of symbols, "that if all the world's traditions were cut off at a single blow, the whole of mythology and the whole history of religion would start all over again with the next generation."[45] Much of Jung's writing in the area of the psychology of religion was concerned with the identification of the larger archetypal contexts into which specific symbols and doctrines, such as the Trinity and the Mass, can be placed. This type of examination, Jung hoped, would enrich the spiritual experiences of individuals both within and outside established religion by enabling them to see the living, psychic immediacy of these symbols and doctrines, which are produced spontaneously by the unconscious. Jung's efforts along these lines were, of course, not always well received, particularly by those for whom such revelations constitute unique and absolute truth. Jung, however, was not deterred and continued to make public those insights from his psychological work that he believed would serve to reawaken the spirituality of an age so intent on dispossessing itself of a genuinely invigorating symbolical life. In his book *The Psyche as Sacrament*, John Dourley, drawing a parallel with the work of Tillich, comments on this specific contribution of Jung's:

> Both [Tillich and Jung] call for a rediscovery of the nature of religion itself, as the precondition for the revitalization of any particular religion. . . . This in fact would mean the recognition of the individual soul and the psyche as the place of ac-

cess to the divine, and the source from which man's symbols and their attendant numinosity arise. Not only would such a self-understanding reinvest the symbols of any particular religion with new life and urgency, it would also relate the holders of any specific pattern of religious symbols more empathically to other symbolic expressions. Put simply, the multiplicity of faiths might cease to culminate in religious antipathy . . . [and] come to see themselves as offering to each other a much needed complementarity.[46]

Next to the discovery of the collective unconscious, a finding of no less and perhaps even greater significance to Jung's model of the psyche was his identification of a central, unifying archetype—an archetype around which all other archetypes are grouped and by which they are ordered.[47] Jung termed this point of orientation and meaning for the psyche as a whole, the self. In accordance with the principle of psychic compensation, the self, through the symbol, is "all the time urging us to overcome our unconsciousness." This, of course, is no easy task, since, as Jung relates, speaking no doubt from many years of clinical experience: "Human nature has an invincible dread of becoming more conscious of itself." The self, Jung explains, "demands sacrifice by sacrificing itself to us."[48] This is a particularly important statement because it draws attention to an aspect of the ego-self relationship that is often overlooked. Great attention is usually given to the sacrifice made by the ego as it struggles to integrate the compensatory material with which it is presented. We tend, however, to overlook the fact that the self too is making a sacrifice as it works, through the symbol, to express itself in the more limiting world of the ego.

With regard to its phenomenology, "the symbols of the self," Jung explains, "cannot be distinguished empirically from a God-image,"[49] for both serve to fulfill the same purpose, which is to give expression to a transcendent level of wholeness and unity that exists independently of consciousness.[50] The figures of Christ and the Buddha, the child, mandala-like patterns, quaternity configurations, various theriomorphic representations such as the bear, horse, bull, or snake, insects like the beetle, plant symbols like the flower, geographical phenomena like mountains and even cities are but a few examples of the great range of the self's symbolism. The self's forms are myriad, ranging "from the highest to the lowest," yet they consistently have as their common link, when viewed in the specific context in which they are presented, their noticeable transcendence of the position of ego-consciousness much "in the manner of a daimonion."[51]

If, then, the symbols of the self are identical with the images of God, are we to understand the archetype of the self to be for Jung equivalent to God within? The answer to this is yes, we are. Writing with reference to the self, Jung states: "It might equally be called the 'God within us.' The beginnings of our whole psychic life seem to be inextricably rooted in this point, and all our highest and ultimate purposes seem to be striving towards it."[52] For Jung the self is the source and goal of our psychic lives. Indeed it is the "a priori existent" out of which the ego has evolved[53] and, as the process of individuation indicates, that toward which the differentiated ego strives. As the point of orientation and meaning for the psyche as a total phenomenon, as the source and goal of our psychic life, the self, it should be emphasized, in summary, like all archetypes, is not a fixed image, but a dynamic ground out of which a vast symbolism emerges. Accordingly, Jung explains, just as "the ancients saw the *imago Dei* in man not as a mere imprint, as a sort of lifeless, stereotyped impression, but as an active force,"[54] so too are we to view the archetype of the self.

Experiential Dimension

The very high value that Jung places on experientially based knowledge is something that cannot be overestimated, particularly as regards his critique of religion. Certainly Jung's great respect for the religious systems of the East such as Taoism, Zen Buddhism, and Indian yoga stems from his understanding that they offer, through their respective methods leading to the systematic unfoldment of personality, so much more to the individual on the experiential level than Christianity. The outstanding attraction of these Eastern systems for Jung is that they call for the cultivation of knowledge, particularly self-knowledge, through direct experiential involvement. Ironically enough, however, the very concern that led Jung to have such high regard for these systems in the first place— his concern with the primacy of experientially based knowledge— was that which led Jung ultimately to be skeptical about the contribution that these same systems could make to the spiritual needs of people in the West. Jung's concern was that the wholesale adoption of Eastern methods would, in practice, serve to alienate individuals from the ground of their own authentic being and thus produce the very reverse of that which these systems seek to achieve, namely, the unfoldment of the genuine personality. This was the key factor that led Jung to urge caution. "If we snatch these things directly from the East," Jung writes,

> we have merely indulged our Western acquisitiveness, confirming yet again that "everything good is outside," whence it has to be fetched and pumped into our barren souls. It seems to me that we have really learned something from the East when we understand that the psyche contains riches enough without having to be primed from outside, and when we feel capable of evolving out of ourselves with or without divine grace.[55]

Experientially based knowledge versus faith and belief is certainly a recurring theme in Jung's writings on psychology and religion. The former, for Jung, is the essential basis of genuine religious experience and wells up from within. The latter, on the other hand, is often characterized by Jung as something extraneous, hence a sterile and lifeless substitute for that which is obtained through direct experience. Jung's very pronounced partiality toward experientially based knowledge is perhaps most clearly evidenced in Jung's frequently voiced call for a new understanding of the concept of the *imitatio Christi*. "The *imitatio Christi*," Jung writes in his commentary on the Chinese text *The Secret of the Golden Flower*, "has this disadvantage: in the long run we worship as a divine example a man who embodied the deepest meaning of life, and then, out of sheer imitation, we forget to make real our own deepest meaning—self-realization." Rather than simply believing in Christ and neutralizing through that belief our own unique strivings, or in faith simply copying in our own lives what for Christ was his own unique destiny, what we really must do, Jung explains, is to accept the *imitatio Christi* as a challenge to realize our deepest, personal meaning "with the same courage and the same self-sacrifice shown by Jesus."[56] What we really must do, simply stated, is to exchange faith and belief for experientially based knowledge.

The road of experiential knowledge that Jung spent most of his life leading people along is clearly not a road that is readily walked. As Jung relates, for many "the steep path of self-development is . . . as mournful and gloomy as the path to hell."[57] Although the path of self-development certainly seems like hell, there can be no question that for Jung the real living hell was to be found in the lives of those for whom faith and belief had all but disappeared and the subsequent challenge for greater self-knowledge ignored. Jung's analytical practice surely made him witness to the great desperation of such individuals. It was the case, however, that the most indelible impression of this hellish meaninglessness came not from his analytical practice, but from his observation of his own father, Johann Paul Achilles Jung, a Swiss Reformed pastor. "My memory of my father," Jung writes in his autobiography, "is of a sufferer stricken with an Amfortas wound, a 'fisher king' whose wound would not heal—that Christian suffering for which the alchemists sought the panacea. I as a 'dumb' Parsifal was the witness of this sickness during the years of my boyhood, and, like Parsifal, speech failed me."

Commenting retrospectively about what he could not have understood as a young man, Jung could say that even though his father had believed his suffering to be personal in nature, it really was not, but was representative of "the suffering of the Christian in general." The suffering that afflicted his father, Jung could understand retrospectively, was specifically a consequence of the *imitatio Christi* in its more concrete form. "He wanted to rest content with faith," Jung writes, "but faith broke with him. Such is frequently the reward of the *sacrificium intellectus*." From such suffering, Jung could also reflect in alluding to the influence that his father's "unhealing wound" was to have on his own life, there arises a great debt which is to be "paid for heavily in the next generation."[58] Elaborating on this important point, Murray Stein states: "While Paul Jung suffered the spiritual plight of modern man dumbly and blindly, his son Carl Gustav would take it on as a conscious problem in desperate need of resolution. Healing the spiritual sources of his father's suffering became in many ways Jung's vocation."[59] The spiritual suffering that Jung witnessed in the person of his father, a suffering that was very possibly heightened in Jung's mind by his father's early death at the age of fifty-four when Jung was himself only twenty-one, shaped what was to become a central issue in Jung's psychology of religion—the need to realize a spirituality that could grow out of an experientially based knowledge, a spirituality based on a genuine self-knowledge.

Having developed an understanding of the very high value that Jung attaches to experientially based knowledge, we shall now examine how, in practice, such knowledge is acquired through the dialogue that takes place between the conscious and unconscious in the individuation process. The concept in analytical psychology that deals most directly with this problem is the process Jung has termed the "transcendent function."

As previously indicated, Jung understands the psyche to be a self-regulating system. Accordingly, in this model every conflict is understood to stimulate "the mind to activity for the purpose of creating a satisfactory solution." When, for example, the conscious attitude is in conflict with the unconscious as a result of a particular position it has assumed, the unconscious becomes activated to compensate this position. What then follows is a dialogue in which both sides exchange points of view. This exchange continues until a compromise that takes both positions into account is reached. In this way, a third, transcendent position is attained.[60] The transcendent function, therefore, describes how out of the conscious-unconscious dialogue a new position, the third, emerges. Even though the emergence of the transcendent third is an ongoing phenomenon of dream analysis, we shall not be directly concerned here with this particular manifestation of the transcendent function. Rather, we shall be exploring this phenomenon in relationship to the psychological procedure that was developed by Jung to enable individuals, directly and consciously, to produce the transcendent function. This procedure is called active imagination.

Active imagination is a practical technique that is consciously employed by an individual to facilitate the transcendent function. In active imagination, the analysand takes a particular emotional state,[61] dream image, or hypnagogic impression as the starting point.[62] While focusing on this psychic event, the analysand is encouraged to give the unconscious "free rein" so that it can go about the task of elaborating the central theme. "This," Jung relates, "according to individual taste and talent, could be done in any number of ways, dramatic, dialectic, visual, acoustic, or in the form of dancing, painting, drawing or modelling."[63] In Jung's own case we know from his autobiography that during the time of his "creative illness" he used the image of a "steep descent" to enable him to "seize hold of his fantasies" and consciously enter the unconscious, where he could learn more about these contents.[64] Whatever medium is used, it is essential that the unconscious is given the chance to express its point of view without restraint and that the resulting symbolical transformations are carefully studied by the analysand. Drawing an analogy between this process of symbol transformation and the work of the medieval alchemists who were themselves concerned with the transmutation of base metals into gold, Jung writes: "Like [the] apprentice, the modern man begins with an unseemly prima materia which presents itself in unexpected form—a contemptible fantasy which, like the stone the builders rejected, is 'flung into the street' and is so 'cheap' that people do not even look at it. He will observe it from day to day and note its alterations until his eyes are opened."[65]

Quite often the psychic material that is initially regarded as insignificant turns out to hold the key to one's psychic progress. It is not uncommon, for instance, for a dream that was considered at first glance to be absolutely meaningless, "so 'cheap' that people do not even look at it," to be later seen, after a more careful examination, to contain information of great value to one's individuation. In light of the fact that the unconscious is always, so to speak, a step ahead of consciousness, this type of development is not surprising. It is of the greatest importance, therefore, in dealing with the symbolical material of the unconscious, that the xenophobic tendency of consciousness to reject and even eliminate the unknown, the stranger, is properly checked. This is particularly the case with active imagination, where the symbolical images must be given the freedom to "develop according to their own logic"[66] until a more or less complete statement of the central theme is produced. With the development of this central theme, the first stage of the transcendent function is thus completed.[67]

The question now arises as to how the ego will relate to this newly acquired psychic material. "This," Jung explains, "is the second and more important stage of the procedure, the bringing together of opposites for the production of a third: the transcendent function." At this second stage, the ego must be the one to lead the process of integration.[68] Usually, this is accomplished in two specific ways. First, the ego must take a more active role in the psychic drama that is taking place in the process of active imagination itself. Second, having given careful consideration to the insights achieved in this manner, the ego must not only decide how these insights are to be "carried out in practice," but it must actually do so.

It is not uncommon for the analysand simply to observe the images that arise in the course of active imagination without fully appreciating his relationship to them. It is imperative, however, if further progress is to be made, that he come to realize that "his fantasy is a real psychic process which is happening to him personally." As Jung relates, "Although, to a certain extent, he looks on from outside, impartially, he is also an acting and suffering figure in the drama of the psyche. This recognition is absolutely necessary and marks an important advance."[69] Accordingly, the ego must now assume a more assertive attitude in its involvement with the images that emerge in active imagination, for only through such genuine involvement will it attain the degree of commitment that is required to facilitate genuine transformation. The ego thus enters into the process and expresses, in the course of its involvement with the figures it encounters, the full heights and depths of its own knowledge. Commenting on this, Jung states:

> If you place yourself in the drama as you really are, not only does it gain in actuality but you also create, by your criticism of the fantasy, an effective counterbalance to its tendency to get out of hand. For what is now happening is the decisive rapprochement with the unconscious. This is where insight, the *unio mentalis*, begins to become real.[70]

In taking the final step toward the realization of the transcendent function, the ego is now required to meet the ethical consequences of its newly acquired insights which, as Jung relates, "demand to be carried out in practice." This is the point where one's moral endowment is put to the test.[71] Insight and action must now be united. Furthermore, it is a point where one's patience will be greatly tried. Indeed, as the individual works to unite the insights he has achieved with his life, it is quite likely that the clash of reality will repeatedly force him to return to the process of active imagination to discover "the blind spots in his psychic field of vision."[72] Only when a satisfactory compromise of the views exchanged between the conscious and unconscious is realized, that is to say, brought into practice, will the process Jung describes as the transcendent function be completed.

The process of active imagination, which serves, like the individuation process, to lead one toward a greater level of conscious relationship to the self, is clearly not without danger. Indeed, as with the individuation process, it is vital that in active imagination the integrity of the ego be at all times carefully guarded, for, as Jung explains, the liberated unconscious may very well "thrust the ego aside and overwhelm it."[73] This is particularly a concern as the individual becomes entangled with the deeper archetypal layers of the psyche. Here the great danger is that the ego will become identified with the contents it encounters and like the psychotic fall under the direct influence of the collective unconscious.[74] At this point, the actual posture that the ego assumes when it is confronted with the contents of the collective unconscious is, for Jung, the pivotal factor that determines whether the experience of the unconscious will be beneficial or harmful, health-promoting or pathological in character. Commenting on this, Jung writes: "The constellation of the archetypal images and fantasies is not in itself pathological. The pathological element only reveals itself in the way the individual reacts to them. . . . The characteristic feature of a pathological reaction is above all, *identification with the archetype*."[75] In his journey inward, the analysand is confronted with and forced to integrate the same fantasy material to which the psychotic "falls victim." His way of dealing with these contents will be the single most important factor keeping his "creative illness" from becoming what we might characterize as an "uncreative illness." Everything depends on the adaptive skill of the analysand, that is, on his ability to integrate the compensatory psychic material without succumbing, as does the psychotic, to it. On the one hand, he must close himself off and thus avoid the temptation to identify with these transpersonal archetypal powers—to usurp their power mentally. This he will do by regarding only that which he has brought into relationship to life, that which he has grounded in reality, as his own. On the other hand, he must open himself up so that the powerful compensatory message of the archetypal psyche has sufficient space to be received at the level of ego-consciousness. "Very often," von Franz writes, "the reason for schizophrenia is not so much the invasion of the unconscious, but that it happens to someone who is too narrow for the experience, either mentally or emotionally. People who are not broad-minded enough and have not enough generosity and heart to open up to what comes are exploded by the invasion." As an example of how the problem arising from such a dangerously narrow conscious outlook was actually depicted by the unconscious, von Franz cites a dream in which "an angel of God" had fallen into the confining backyard of a Paris hotel. The angel's positioning was such in relationship to the building that if it were to move to free itself, "if it made the smallest movement, the whole building would collapse." The collapse of the building would signify, von Franz explains, the outbreak of schizophrenia which did in fact take place shortly after this dream.[76]

The difficult challenge facing the analysand, then, is how to integrate the contents of the unconscious, how to bring them into relationship to life itself. As we have seen, one must not, in the course of doing this, become identified with the transpersonal powers of the archetypal psyche. On the other hand, as also indicated above, one must at the same time do real justice to the compensatory messages of these archetypal contents, which seek to expand the base of consciousness and demand to be acknowledged. In the following passage Jung uses the symbolism of mythology to characterize the type of skill and insight that is required in the individuation process to meet this challenge: "In myths the hero is the one who conquers the dragon, not the one who is devoured by it. And yet both have to deal with the same dragon. Also, he is no hero who never met the dragon, or who, if he once saw it, declared afterwards that he saw nothing. Equally, only one who has risked the fight with the dragon and is not overcome by it wins the hoard, the 'treasure hard to attain'."[77]

The hero must conquer the same "dragon" to which the psychotic has fallen victim. He is the one who goes alone to seek it out when others, choosing to cling to their present level of security, remain behind. Finally, the hero is the one who undertakes the battle and ultimately is given, because of his sincerity, the strength to overcome the dragon and take possession of the "treasure hard to attain." The winning of the "treasure hard to attain" is, of course, an allusion on the part of Jung to an experience of the archetype of total unity, the self, the goal of the process of individuation.

One of the very important aspects of Jung's description of the self, particularly as regards the experiential dimension, is Jung's characterization of the functional emergence of the self. In that this characterization seems at times to be in conflict with Jung's description of the self as an archetype, it has been a source of considerable confusion. It is clear that Jung's characterization of the self falls into two general categories. First, Jung speaks of the self as the source and goal of our psychic development, the unchanging archetype of wholeness that from the very beginning has served as "the *secret spiritus rector* of our fate."[78] We examined this conceptualization of the self in the previous section dealing with the doctrinal dimension of Jung's psychology of religion. In contrast to this description, Jung, in wanting to emphasize that on an experiential level knowledge of the self is something that is gradually achieved through conscious effort, has in some instances described the self as something that is created out of the individuation process. A very serious misunderstanding of what Jung means by the self results when this latter description is understood not solely as a description of the functional emergence of the self, but as a description of its actual beginning. In the following passage, Jung presents one of his best descriptions of these two important ways of viewing the self. Writing with reference to the individuation process, Jung states:

Conscious realization or the bringing together of the scattered parts is in one sense an act of the ego's will, but in another sense it is a spontaneous manifestation of the self, which was always there. . . . Up to a point we create the self by making ourselves conscious of our unconscious contents, and to that extent it is our son. This is why the alchemists called their incorruptible substance—which means precisely the self—the *filius philosophorum*. But we are forced to make this effort by the unconscious presence of the self, which is all the time urging us to overcome our unconsciousness. From that point of view the self is the father.[79]

Above all else the self is for Jung the goal and source of our psychic existence, the central archetype of orientation and meaning, "God within." From an experiential viewpoint, however, it is very important, as Jung emphasizes, that we never overlook or undervalue the fact that the self emerges out of the unconscious very much through the conscious efforts of the individual.

The emergence of the self in the individuation process can be the source of a radical change of personality, and its sudden emergence may very well come upon one with the force of a full-scale conversion experience. There can be no question that for Jung his own experience of the emerging self came to him with the intensity of a religious conversion. In his autobiography, Jung describes the critical turning point in his understanding as being reached suddenly in 1927 through a dream. This was the point at which he developed a sense of absolute certainty about the self.

In the dream, it was winter and Jung was in a dark, sooty city where it was raining. The city was Liverpool, a symbol of the "pool of life" in that an ancient view regards the liver as the "seat of life." Accompanied by several Swiss, Jung had approached the city, which was on a plateau, from the harbor, passing through an area that reminded him of the Totengasschen (Alley of the Dead) in Basel. Reaching the plateau, Jung could see a broad square, around which were the individual quarters of the city. Each quarter, moreover, like the broad central square, had its own center point. There was, however, a key difference between the center point of the main square and those of the secondary areas where "other Swiss" had settled. Whereas the secondary areas had a large street lamp for their center point, the central square, which Jung approached, had at its center a small island surrounded by a pool of water, upon which "stood a single tree, a magnolia, in a shower of reddish blossoms. It was as though," Jung writes, "the tree stood in the sunlight and were at the same time the source of light." This dream, which Jung depicted in a mandala he titled " 'Window on Eternity,' " had come to him "as an act of grace," and through it he had been given a subjective certainty that he had previously lacked about his concept of the self.[80]

A description of the experience of the emergence of the self can never live up to the richness and depth of the experience itself. It always falls short of conveying the "subtle feelings which are, none the less, infinitely important for the life and well-being of the individual."[81] As with other conversion experiences whose full spiritual meaning remains accessible only to the subject himself, the depth of Jung's experience of the self at the time of the Liverpool dream can never be known to us as observers. We do know, however, that although Jung had for ten years been growing in his understanding of what he had begun to recognize as a point of orientation for the psyche as a whole, it was only after the Liverpool dream that he would formally write about the self and, moreover, draw on the testimonies of religious figures to describe what the experience of the emergence of the self is like. Comparing the experience of the emergence of the self to St. Paul's experience of Christ as expressed in Paul's testimony " 'Yet not I, but Christ liveth in me,' " Jung in 1929 could thus write:

> The symbol "Christ" as "son of man" is an analogous psychic experience of a higher spiritual being who is invisibly born in the individual, a pneumatic body which is to serve as a future dwelling, a body which, as Paul says, is put on like a garment ("For as many of you as have been baptized into Christ have put on Christ"). . . . It is, in a sense, the feeling that we have been "replaced," but without the connotation of having been "deposed." . . . It is as if the guidance of life had passed over to an invisible centre. . . . "I live" becomes the objective "It lives me."[82]

Ethical Dimension

There can be no question that for Jung the analysis of the unconscious confronts one with very specific moral challenges, which have to be directly addressed as such. Although Jung never laid down anything like a comprehensive ethical code to serve as a guide for those individuals working within the system of analytical psychology, we can, nevertheless, in examining his writings, uncover the salient features of the ethical dimension of his psychology of religion.

The most general, yet nonetheless important, moral challenge with which the individual is confronted is the moral challenge to accept consciously the responsibility of the individuation process itself. In that the individuation process is experienced as a task "imposed on us by nature," the task of individuation must, Jung suggests, be received "as a binding personal commitment."[83] Individuation is for Jung the challenge to become what one is virtually destined to become. It is the challenge to fulfil consciously the unique pattern of development that has existed in potential from the beginning and that nature now strives, through its compensatory activities, to lead one to realize.[84] Accordingly, within the Jungian worldview, the great and very real sin is the sin of unconsciousness.

A second feature of the ethical dimension of Jung's psychology of religion concerns a point made in the preceding section dealing with the experiential dimension. I am referring here to the need to ground in reality the insights one achieves through the encounter with the unconscious. "With the advance towards the psychological," Jung writes, "a great change sets in, for self-knowledge has certain ethical consequences which are not just impassively recognized but demand to be carried out in practice."[85] It is clear that for Jung this problem of making a reality of the insights one achieves through one's confrontation with the psychic material of the unconscious was a concern of the greatest ethical importance, and approached with exacting seriousness. "No matter how deeply absorbed or how blown about I was," Jung explains in his autobiography, "I always knew that everything I was experiencing was ultimately directed at this real life of mine. I meant to meet its obligations and fulfill its meanings."[86] For Jung the current of the unconscious ultimately seeks to find its way into reality. The flow of psychic energy is ultimately into life. On a rather small scale, there thus arises the ethical responsibility to bring the specific insights one achieves into reality. On a somewhat more grand scale, with the conscious emergence of the self, which may come to one with the intensity of a full religious conversion, there arises the ethical responsibility to communicate this experience directly to others. The feeling one has about such a religious experience, Jung suggests, is that one is "unable to remain alone with it."[87]

A third moral challenge, which is identified by Jung as being particularly demanding, is the problem of coming to terms with what he describes as the shadow. The shadow, which constitutes something of a secondary personality living in the unconscious, is the personification of the "hidden, repressed, [and] for the most part inferior and guilt-laden" aspects of the individual.[88] Accordingly, the shadow contains many of those qualities that one is all too ready to recognize in others but less able and willing to discover in oneself. Although one would suspect that these hidden traits are completely malicious and negative, it is not the case that they are. The shadow contains positive as well as negative traits and, moreover, consists of both personal and transpersonal elements.

With "shadow work," the basic objective is to bring these hidden aspects of the secondary personality within the scope of consciousness. Accordingly, as these psychic contents are raised to consciousness, one is able to withdraw that which previously was unconsciously projected onto others. This process of withdrawing one's projections is viewed by Jung to be of special importance for two reasons: first, because projections themselves "falsify the nature of the object," and second, because they contain items that are actually part of the individual's personality and should, therefore, be consciously restored to it.[89]

With the penetration of the shadow considerable negative side effects will be produced giving rise to "a good deal of confusion and mental darkness." Personality crises that were never experienced previously arise. The shadow, Jung explains, contains painful elements that initially entered its "wholesome darkness" with hopes of never again seeing the light of consciousness, and, accordingly, the "veils of illusion" must be removed with the greatest care.[90] Increasingly, one discovers that the peace and false sense of security that ignorance provides are the dear prices that one must pay for genuine self-knowledge. Clearly, one does not readily accept the painful inferior aspects of one's personality that this type of work brings to light. And, we should add to this, one does not always readily accept hidden talents, for these too present burdens of a different sort. Yet ultimately, one must come to accept these negative and positive personality traits that previously were recognizable only in others. Therefore, if shadow work is to be successful, considerable moral strength is required. As Jung relates: "The shadow is a moral problem that challenges the whole ego-personality, for no one can become conscious of the shadow without considerable moral effort."[91]

It should be noted here that the integration of the shadow is regarded by Jung as a prerequisite for the emergence of the contra-sexual image in its completeness, that is to say, for the full emergence of what Jung terms the anima in men and the animus in women.[92] In their undifferentiated states, the anima and animus are but weak imitations of the feminine principle of Eros, characterized by Jung as interweaving and relatedness, and the masculine principle of Logos, characterized by Jung as differentiating knowledge. Drawing attention to this point, Jung writes: "The anima of the man consists of inferior relatedness, full of affect . . . [and] the animus of woman consists of inferior judgements, or better said, opinions. . . . On a low level, the animus is an inferior logos, a caricature of the differentiated masculine mind, just as the anima, on a low level, is a caricature of the feminine eròs."[93] In their undifferentiated states, the anima and animus are contaminated with the inferior traits of the shadow and, therefore, are very underdeveloped expressions of their respective feminine and masculine principles. The unintegrated masculine shadow contaminates the anima with its inferior masculine traits, just as the animus is contaminated with inferior unintegrated aspects of the feminine shadow. A key objective of analytical work is, then, to facilitate the emergence of the complete contrasexual image. Ultimately, the goal is for men and women equally to be consciously related to both the masculine and feminine principles. Paradoxically, however, this is primarily achieved, particularly in the earlier stages of analytical work, not so much through direct involvement with someone of the opposite sex, but rather through the integration of the contents of one's own shadow.

Having the moral fortitude to acknowledge and accept the inferior personality within and in so doing ceasing to use others as the receptacles of our dark projections is a task that Jung regarded as of particular importance to the modern age. Wars, racism, and bigotry, Jung believed, arise out of the projections of the undifferentiated elements of the shadow. Individuals, accordingly, must assume the ethical responsibility to come to terms with the dark elements situated within their own natures, both personal and transpersonal, if there is ever to be an end to these sinister social and political problems. This, Jung repeatedly emphasized, is something not to be taken lightly, for left unchecked the projected darkness of the shadow could well precipitate the destruction of our civilization. People in the West, Jung wrote shortly before his death in 1961,

> have begun to realize that the difficulties confronting us are
> moral problems, and that attempts to answer them by a policy

of piling up nuclear arms or by economic "competition" is achieving little, for it cuts both ways. . . . It would be much more to the point for us to recognize our own shadow and its nefarious doings. If we could see our shadow . . . we should be immune to any moral and mental infection and insinuation. As matters now stand, we lay ourselves open to every infection, because we are really doing practically the same thing as *they.* Only we have the additional disadvantage that we neither see nor want to understand what we ourselves are doing, under the cover of good manners.[94]

Through his method of the integration of the shadow under the direction of the self Jung believed that he had developed a type of vaccine that would go far in protecting mankind from outbreaks of serious psychic infections such as bigotry, radical nationalism, racism, and war. Having what he believed to be the vaccine in hand, the source of real frustration for Jung was, however, what we might describe as the problem of its distribution. The problem of how the vaccine might be made available, and the additional problem of whether time would provide sufficient allowance for its distribution, were two problems that were unquestionably of great concern to Jung right up to the very end of his life.

For those who consciously assume the burden of the integration of the shadow there emerges a more reality-based moral framework. This new moral framework is one that does not seek a perfectionistic absolute goodness by splitting off the darkness of one's nature, thereby making the latter far more destructive than it otherwise would be. Rather, it is a framework that encompasses both the dark and light factors, valuing, in this way, wholeness over perfection. For Jung the light and dark principles are equally real factors in nature. Both entwine in the compensatory pattern of the whole, and the great task of modernity is to find a moral position that is commensurate with this reality. Commenting further on this point, Jung writes:

Integration cannot take place and be put to a useful purpose unless one can admit the tendencies bound up with the shadow and allow them some measure of realization—tempered, of course, with the necessary criticism. This leads to disobedience and self-disgust, but also to self-reliance, without which individuation is unthinkable. The ability to "will otherwise" must, unfortunately, be real if ethics are to make any sense at all. Anyone who submits to the law from the start, or to what is generally expected, acts like the man in the parable who buried his talent in the earth. Individuation is an exceedingly difficult task: it always involves a conflict of duties, whose solution requires us to understand that our "counter-will" is also an aspect of God's will.[95]

No doubt Jung's most serious point of contention with Christianity was with what he regarded as its failure to recognize that that which we experience as the dark and evil aspects of nature are as much a manifestation of God as that which we regard as the good. Jung, as is well known, took particular issue with the Catholic doctrine of the *privatio boni*, which characterizes evil as the privation of good. This doctrine, Jung felt, completely deprives evil, which is certainly real enough for anyone living in this world, of its substance.[96] Rather than the *privatio boni*, Jung favored the Chinese theory of the yin and yang which he regarded "to be closer to the truth" in its characterization of the reality of evil and in its description of the interplay in phenomenal reality of the light and dark forces. Jung found the yin/yang theory especially suitable because "it does not damage monotheism in any way, since it [ultimately] unites the opposites just as yang and yin are united in Tao (which the Jesuits quite logically translated as 'God')."[97]

In contrast to the Chinese worldview, the problem for Jung with the Christian one, which he regarded as being based on "a flight from nature," is that it has given rise to a morality that stands as an actual obstacle, a moral barrier, to the integration of the opposites.[98] The problem of this moral obstacle, Jung believed, is particularly evidenced in the split that is to be found in Christianity between the body and the spirit—a position that has done among other things great injury to the feminine principle and left sexuality split off from the higher consciousness that emerges through the pursuit of self-knowledge. What is really needed, Jung believed, and indeed what is actually being widely sought by people today, is for this oppressive moral barrier to be shattered and a new morality produced that reconciles the individual to nature. In the search for this new understanding, we arrive at what is perhaps the greatest moral problem of the analysis of the unconscious. It is the moral problem of coming to terms with the dark forces of nature—forces that for Jung demand, like all other manifestations of God, to be consciously integrated.

Social Dimension

Developing an understanding of the social dimension of Jung's psychology of religion is not something easily accomplished, as this aspect of the Jungian worldview lends itself to very divergent interpretations. It could be argued, for example, that from the Jungian perspective the collective consciousness, by which Jung means the societal consciousness (not to be confused with the collective unconscious), is a menacing element and the further removed one is from it, the better off one is. With this position one would have to look hard to find any notion of social responsibility. On the other hand, it could be argued that in the Jungian worldview there is a very definite sense of social responsibility, albeit a unique and different one. This argument, I believe, is closer to the truth of Jung's position as it exists in the context of his writings as a whole. With this second interpretation, the qualifying factor is that social action is to arise out of the pursuit of one's psychological wholeness. There must, therefore, be no blind sacrifices of one's personal values and insights to those of the collective consciousness. Psychological wholeness and social action are to be inseparably linked.

In the above, we have two positions which are seemingly incommensurable. It is the case, however, that these two positions have a common denominator, for both are attempts to resolve the same problem: the problem of how the introvert is to come to terms with the potentially self-alienating phenomenon of the collective consciousness. With the first position described above, there is the reaction of panic and fear and the need for safe distancing. With the second position, however, there is an attempt at striking a compromise, without, of course, bargaining away too much in the process. For the introvert the collective consciousness presents a particularly unique challenge, and this is the problem with which the social dimension of the Jungian worldview is largely concerned. Commenting on the differences that exist in the points of view of the introvert and extravert as regards their sense of relationship to the collective, Jung writes:

The man with the extraverted attitude bases himself primarily on social relationships; the other, the introvert, primarily on the subjective factor. The former is largely unaware of his subjective determinacy and regards it as insignificant; as a matter of fact, he is frightened of it. The latter has little or no interest in social relationships; he prefers to ignore them, feeling them to be onerous, even terrifying. To the one, the world of relationships is the important thing. . . . The other is primarily concerned with the inner pattern of his life, with his own self-consistency.[99]

Whereas the introvert's life meaning is found in relationship to the inner world, the world of the unconscious, the extravert is an individual whose meaning emerges through his encounter with the outer objects and events of his life. Jung was himself, of course, a radical introvert, and there can be no question that his psychology bears the stamp of the introvert. "My life," Jung begins his autobiography, immediately drawing his reader's attention to his introverted orientation, "is a story of the self-realization of the unconscious. Everything in the unconscious seeks outward manifestation, and the personality too desires to evolve out of its unconscious conditions and to experience itself as a whole."[100] One of the most striking features in Jung's autobiography is the absence of outward events, particularly his relationships with friends and colleagues, and one is led to believe that his outward life was, as Jaffé misleadingly asserts, "relatively uneventful." This, however, was not at all the case, for judged by the standard of the lives of most individuals, Jung's outward life was indeed very eventful. The real point to be made here, and this is the point that Jaffé wishes to make, is that the outward events primarily had meaning for Jung when they were viewed in relationship to his inner development. From the point of view of the introvert, these "external incidents appear merely as milestones, over which Jung's spiritual development arched in broad curves."[101]

The primary problem, then, that Jung grapples with in the social dimension of his psychology of religion is the problem of how the introvert is to come to terms with the collective and hopefully contribute to it without sacrificing his own search for wholeness in the process. For many, with the apparent absence here of self-sacrifice in the normal sense of the word, this position of Jung's may not meet the requirements of genuine social consciousness, yet for Jung we must understand that it does. To understand better the fine line that one is required to walk to meet these objectives, we shall now turn to examine more specifically the problem of individual versus collective functioning as it exists in the Jungian worldview.

One of Jung's greatest concerns with mass social and political movements was with what he perceived to be their vulnerability to possession by archetypal forces. This problem, Jung believed more-over, demands our closest attention because it is a problem specific to the modern period. Prior to the Reformation, Jung told his audi-ence during his Terry Lectures at Yale University, the Catholic church provided a protective shield against the type of archetypal psychic epidemics that have arisen in recent history, such as the "murderous outburst of Bolshevistic ideas" and the developments, then underway in 1937, in Nazi Germany.[102] These events, Jung ex-plained, stem from collective archetypal inflations that in the pre-Reformation period would have been contained by the highly structured spiritual retort of the Catholic church. In the absense of such a spiritual container for the archetypal forces of the psyche, these religiously charged energies, Jung argued, are destructively released in mass movements taking full possession of their adherents.

With regard to Jung's above argument, a point that consider-ably undermines his view about the protective role played by the Catholic church is the fact that the pre-Reformation period was not itself immune to such psychic epidemics. This point is taken up by Volodmyr Odajnyk in his book *Jung and Politics*. As Odajnyk ex-plains, "Such epidemics are not a unique product of the present century, and they need not always take a political form. The Cru-sades and the numerous millenarian movements of the Middle Ages are also instances of mass psychic inflation. The presence of a religion that allows for the expression of irrational and unconscious forces is not alone sufficient to prevent mass psychoses; the move-ments simply take a religious form." The important point, however, to which Jung has drawn our attention, Odajnyk goes on to explain, is that a definite relationship exists between the appearance of mass social, political, and religious crises and the activation of archetypal forces which, when left unchecked, will take the form of highly de-structive psychic epidemics.[103] What we must therefore attempt to do is to discover how we can arrest these dangerous developments before they reach levels where they are completely out of control. With regard to the psychological dimension of this problem, the Jungian understanding offers considerable help.

For Jung, the individual in the mass invariably loses ground both morally and spiritually.[104] In the group, Jung suggests, an in-ferior collective intelligence and morality emerges that tends to plunge to even lower depths as the size of the group increases.[105] With the increase in the size of a group, moreover, there is a corre-sponding decrease in individual consciousness until it reaches the point as with very large groups where individual consciousness is virtually eliminated. "The bigger the group," Jung explains, "the more the individuals composing it function as a collective entity"[106] and, we could add as Jung would, the lower also their level of collective morality and intelligence.

In dealing with the collective consciousness, the Jungian watchword is vigilance—vigilance against unconscious identification with the values of the collective, which stand directly in opposition to the highly differentiated and personalized values that are characteristic of the process of individuation. "The criterion of adulthood," Jung writes, reflecting this sentiment, "does not consist in being a member of certain sects, groups, or nations, but in submitting to the spirit of one's own independence."[107] In contrast to the relative ease with which one can slip into a state of collective identification, the differentiation of the personality is an intensely demanding undertaking. Collective functioning and thinking is always an easier route for the individual and, accordingly, "there is always a great temptation to allow collective functioning to take the place of individual differentiation of the personality." There is also the danger, after having gained a good deal of ground in the struggle for a higher level of consciousness, of backsliding, that is to say, surrendering one's spiritual insights, acquiescing to the collective consciousness out of laziness or simply to avoid further conflict. Jung suggests that Peter's denial is something of a symbol of such a regression.[108] In his denial of Jesus when confronted by the hostile collective, what Peter in effect did, Jung would argue, was to deny his unique spiritual understanding, the higher consciousness he had achieved through his relationship with Jesus.

For Jung spiritual wholeness arises primarily out of one's unique and highly personalized encounter with the unconscious, and we could thus say with Goldbrunner that essentially Jung leads his analysands "to individual religion as the way of salvation."[109] Individuation does indeed present what is perhaps an unprecedented opportunity for the differentiation of the personality and a highly personalized experience of spiritual wholeness. It is important to realize, however, that Jung never believed that one can individuate cut off from society and the warmth and conflicts of genuine human interaction. Jung certainly never advocated withdrawal from the world as we find in certain religious traditions. The realities of social contact and friendship are essential to the individuation process. Jung, as Barbara Hannah reports, often made the point that one cannot individuate on Mt. Everest.[110] Individuation is a process of differentiation, but it is also a process of gathering in through the penetration of one's own personality. As one's experience of oneself broadens, so too does one's experience of relationship to others. Jung thus writes about individuation that it "does not shut one out from the world, but gathers the world to oneself."[111]

Although it is the case that within the Jungian worldview spiritual wholeness primarily is sought through a highly personalized encounter with the unconscious, Jung, nevertheless, did appreciate the fact that for some individuals the group itself would serve as the vehicle of their religious awakening. An interesting point related to this is that Jung himself played a critical role in the sequence of events that led up to the formation of Alcoholics Anonymous. "Alcohclics Anonymous," as Ellenberger puts it, "indirectly owes its origin to Jung."[112]

Around 1931, Jung treated an American patient, Roland H., who was suffering with an alcohol problem. The therapy, it seems, lasted for about one year, but little ground was gained, for shortly afterward he relapsed. Roland H. then returned to Jung seeking further treatment. Jung, however, told him that analytical therapy was not the answer to his problem. Roland H. then asked if Jung saw any hope whatsoever for his problem; to which Jung replied that he could see hope only in the possibility of a spiritual experience that might serve to "remotivate him entirely." With this advice of Jung's in mind, Roland H. joined the Oxford Group and was subsequently the subject of a conversion experience. Roland H. then turned to helping other alcoholics. In November of 1934, one of the men helped by Roland H., Eddy, contacted his friend Bill, who also had a drinking problem and was considered to be beyond help. "Bill subsequently had a religious experience and a vision of a society of alcoholics transmitting their experience from one to the other. Eddy and Bill then founded the Society of Alcoholics Anonymous whose subsequent development is known."[113]

Some thirty years later, in response to a letter sent to him by William G. Wilson, "Bill W.," Jung could reflect again on the case of Roland H. The alcohol problem of Roland H., Jung wrote in his letter dated January 30, 1961, "was the equivalent on a low level of the spiritual thirst of our being for wholeness." Roland H., Jung told his correspondent, was seeking a spiritual experience that had to happen to him in reality. There are, Jung continued, three possibilities for such an experience: first, through an act of grace, that is, a completely spontaneous religious conversion; second, "through a personal and honest contact with friends," such as is found in groups like Alcoholics Anonymous; and third, through an educational experience that is "beyond the confines of mere rationalism," such as is found in the analysis of the unconscious. "I see from your letter," Jung commented to Bill W., "that Roland H. has chosen the second way, which was, under the circumstances, obviously the best one."[114]

In conclusion, it should be emphasized that Jung does not subscribe to the position that the individual has no responsibility to the collective. Jung believes that the individual most certainly does. The actual way in which this social responsibility is to be fulfilled is, however, that which particularly distinguishes Jung's position. From the Jungian perspective progressive social change can only grow out of the genuine psychological wholeness of the individual. Jung, von Franz states, "never got tired of emphasizing again and again that every change must begin with the individual himself and not with trying to improve other people; the latter he regarded as a display of the power complex."[115] One can only uplift others morally and spiritually when one is in possession of the genuine thing oneself. The objective, then, is for the individual to develop himself in such a way that he will have sufficient self-understanding and wisdom to thus influence the social order. It is the case, however, that in order for this approach to be successful, the process of self-preparation itself must be undertaken, as Jung emphasizes, with great exactness, so that when it comes to the test, when one stands face-to-face with the collective, one is as organized in one's individuality as the society concerned is itself organized in its collective consciousness.[116]

Mythological Dimension

One of the lamentable trends of the modern period, Jung felt, is the tendency to view the mythological dimension of experience, particularly the mythological dimension of religious experience, as something that is irrelevant, meaningless, and expendable. In great contrast to this, for Jung myth is the unique bearer of the truths of the various religious and secular worldviews and in this way is irreplaceable. Just as psychic development requires symbols that point beyond themselves, thus drawing the individual to higher levels of consciousness, so too, Jung believed, do our worldviews require the presence of myths that as collective symbolical representations direct us toward higher levels of understanding.

It is clear that for Jung the Christian myth held particular significance. Not only did he view it as the central religious myth of the Western worldview, but he saw in it, moreover, a type of definitive symbolical depiction of his own concept of the individuation process. Given this, it is not surprising that Jung, after having watched the Christian myth sink to great depths of neglect in recent times, took it upon himself to salvage this myth, using as the instruments of this work his analytical insights. Specifically, this salvage operation entailed demonstrating the importance of the Christian myth "as an expression of intrapsychic processes."[117]

Essentially, what Jung sought to do was to free the Christian myth from its dependence on a distant historical context by uncovering its immediate, living, archetypal reality as found in the symbolisms of the unconscious processes. The myth of the Incarnation of God, the suffering of the God-man in this world, his crucifixion and resurrection is, Jung sought to demonstrate, a living archetypal drama that is actually being enacted in the lives of us all. From the Jungian perspective this archetypal drama so magnificently depicted in the Christian myth is indeed the ongoing struggle of the conscious and the unconscious, the ego and the self. It is at once the suffering and the joy associated with both the ego's struggle for higher levels of consciousness and the self's relentless desire for incarnation in this life. Commenting on this, Jung writes:

> Because individuation is an heroic and often tragic task . . . it involves suffering, a passion of the ego: the ordinary, empirical man we once were is burdened with the fate of losing himself in a greater dimension and being robbed of his fancied freedom of will. He suffers, so to speak, from the violence done to him by the self. The analogous passion of Christ signifies God's suffering on account of the injustice of the world and the darkness of man. The human and divine suffering set up a relationship of complementarity with compensating effects. Through the Christ-symbol, man can get to know the real meaning of his suffering. . . . The cause of the suffering is in both cases the same, namely, "incarnation," which on the human level appears as "individuation." . . . The drama of the archetypal life of Christ describes in symbolic images the events in the conscious life [life of the ego]—as well as in the life that transcends consciousness [life of the self]—of a man who has been transformed by his higher destiny.[118]

Given the very great differences in the points of view of the ego and the self, it is not surprising that the entrance of the latter from the archetypal world into the world of ego-consciousness often results in experiences of tremendous conflict and chaos. From the point of view of the ego, these unexpected compensatory intrusions of the omnipotent and omniscient self into its world can very well appear as acts of violence against it. The *"experience of the self,"* Jung writes with this in mind, *"is always a defeat for the ego."*[119] The only real thing in doubt, it seems, is how great a defeat the ego must suffer. With regard to the self's experience, there too is a suffering, but this time it is the suffering that stems from the surrender of an otherworldly, undifferentiated state of perfection in favor of the search for differentiation and conscious wholeness amidst the darkness, limitations, and imperfection of a time- and space-bound existence. This suffering is perhaps that to which William Blake refers when he writes in his poem addressed to God, "If you have form'd a Circle to go into, Go into it yourself and see how you would do."[120] For Jung, this suffering, the suffering associated with the descent of the self into life, is the very suffering associated with the humanization of God in the person of Christ.

Speaking with an acquaintance at his home in Kusnacht in 1938, Jung, reflecting on this problem of suffering, commented that in the East the objective is to eliminate suffering "by casting it off," whereas in the West people resort to drugs seeking to suppress it. Suffering, Jung continued, is a serious problem and we must seek to overcome it, yet in actual fact the "only way to overcome it is to endure it." This, Jung told his guest as he pointed to a stained glass depiction of the crucifixion of Christ, we learn "only from him."[121]

For Jung it is the case that in this life the clash of the opposites is relentless. This struggle will never be eliminated, for it is part of the reality of the life process itself. "Complete redemption from the sufferings of this world," Jung accordingly writes, "is and must remain an illusion."[122] There is, however, a way to keep suffering from dominating one's life completely. This we can do, Jung argues, by accepting suffering as a necessary concomitant of our spiritual rebirth. The neurotic, by contrast, loses all touch with the meaning underlying his suffering and thus falls into ever more fearful depths of regression, moving at the same time further away from the place where his redemption must be secured, this life.[123] " 'Redemption,' " Jung explains, "does not mean that a burden is taken from one's shoulders which one was never meant to bear."[124] Redemption means, rather, to bear that burden with consciousness, that is to say, in conscious relationship to the personal and archetypal meaning that is seeking to find its way into this world through such suffering.

One cannot help but think here of the observations of the psychiatrist Viktor Frankl, who spent three years in Nazi concentration camps. Death, Frankl observed, came quickly to those for whom life had been completely deprived of meaning. The key to survival, Frankl came to see, was for the individual to find amidst the suffering with which he was surrounded and personally endured daily a meaning that was uniquely his own. Nietzsche, Frankl writes, expresses the essential point when he states, " 'He who has a *why* to live for can bear with almost any *how*.' " "Life," Frankl reflects, expanding further on this idea,

> ultimately means taking the responsibility to find the right answer to its problems and to fulfil the tasks which it constantly sets for each individual. . . . No man and no destiny can be compared with any other man or any other destiny. No situation repeats itself. . . . Sometimes the situation in which a man finds himself may require him to shape his own fate by action. At other times it is more advantageous for him to make use of an opportunity for contemplation. . . . Sometimes a man may be required simply to accept fate, bear his cross. . . . When a man finds that it is his destiny to suffer, he will have to accept his suffering as his task. He will have to acknowledge the fact that in his suffering he is unique and alone in the universe. No one can relieve him of his suffering or suffer in his place. His unique opportunity lies in the way in which he bears his burden.[125]

As with Frankl, for Jung the cross is the place where at once there is to be found both intense suffering and fulfilment. In the symbol of Christ on the cross, Jung believes moreover, we enter a sacred mandala in which man and God, the ego and the self, unite in both their sufferings and in their experiences of the ultimate fulfilment of their deepest meanings. Here the desire of the self for incarnation painfully assumes its most finite form. Nailed to the cross, it voluntarily submits itself to the suffering of time- and space-bound reality. Here the desire of the ego for self-knowledge attains its point of complete balance as it holds in consciousness the tremendous tension of the powerfully constellated opposites while opening itself at the same time to the wholeness of the personal

.rchetypal meaning of its suffering and unique destiny. Here is the point in space and time where the ego and the self, amidst suffering and imperfection, conjoin in a sacred circle of meaning and attain fulfilment, the resurrection.

Conclusion

It is clear that Jung's way of interpreting the Christian myth, his way of salvaging it with psychological insight, is something that is welcomed by some and a source of considerable concern for others. For some Jung opens up a new dimension of meaning; the Christian myth is now shown to stand in special relationship to the psychological experiences of each individual. For others, however, it is feared that Jung's interpretation closes off a level of meaning that they before took great comfort in; is it the case, they wonder, that Jung's interpretation inadvertently, or even possibly deliberately, serves to discredit the objective reality of the events described?

The problem raised here is a problem, of course, that is not confined to Jung's treatment of the Christian myth; it is rather a problem that is central to Jung's psychology of religion as a whole, as presented in this chapter. The central problem of Jung's intrapsychic model of the psychology of religion is that in opening up a completely new dimension of meaning through interpreting religious experience as a phenomenon of psychological processes, it also seems to cut off, with the same stroke, the level of meaning associated with the objective reality of these events. With reference to this problem, Homans speaks of a type of "double movement of reduction and retrieval" in Jung's psychology of religion. There is a reductive movement, but it is, Homans suggests, a movement that Jung regards as necessary for the new emergence of religious meaning:

> By applying his core process [individuation] to traditional Christianity, Jung in effect created a double movement of reduction and retrieval of meaning. In one sense he *was* reductive. . . . All the major tenets of Christianity were interpreted as instances of archetypes in the collective unconscious. . . . But Jung's psychology contained a second movement. . . . Once the reductive movement had been made—once the psychological meaning of doctrine had been disclosed—then Jung proceeded to clothe these constructs with positive meaning and value. . . . He claimed that the archetypes and the individuation process, though not part of the vocabulary of the

traditional Christian, nevertheless captured the hidden essence of that tradition.[126]

Jung's approach may indeed open up new levels of religious meaning and understanding; nevertheless, the problem of whether or not Jung's psychology of religion reduces religious experience strictly to intrapsychic processes is a problem that for many represents a sizable question mark about how Jung's contribution is ultimately to be received. There are some who have no doubt that for Jung religious experience is strictly a phenomenon of the processes of the conscious and the unconscious. From this group there has arisen the accusation against Jung of psychologism, by which is meant the tendency to reduce religious experience strictly to the intrapsychic level. About this charge David Wulff writes: "Freud won the disapprobation of theologians for presuming to judge religion an illusion. . . . Jung has likewise been sharply criticized for foreclosing the question of religion's objective validity."[127] Similarly, G. S. Spinks remarks with reference to Jung's emphasis on the psychical reality of God through his concept of the self, "How these psychological facts are to be related to 'objective' truth is a question that remains unanswered."[128] Raymond Hostie, on the other hand, feeling that Jung's position on this matter is too unclear to draw conclusions, makes the point that some of Jung's "disciples have not been afraid to exploit his ambiguities in favour of an out-and-out psychologism."[129]

Those familiar with Jung's writings in the area of the psychology of religion know that the charge of psychologism was no small source of annoyance for Jung. Indeed, there are few papers written by Jung dealing with the psychology of religion wherein the author does not take up his own defense against what he regarded as this highly malicious and groundless charge. In his commentary on *The Tibetan Book of the Great Liberation*, Jung, for instance, questions the motives of his accusers. This accusation, Jung argues, stems from the common fear in the West of experiencing the religious dimension within. "Anyone," Jung bitterly writes, "who dares to establish a connection between the psyche and the idea of God is immediately accused of 'psychologism' or suspected of morbid 'mysticism.' "[130] Jung clearly felt that he was greatly maligned by the charge of psychologism. The question we might now address is then, was he?

In his defense against the charge of psychologism Jung often would make the point that his science is a "science of mere phenomena without any metaphysical implications."[131] It is a science, Jung would have us believe, that concerns itself solely with the empirical facts, the observable phenomena of religious experience as opposed to metaphysical or philosophical problems. "Inasmuch as religion," Jung writes in his own defense, "has a very important psychological aspect, I deal with it from a purely empirical point of view, that is, I eschew any metaphysical or philosophical considerations."[132] What Jung is here saying, in effect, in using this as his defense against the psychologism charge is that his concern is solely with the study of religious symbols as they spontaneously arise in the course of the individuation process. He is not concerned with attempting to account for the origins of these symbols, but rather satisfied simply to study them as they present themselves. The fact of their presence in the psyche, Jung argues, is of great import for both psychology and religion. It is a psychological presence, Jung suggests, we can note without at the same time doing any damage to traditional religious notions of their origin.

Well, if this was Jung's position there would really be no grounds for the accusation of psychologism. As has already been demonstrated in this work, however, this was not the extent of Jung's analysis of the symbols of religious experience, for Jung concerns himself with accounting for the origins of these religious symbols, and he does this through his concept of the archetypal unconscious. And it is this further step that Jung takes that really creates the problem. "Psychology," Jung writes, giving expression to what some consider to be the more alarming side of his psychology of religion, " . . . treats all metaphysical claims and assertions as mental phenomena, and regards them as statements about the mind and its structure that derive ultimately from certain unconscious dispositions."[133] These "unconscious dispositions" are, of course, the archetypes. Goldbrunner, accordingly, perceiving this line of argument in Jung's work, has no hesitation himself in supporting the psychologism charge. "If we remove the husks of the various religions," Goldbrunner writes about Jung's psychology of religion, "what remains is the autonomous, purposeful, one might say, absolute life of the psyche as the divine ground. . . . All assertions about the other world, the world beyond, the Kingdom of God, grace and miracles are projections of unconscious spiritual contents. . . . In the language of science this thinking of Jung's must be called psychologism."[134]

It is one thing for Jung to say that he is solely concerned with the study of the phenomenology of religious experience, and yet another thing to assert that religious experience ultimately derives from the archetypal level of the psyche. It is this latter position that gives credence to the charge of psychologism. In defense against the charge of psychologism, Jung cannot claim to be confining his venture into the psychology of religion to the study of the phenomenology of its symbols. Jung goes beyond that level of interpretation. Clearly, in reducing religious phenomena to the archetypes of the collective unconscious, intrapsychic factors, Jung gives us what Smart refers to as a projectionistic theory of religion, something Smart notes that sociology serves up in a somewhat different form in that it sees the projection as arising not from unconscious factors but from social ones.[135]

If the model of Jung's psychology of religion that we have been examining in this chapter were Jung's sole model by which he accounts for religious experience, the charge of psychologism would, I believe, be justified. It is not the case, however, that this is his only model. In this chapter, we have been examining what I have for the purposes of this study described as the intrapsychic model of Jung's psychology of religion. Certainly for most individuals, after having been very much led to believe so by Jung himself, this is understood to constitute Jung's one and only model of his psychology of religion. This is the model to which they refer in their analyses of Jung's position. As we now turn to study the synchronicity concept, the assumption that this is Jung's sole model of religious experience shall be proven wrong and the attendant accusation of psychologism shall be shown to be unjustified, for we shall see that through the synchronicity concept a completely new frontier in Jung's psychology is opened up leading us into a new, largely uncharted area of his psychology of religion beyond the strictly intrapsychic model.

The Synchronicity Theory: A Systematic Study 🍎

In chapter 1 of this work, in the section dealing with the doctrinal dimension of Jung's psychology of religion, consideration was given to Jung's theory of the archetype. The archetype, it was pointed out, is a factor in the unconscious that produces symbols related to its ground theme. In that these representations, the archetypal images, are but variations of the archetype's ground theme, it is of the greatest importance that these specific images not be confused with the archetype as such. In addition to this, it was also explained that taken as a total phenomenon, the archetypal unconscious is, among other things, regarded by Jung as the matrix of the numerous symbols of the religions and myths of mankind.

In this chapter, we shall begin by turning once again to Jung's concept of the archetype, this time to investigate Jung's description of the archetype as a "psychoid" factor. Jung's writings on the psychoid aspect of the archetype, which were very much shaped by his study of synchronistic phenomena, constitute the climax of his theorizing about the archetype. Accordingly, like the synchronicity theory itself, they stand on the farthest reaches of Jung's thought.

Central to Jung's theory of the psychoid archetype is his long-held view that in the collective unconscious there are two complementary types of energies at work: one of which gives rise to typical patterns of behavior, the other of which gives rise to typical patterns of perception and understanding. In his earlier writings, Jung associated these innate tendencies with the instincts and archetypes, respectively. With the development of his concept of the psychoid archetype, however, Jung came to locate these two energies within the archetype itself.

Reflecting his earlier formulation, Jung, in 1919 in his essay "Instinct and the Unconscious," described the collective unconscious as consisting of both instincts and archetypes. *"Instincts,"*

Jung explained in his essay, *"are typical modes of action, and wherever we meet with uniform and regularly recurring modes of action and reaction we are dealing with instinct. . . . Archetypes are typical modes of apprehension, and wherever we meet with uniform and regularly recurring modes of apprehension we are dealing with an archetype."*[1]

One of the outstanding features of Jung's paper "Instinct and the Unconscious" is the high degree of complementarity he ascribes to the instincts and archetypes. "It seems to me," Jung writes about the instinct and archetype, "that both are aspects of the same vital activity, which we have to think of as two distinct processes simply for the purpose of better understanding."[2] In illustration of his point, Jung cites the "incredibly refined instinct of propagation in the yucca moth," which only once in its life, and on the sole evening in which the flowers of the yucca plant open, must shape the pollen of one flower into a pellet and insert in into the pistil of a second flower. It is as if the yucca moth, Jung writes, drawing his reader's attention to the mutual complementarity of instinct and archetype, "must carry within it an image, as it were, of the situation that 'trigger's off' its instinct. This image enables it to 'recognize' the yucca flower and its structure."[3]

In his book *Archetype*, Anthony Stevens provides what is perhaps an even better example of Jung's above characterization of the complementary interplay between an innate pattern of behavior (instinct) and an innate pattern of perception (archetype). "If you hatch out a clutch of baby chicks," Stevens explains, "and then pull a wooden model of a flying hawk over their heads they will crouch down against the ground and emit cries of alarm. This is an ancient defensive response, and it is innate. Moreover, one can raise generations of chicks without ever exposing them to a hawk—real or wooden—without extinguishing the response." In 1939, Stevens continues, David Lack, a British ornithologist, sent thirty caged finches from the Galapagos Islands to a colleague in California. In the Galapagos Islands, the finches had been spared for thousands of years from exposure to predatory birds simply because on the islands there were none. Still, when the finches arrived in California and saw a predatory bird "such as a raven or a red-tailed hawk," the finches cringed and cried out in alarm. "The 'predator archetype,' " Stevens concludes, "had lain dormant in the 'collective unconscious' of these birds for something approaching a million years. Yet, when the appropriate stimulus was encountered in the environment, the archetype was at once activated, with its related behavior patterns and, one may infer, the experience of fear."[4]

Much as the "predator archetype" lay dormant in the finches yet came fully into play when they were confronted with outward danger, Jung maintains that in the psyches of human beings there too are innate patterns of behavior and meaning which, in accordance with the compensatory needs of the individual, similarly become activated to facilitate human adaptation. "Just as his instincts compel man to a specifically human mode of existence," Jung explains, "so the archetypes force his ways of perception and apprehension into specifically human patterns."[5] In the course of decades of work as an analyst, Jung observed and studied the spontaneous emergence of such patterns, which followed themes of universal significance such as dismemberment and renewal, wholeness and self-realization, the God-man, the hero, the mandala, initiatory ordeals and rites of passage, the great mother, death and rebirth, the wise old man, the hostile brothers, the birth of the hero, the trickster figure, and spiritual journeys of ascent and descent, to name but a few examples. These themes, which were paralleled in the myths and religious symbols of mankind yet arose spontaneously in the dreams and visions of his patients, were the factors upon which Jung built his theory of the collective unconscious. Just as Lack's colleague in California had witnessed in the finches the emergence of a pattern of behavior and apprehension that was not based on any process of learning but nevertheless was essential to the maintenance of their survival, so too Jung had witnessed over the years the spontaneous, compensatory emergence of equally innate patterns of behavior and apprehension—patterns that served in times of crisis to direct his analysands to points of balance—patterns that more generally intervened to bring about a higher synthesis of the personality through the provision of universally valid courses of action and thought.

In his essay "Instinct and the Unconscious," Jung therefore describes the collective unconscious as consisting of the discontinuous yet functionally complementary instincts and archetypes. This model seemed to work well for Jung in the beginning; however, in 1946 Jung felt that a further revision of his theoretical model of the archetype was needed. This revision, which constitutes Jung's final position on the nature of the archetype, was outlined in the essay "On the Nature of the Psyche."

In his paper "On the Nature of the Psyche," Jung returns to the theme of the functional complementarity of instinct and archetype as outlined in his "Instinct and the Unconscious"; his discussion of this theme, however, is given a significant theoretical twist.

Rather than characterize instinct and archetype as complementary but discontinuous factors as he did in "Instinct and the Unconscious", in his new theoretical model, Jung views these two factors as part of a continuum. Laying the groundwork for this theoretical shift, Jung writes: "Archetype and instinct are the most polar opposites imaginable, as can easily be seen when one compares a man who is ruled by his instinctual drives with a man who is seized by the spirit. But, just as between all opposites there obtains so close a bond that no position can be established or even thought of without its corresponding negation, so in this case also 'les extremes se touchent.' "[6] We need only think, Jung further explains, drawing attention to the affinity of the opposites of instinct and spirit, of the close relationship that emerges in religious phenomenology between what are supposed to be the "deadly enemies" of physical and spiritual passion. In reality, Jung suggests, these "enemies" are indeed "brothers-in-arms, for which reason it often needs the merest touch to convert the one into the other."[7]

Essentially, what Jung is attempting to develop and indeed achieves in his paper "On the Nature of the Psyche" is a theoretical model that more accurately portrays the compensatory interplay of the innate patterns of action and the innate patterns of apprehension or meaning in the collective unconscious. Accordingly, rather than speak of the complementary yet discontinuous opposites of instinct and archetype as he did in "Instinct and the Unconscious," Jung proposes that the psychoid archetype be regarded as a continuum within which is contained the instinctual tendency, that is, the innate pattern of action, and that which he previously referred to as the archetypal tendency but now characterizes as spirit, that is, the innate pattern of meaning. The archetype itself is, then, now understood by Jung to be something of a progressive synthesis of the two factors of instinct and spirit.

Using color symbolism to emphasize his point, Jung explains that if we are to associate instinct with the color red and spirit with the color blue, then the appropriate color for the psychoid archetype would be violet. "Violet," Jung writes, "is the 'mystic' colour, and it certainly reflects the indubitably 'mystic' or paradoxical quality of the archetype in a most satisfactory way. Violet is a compound of blue and red, although in the spectrum it is a colour in its own right."[8] Violet is the appropriate color for the archetype because although the archetype contains within it the energies of pure instinct and pure spirit, it is a numinous dynamism that transcends the tensions of these opposites. As a psychoid factor, the archetype, therefore, is understood to constitute a spiritual force in its own right—spiritual not in the sense of pure spirit, but rather as a dynamism of spirit that is grounded in instinct.

Certainly one of the key factors behind Jung's above-described formulation was his understanding that instinct is never integrated directly but is raised to consciousness only indirectly through the archetypal image "which signifies and at the same time evokes the instinct, although in a form quite different from the one we meet on the biological level." This is necessarily the case because as one moves closer to the condition of pure instinct, the light of consciousness diminishes proportionately. In the extreme, pure instinctuality eliminates consciousness completely.[9] There is a fine point to be made here in connection with attempts to heighten body experience. The common tendency is to give free rein to the instincts. This, however, only serves to pull the individual, as Jung relates, into "unconsciousness without taking . . . anything of the light of the spirit into the darkness of the body."[10] Rather than give free rein to the instincts, what the individual must do is to follow the lead of the compensatory images of the unconscious, and utilizing the light of consciousness, actively bring about a conscious synthesis of instinct and spirit. In giving theoretical expression, therefore, to the important point that the assimilation of instinct takes place through the archetypal image, and that the compensatory activities of the unconscious ultimately seek to facilitate a spiritual wholeness, characterized as a state in which spirit is grounded in instinct, Jung situated the energies of instinct and spirit in the continuum of his expanded model of the archetype.

A second key development that prepared the way for Jung's interlinking of the energies of instinct and spirit in the continuum of the archetype was Jung's recognition of the archetype as a psychoid, that is to say, psychophysical factor. This particular theoretical development was a direct outcome of Jung's observations of synchronistic phenomena—observations that led Jung to take the critical step of situating the physiologically based instinct and the archetypal image within the same psychophysical continuum. "Since psyche and matter," Jung writes,

> are contained in one and the same world, and moreover are in continuous contact with one another and ultimately rest on irrepresentable, transcendental factors, it is not only possible but fairly probable, even, that psyche and matter are two different aspects of one and the same thing. The synchronicity phenom-

ena point, it seems to me, in this direction, for they show that the nonpsychic can behave like the psychic, and vice versa, without there being any causal connection between them.[11]

It is clear that Jung believed that through his study of synchronistic phenomena, which pointed toward an identity of psyche and matter, he was travelling along a path that ran parallel with the one being followed by researchers in the area of modern physics. Both analytical psychology, through its study of the psyche and synchronistic phenomena, and microphysics, through its investigation of the unknown side of matter, have, Jung felt, "developed concepts which display remarkable analogies."[12] Of particular interest to Jung were the contributions made by physics to our understanding of the nature of the phenomenal world.

It is certainly the case that the findings of the new physics have served to refute many of the basic concepts of the Newtonian worldview. In modern physics, space and time are not absolute, the notion of elementary solid particles has been shattered, and along with it the concept of the "strictly causal nature of physical phenomena."[13] In contrast to the mechanistic world of classical physics, which is based on the concept of solid bodies moving in empty space,[14] modern physics "reveals a basic oneness of the universe."[15] Physics, Jung explains, has revealed that "the phenomenal world is an aggregate of processes of atomic magnitude" in which both light and matter have a dualistic nature. On the level of atomic magnitudes, "light and matter both behave like separate particles and also like waves." These findings have forced physicists to abandon, Jung continues, "on the plane of atomic magnitudes, a causal description of nature in the ordinary space-time system, and in its place to set up invisible fields of probability in multidimensional spaces."[16]

According to the findings of modern physics, therefore, the phenomenal world, viewed at the microphysical level, is understood to constitute a "dynamic, inseparable whole" in which the traditional concepts of isolated objects, space and time, cause and effect no longer have meaning.[17] It is clear that these discoveries were regarded by Jung to be of particular importance to his own work. By complementing his own conclusions with respect to his investigation of synchronistic phenomena, the new worldview demanded by the findings of modern physics would, Jung believed, contribute to the acceptance of his revised theoretical model of the archetype.

Through his observations of synchronistic phenomena, Jung determined that the psyche does at times, "as the knowledge of future or spatially distant events shows,"[18] function outside the normal space and time framework. In the unconscious, space and time appear to be relative, that is, "knowledge finds itself in a space-time continuum in which space is no longer space, nor time time."[19] Commenting further, Jung states: "We conclude . . . that we have to expect a factor in the psyche that is not subject to the laws of time and space . . . [and] this factor is expected to manifest the qualities of time- and spacelessness, i.e., 'eternity' and 'ubiquity.' Psychological experience knows of such a factor; it is what I call the archetype."[20] Related to this, Jung observed, through his study of the intrapsychic processes and the equivalent external psychic or physical processes characteristic of synchronistic phenomena, that an archetype "underlies not only the psychic equivalences but, remarkably enough, the psychophysical equivalences too."[21] This tendency of the archetype "to behave as though it were not localized in one person but were active in the whole environment,"[22] led Jung to conclude that there is through the archetype a partial identity of psyche and matter, hence its description as a psychoid factor. Taken as a whole, the above findings, therefore, led Jung to characterize the archetype as constituting, at the microphysical level, a psychophysical continuum of meaning in which the traditional concepts of space, time, and causality simply do not exist.

It is clear, then, that the space-time world of the archetype is understood by Jung to be analogous to the subatomic world of microphysics where, as noted previously, the relativity of space and time has been firmly established. Physics and psychology, Jung believed, have reached the same frontier. The "seeming incommensurability" of psyche and matter is now bridged, Jung relates, "from the physical side by means of mathematical equations, and from the psychological side by means of empirically derived postulates— archetypes."[23] Both disciplines, using their respective methodologies, have thus uncovered what appears to be the *unus mundus*, that is, the unitary world.[24] Physics, which is in the main mathematical, has provided a quantitative analysis. Psychology, through the concept of the archetype, now has provided a qualitative one, for as a dynamism of spirit which is grounded in instinct, the archetype is a dynamic pattern of unique spiritual meaning.

In summary, we should emphasize, therefore, that in the final stage of its theoretical unfoldment, the archetype is no longer understood to be a strictly intrapsychic factor, but rather is regarded by Jung as constituting a psychophysical continuum of meaning which, being unrestricted by spatial or temporal limitations, is active in nature as a whole. Having thus established this critical point, we shall now turn to investigate Jung's position on the subject of synchronicity.

As indicated in the introduction, Jung's presentation of the synchronicity concept was greatly obstructed by the fact that he never developed a theoretical framework that would provide him with the means to discuss his position systematically. Progoff, putting his finger on this very critical point, writes about Jung: "His vision was so rich and essentially valid, but he could not reduce it to a form that he could communicate, and he could not say the things that needed to be said in order to reflect his vision."[25] The essential problem to which we must now turn our focus, therefore, is the problem of developing a theoretical model that gives full expression to Jung's position. Given the shortcomings of Jung's own endeavours along this line, this theoretical model will have to be primarily constructed not from Jung's theory, but from the praxis, that is to say, primarily from the study of how Jung, in practice, identified and interpreted synchronistic phenomena both for his analysands and for himself.

I shall begin by making two points concerning the general classification of the phenomena to be studied. This will be followed by the presentation of a descriptive framework that has been designed to identify the essential characteristics of what I refer to as the synchronistic event. This descriptive framework will then be put to use in the detailed examination of two case histories.

As was explained above, the macrophysical world of ego-consciousness is characterized by the coordinates of absolute space and absolute time. Conversely, in the microphysical world of the archetype, space and time are inseparably linked in a four-dimensional space-time continuum. It is the case that Jung touches on both these worlds in his discussion of the synchronicity concept. There is a problem, however, with Jung's presentation. The problem is that Jung does not specifically indicate on which of these two levels he is focusing his discussion at a given time. Accordingly, just as Jung's failure to distinguish consistently the archetypal image from the archetype was the source of endless confusion, so too is Jung's blending of the conscious and unconscious levels in his discussion of the synchronicity concept a serious obstacle to understanding, and not just for his reader, but for Jung himself. This is particularly evident, as we shall see shortly, with Jung's discussion of the time factor.

I would like to submit, therefore, that the term synchronicity be used specifically to describe the acausal connecting principle in the space-time world of the archetype. I would like also to propose that the conscious counterpart to this acausal connecting principle be termed the synchronistic experience or event. As explained here, then, whereas synchronicity is a phenomenon of the microphysical space-time world of the archetype, the synchronistic event, in contrast to this, takes place in the space- and time-bound macrophysical world of ego-consciousness.

My second point concerning the general classification of our subject material is that Jung's synchronistic examples fall into two distinct categories. This again is a point not identified by Jung. As we have seen, the archetype, which was previously regarded by Jung as a strictly intrapsychic factor, came to be regarded as a psychophysical continuum present in nature as a whole. Accordingly, the compensatory relationship that is understood to exist between the ego and the archetype on the intrapsychic level now is to be found as well in the interactions of the ego and the archetype that take place outwardly. That nature, through the psychoid archetype, compensates consciousness both inwardly and outwardly is certainly one of the central points of the synchronicity theory. It is not, however, always the case with synchronistic events that this compensatory activity is experienced by the subject both inwardly and outwardly. We should, therefore, recognize two types of synchronistic experiences, one in which the compensatory activity of the archetype is experienced both inwardly and outwardly, and a second type in which the compensatory activity of the archetype is experienced outwardly only.

With respect to the first type of synchronistic event, where the compensatory images are experienced both inwardly and outwardly, we could use as a simple example several dreams Jung had about Churchill during the war. It seems that Jung dreamt about Churchill whenever the British prime minister was in the vicinity of the Swiss border, even though Jung had had no prior knowledge that such visits were to take place. Only following Churchill's departure, when the newspapers would announce that the British leader had been in the area of the Swiss border, was Jung able to recognize the synchronistic aspect of his dreams. With regard to the compensatory meaning of these experiences, Jung had told Hannah that Churchill was a symbol of the extravert in himself. The paralleling of these inner and outer compensatory events would refer, then, to the development of that specific extraverted aspect of Jung's personality that Churchill symbolized.[26] The compensatory development that Jung was being led toward inwardly, through the dream, was, therefore, being synchronistically paralleled outwardly in the actual event of Churchill's visit.

Concerning the second type of synchronistic experience described above, where the compensatory event is experienced outwardly only, we could take as an example an experience that Jung had immediately following the death of his mother. Perhaps more than any other experience, death confronts us with the reality of just how different the points of view of the ego and the self are. From the point of view of the ego, "death is indeed," Jung relates, "a fearful piece of brutality; there is no sense pretending otherwise. It is brutal not only as a physical event, but far more so psychically: a human being is torn away from us, and what remains is the icy stillness of death." In extreme contrast to this, from the perspective of the self death is regarded as an occasion for joyousness. From the point of view of the self, our physical death is not viewed, as it is by the ego, principally as a time of loss, rather, it is viewed as a time of gain, for it is finally to be united with that from which it has been separated. Accordingly, death is often represented from the perspective of the self as a wedding. "In the light of eternity," Jung explains, "it [death] is a wedding, a *mysterium coniunctionis*. The soul attains, as it were, its missing half, it achieves wholeness."

Given these very great differences between the perspectives of the ego and the self with respect to the experience of death, it follows that synchronistic experiences that seek to convey to the ego the much-needed wholeness of the self's perspective can have a very dramatic compensatory influence. This was certainly the case with Jung as he travelled home by train after having just learned of his mother's death. Grief-stricken with the news, Jung found, however, that the situation with which he was surrounded on the train kept him from being completely overwhelmed by his sorrow. Describing his experience, Jung writes:

> I went home immediately, and while I rode in the night train I had a feeling of great grief, but in my heart of hearts I could not be mournful, and this for a strange reason: during the entire journey I continually heard dance music, laughter, and jollity, as though a wedding were being celebrated. . . . Here was

gay music, cheerful laughter, and it was impossible to yield entirely to my sorrow.[27]

Whereas from the point of view of the ego death appears as a violent annihilation of a human being, from the point of view of the self it appears as a time of union and wholeness, a marriage. Accordingly, as Jung journeyed home laden with the burden of the ego's sense of loss, he found his experience of sorrow being compensated by a completely opposite feeling—a feeling of celebration that was actually present in the environment. The joyousness with which his grief was surrounded on that journey home was, Jung realized, the wholeness of the self being synchronistically manifested.

Both the first type of synchronistic experience, where the compensatory event is experienced both inwardly and outwardly, and the second type, where the compensatory event is experienced outwardly only, give expression to the interrelatedness of the individual, through the psychoid archetype, with the events of nature as a whole. The first type is, however, different from the second type of synchronistic event in one important respect. With the first type of synchronistic event we have the additional idea that the individual, through the compensatory content that emerges from the unconscious, has access to what Jung refers to as an "absolute knowledge." By looking within, or through the spontaneous emergence of the compensatory content, the individual achieves specific knowledge concerning the events of the outer world. Of the two case histories to be examined in detail in this chapter, the first one describes such an experience of "absolute knowledge," while the second case history provides a detailed look at a synchronistic experience in which the compensatory activity of nature is experienced outwardly only.

Before turning to examine directly these case histories, I would like to outline briefly the descriptive framework that will be used in our investigation of these synchronistic experiences.

We find in Jung's paper "On Synchronicity" a descriptive framework that seeks to identify the essential features of the synchronistic event. This model, it should be noted, is the most complete summary ever developed by Jung to outline these features. "All the phenomena I have mentioned," Jung writes, "can be grouped under three categories:"

1. The coincidence of a psychic state in the observer with a simultaneous, objective, external event that corresponds to

the psychic state or content (e.g., the scarab), where there is no evidence of a causal connection between the psychic state and the external event, and where, considering the psychic relativity of space and time, such a connection is not even conceivable.

2. The coincidence of a psychic state with a corresponding (more or less simultaneous) external event taking place outside the observer's field of perception, i.e., at a distance, and only verifiable afterward (e.g., the Stockholm fire).

3. The coincidence of a psychic state with a corresponding, not yet existent future event that is distant in time and can likewise only be verified afterward.

In groups 2 and 3 the coinciding events are not yet present in the observer's field of perception, but have been anticipated in time in so far as they can only be verified afterward. For this reason I call such events *synchronistic,* which is not to be confused with *synchronous.*[28]

It should be noted that the two examples to which Jung refers, the scarab case history, which we will soon examine, and Swedenborg's vision of Stockholm burning, both belong to the category of the first type of synchronistic event I have identified above, for here a specific unconscious content corresponds to the content of the outward synchronistic event. These are the synchronistic experiences of "absolute knowledge."

Certainly one of the problems with Jung's above model is that it only directly addresses itself to this first type of synchronistic experience. It could perhaps be argued that when Jung, in his section 1, speaks of an external event corresponding to "the psychic state or content," he is alluding to the existence of two types of synchronistic experiences. This being so the "psychic content" would be taken to designate the specific compensatory image that emerges out of the unconscious usually in a dream, as with Jung's dream about Churchill. The "psychic state," on the other hand, would refer simply to the conscious orientation around which the compensatory synchronistic activity centers; in our example that would be Jung's state of grief following his mother's death. Support for this interpretation is to be found in a statement Jung makes immediately after the introduction of his above model, when he describes the casting of the *I Ching* as a synchronistic event. "The *I Ching,*" Jung writes, "presupposes that there is a synchronistic correspondence between the psychic state of the questioner and the answering hexagram."[29] When Jung here speaks of the "psychic state of the questioner," he is clearly not referring to the presence of a specific compensatory content which will in turn be mirrored in the casting of the *I Ching*, that is to say, he is not speaking of a situation in which the compensatory content is experienced both inwardly and outwardly. Rather, he is referring to a situation in which the compensatory content is synchronistically represented outwardly only, much as it was when he was travelling home grief-stricken following his mother's death.

Whether or not Jung is indirectly referring to the existence of two types of synchronistic experiences in his outline, we know for a fact that Jung's examples of synchronistic experiences do fall into two specific categories and that his above summary fails to do justice to both types of experiences. In seeking, therefore, to come to terms with the existence of two specific types of synchronistic experiences, the first two points of our model outlining the essential characteristics of the synchronistic event read as follows:

1) The specific intrapsychic state of the subject defined as one of the following:
   a) The unconscious content which, in accordance with the compensatory needs of the conscious orientation, enters consciousness
   b) The conscious orientation of the subject around which the compensatory synchronistic activity centers

2) An objective event corresponds with this intrapsychic state
   a) The objective event as a compensatory equivalent to the unconscious compensatory content
   b) The objective event as the sole compensator of ego-consciousness

The time factor is unquestionably one of the most problematic aspects of Jung's thinking on synchronicity. When we move into our first case history we shall be looking very closely at the various problems that are associated with Jung's discussion of the time factor. Fortunately, in Jung's above outline we have one of his most straightforward descriptions of the way synchronistic events manifest themselves in time and space. Jung's position can be reduced to the following:

3) Even though the intrapsychic state and the objective event may be synchronous according to clock time and spatially

near to each other, the objective event may, contrary to this, be distant in time and/or space in relation to the intrapsychic state

With respect to the question of causality, we see in Jung's outline that there can be "no evidence of a causal connection between the psychic state and the external event." This is certainly one of the key characteristics of the synchronistic event and indeed it is exactly this feature that leads people to regard these events as mere coincidences based on pure chance. The fourth point in our outline shall read then:

4) The intrapsychic state and the objective event are not causally related to each other

Perhaps Jung's most important point concerning synchronistic phenomena is that these events, which superficially viewed appear to be based on mere chance and, accordingly, are characterized as meaningless coincidences, are events that are very meaningful indeed. That Jung regards synchronistic events as very meaningful occurrences is an indubitable truth. When one does seek, however, to determine how exactly these events are understood by Jung to be meaningful, confusion does arise. Here, Jung's exposition is not easily followed. Reflecting this sentiment, Fordham writes about Jung's descriptions of the synchronistic event, "His examples do not always make it evident in what his idea of meaning consists."[30] The fifth characteristic of our outline identifies, then, the meaning that Jung understands to be associated with these experiences.

In examining Jung's descriptions of synchronistic experiences, it becomes apparent that the "meaningfulness" that Jung associates with these experiences acutally consists of four interrelated layers. We should note here that the depth of one's experience of the synchronistic event grows in proportion to the ability of the individual to assimilate consciously these various levels of meaning.

5) The synchronistic event is meaningful
   a) The intrapsychic state and the objective event as meaningful parallels

The first layer of meaning relates to a point that was introduced above but must nevertheless be reintroduced and studied in this particular context. With synchronistic experiences, the subjective and objective events form "meaningful parallels."[31] This is to say, as we have seen above, that the objective event stands in a compensatory relationship to the subjective event either in the sense of mirroring the specific inner compensatory content or forming the sole compensator of consciousness. Clearly one of the real shortcomings of Jung's above descriptive framework is that this first level of meaning is the only one to which he refers.

b) The numinous charge associated with the synchronistic experience

The second layer of meaning concerns the numinous or spiritual charge—the former term being borrowed by Jung from Rudolf Otto—which in varying intensities is associated with the synchronistic experience. As is the case with archetypal manifestations, one often experiences with synchronistic events, which we should recall arise themselves out of an archetypal ground, a type of numinous energy. This numinous charge, it seems, is experienced by the subject primarily on a feeling level. Accordingly, it is that which reaches into "one's heart of hearts," much as it did with Jung, healing his sense of grief. It is that to which Bolen refers when she writes, "Every time I have become aware of a synchronistic experience, I have had an accompanying feeling that some grace came along with it."[32]

c) Import of the subjective-level interpretation

The third layer of meaning describes that which is uncovered when the synchronistic experience is interpreted on the subjective level. In that synchronistic experiences take place within the compensatory framework, they stand in a special relationship to the psychological development of the individual and, therefore, require interpretation on the subjective level. Unfortunately, several of the examples of synchronistic experiences provided by Jung do not lend themselves to detailed interpretation on the subjective level. This problem is very likely attributable to the fact that Jung's examples are often based on his own experiences. Jung, it would seem, chose not to elaborate the relevant subjective information even though he does allude to its importance.

Jung's tendency to deal with the subjective level of meaning in this manner is evidenced in the following excerpt from his autobiography. A few months before the death of his mother, in September 1922, Jung dreamt that his father, whom he had not dreamt about since the time of his death in 1896, wanted "to consult me about marital psychology." However, just as Jung was about to give "a lengthy lecture on the complexities of marriage," he awoke. In commenting on this synchronistic dream, Jung states:

> My parents' marriage was not a happy one. . . . My dream was a forecast of my mother's death, for here was my father who . . . wished to ask a psychologist about the newest insights and information on marital problems, since he would soon have to resume this relationship again. . . . Such was the dream's message. Undoubtedly, I could have found out a good deal more by looking into its subjective meaning—but why did I dream it just before the death of my mother, which I did not forsee? It plainly referred to my father, with whom I felt a sympathy that deepened as I grew older.[33]

Even though Jung explicitly attaches a great importance to the subjective level interpretation of this synchronistic event, he does not provide the relevant subjective information that is crucial to the development of a full subjective interpretation. It is very difficult, therefore, if not impossible, to analyze the subjective import of this synchronistic experience, that is, to know how the synchronistic experience is specifically compensating Jung's conscious attitude.

d) The archetypal level of meaning

The fourth and final layer of meaning is, of course, the archetypal layer. Archetypes, Jung relates, "are perhaps the most important basis for synchronistic events."[34] The archetype, as we have seen, is understood to constitute a psychically relative space-time continuum of meaning that extends into nature as a whole. The fourth layer of meaning refers, then, to the presence of this objective meaning, which exists independently of consciousness.

Summary of the Essential Characteristics of the Synchronistic Event

1) The specific intrapsychic state of the subject defined as one of the following:
    a) The unconscious content which, in accordance with the compensatory needs of the conscious orientation, enters consciousness
    b) The conscious orientation of the subject around which the compensatory synchronistic activity centers

2) An objective event corresponds with this intrapsychic state
   a) The objective event as a compensatory equivalent to the unconscious compensatory content
   b) The objective event as the sole compensator of ego-consciousness

3) Even though the intrapsychic state and the objective event may be synchronous according to clock time and spatially near to each other, the objective event may, contrary to this, be distant in time and/or space in relation to the intrapsychic state
4) The intrapsychic state and the objective event are not causally related to each other
5) The synchronistic event is meaningful
   a) The intrapsychic state and the objective event as meaningful parallels
   b) The numinous charge associated with the synchronistic experience
   c) Import of the subjective-level interpretation
   d) The archetypal level of meaning

Of the different examples provided by Jung of synchronistic experiences, the example that has attracted the most attention is the case of the "golden scarab." The example, Jung relates, concerns a young woman "who, in spite of efforts made on both sides, proved to be psychologically inaccessible." The analytical process, it seems, had become obstructed by what Jung describes as an "animus problem," a state of psychic onesidedness on the part of the analysand that manifested itself in the form of a domineering rationality. "The difficulty lay in the fact," Jung writes, "that she always knew better about everything. Her excellent education had provided her with a weapon ideally suited to this purpose, namely a highly polished Cartesian rationalism."

Seeking to circumvent the obstacle of his analysand's rationalism, Jung attempted to direct his patient into a more feeling level dimension of experience. However, after these attempts to "sweeten her rationalism with a somewhat more human understanding" also proved unproductive, Jung could only hope "that something unexpected and irrational would turn up, something that would burst the intellectual retort into which she had sealed herself." Describing the synchronistic experience that served to do just this, Jung writes:

I was sitting opposite her one day, with my back to the window. . . . She had had an impressive dream the night before, in which someone had given her a golden scarab—a costly piece of jewellery. While she was still telling me this dream, I heard something behind me gently tapping on the window. I turned round and saw that it was a fairly large flying insect that was knocking against the window-pane from outside in the obvious effort to get into the dark room. . . . I opened the window immediately and caught the insect in the air as it flew in. It was a scarabaeid beetle, or common rose-chafer (*Cetonia aurata*), whose gold-green colour most nearly resembles that of a golden scarab. I handed the beetle to my patient with the words, "Here is your scarab."[35]

Through this synchronistic experience, the grip that the young woman's intellectual onesidedness had had on the analytical process was broken. Indeed the influence of the synchronistic experience was such, Jung writes, that "her natural being could burst through the armour of her animus possession and the process of transformation could at last begin to move."[36]

1) *The specific intrapsychic state of the subject*
   a) *The unconscious content which, in accordance with the compensatory needs of the conscious orientation, enters consciousness*

With synchronistic experiences of this type, the unconscious content usually enters consciousness through a dream, intuition, wakeful fantasy, or hypnagogic vision. In this particular case, it is stated that the unconscious content entered consciousness through the woman's dream. As Jung relates in the above passage: "She had had an impressive dream the night before, in which someone had given her a golden scarab—a costly piece of jewellery."

2) *An objective event corresponds with this intrapsychic state*
   a) *The objective event as a compensatory equivalent to the unconscious compensatory content*

We learn from Jung's above account that at the time the young woman was relating her dream to Jung, a large insect began flying up against the window: "It was a scarabaeid beetle, or common rose-chafer (*Cetonia aurata*), whose gold-green colour most nearly resembles that of a golden scarab." The rose-chafer, Jung explains, is "the nearest analogy to a golden scarab that one finds in our latitudes."[37] In keeping, furthermore, with the script of the dream, we see that the "golden scarab" was presented to the woman. When Jung opened the window, he was able to catch the scarab as it entered the room. Then turning to his analysand, he presented it to her with the words, "Here is your scarab."

With this case study, the unconscious content and objective events, for the most part, literally correspond. This is to say, the young woman dreamt of being presented with a golden scarab, and the day following this dream, she actually was. In contrast to this, however, other examples presented by Jung indicate that it is not essential for there to be a literal correspondence between the unconscious content and the objective event. Rather, their correspondence may be of a more figurative nature. This idea of a figurative correspondence is clearly revealed in the following account of a hypnagogic vision that told Jung in no uncertain terms that Richard Wilhelm, the German sinologist, was about to die. Describing his experience, Jung writes: "A few weeks before his [Wilhelm's] death, when I had had no news from him for a considerable time, I was awakened, just as I was on the point of falling asleep, by a vision. At my bed stood a Chinese in a dark blue gown, hands crossed in the sleeves. He bowed low before me, as if he wished to give me a message. I knew what it signified."[38] Here, we see that the subjective image, the vision of the bowing Chinese, does not literally correspond with the objective event, Wilhelm's death. The subjective event does, nevertheless, using a more figurative mode, transmit a message which is as definite. With respect, then, to the requirement that the unconscious content and the objective event correspond, it is apparent that this correspondence may be either literal or figurative in character.

> 3) *Even though the intrapsychic state and the objective event may be synchronous according to clock time and spatially near to each other, the objective event may, contrary to this, be distant in time and/or space in relation to the intrapsychic state*

In the case study of the golden scarab, the objective event is distant in time and space in relation to the intrapsychic state. With respect to the latter, we see from Jung's description that his analysand had dreamt about the golden scarab "the night before." The objective event, however, that is, the actual appearance of the scarab, took place the following day in Jung's office. The objective event, therefore, is not only spatially distant in relation to the subjective event, but it is also distant in time, for within the framework of clock time the subjective event preceded the objective one.

As already pointed out, Jung's discussion of the time element is highly problematical. Here we shall attempt to come to terms with some of the problems associated with Jung's presentation. Further comments will then be given in chapter 4 when we again return to this subject.

As indicated in Jung's above-described summary of synchronistic phenomena, the objective event may be distant in time in relation to the subjective event. The intrapsychic and objective events are thus not always simultaneous within the clock-time framework. This seems straightforward enough. Things, however, do take an unexpected twist when Jung presents definitional statements that contradict this. For example, Jung writes, "Synchronistic events rest on the *simultaneous occurrence of two different psychic states.*"[39] As a second example we could take the following: "Synchronicity designates the parallelism of time and meaning between psychic and psychophysical events."[40] Related to this is the emergence of the erroneous notion that the time element constitutes the central unifying link in the synchronistic experience. This idea, which can be found in Jung's own writings, has since been taken up by a number of individuals following his lead. Zavala provides us with a good example of this mistaken emphasis on simultaneity when he asserts, "The only common characteristic of the two phenomenon forming a synchronistic event is the moment of time in which they take place."[41] We shall return to this specific problem in chapter 4.

The confusion that definitional statements such as the above create is further compounded by Jung's tendency to work his synchronistic case studies, whenever it is possible to do so, into the framework of a clock-time simultaneity. We see this tendency even in the case we are presently examining, where Jung emphasizes the paralleling of his discussion with his analysand about the scarab and the scarab's subsequent appearance over and above the more important paralleling of the dream of the golden scarab and its appearance. By emphasizing the former, Jung is seeking to place the intrapsychic experience, here defined as their discussion about the scarab dream, and the objective event, the actual appearance of the scarab, within the framework of clock-time simultaneity. Thus, following this line of argument, Jung, in his summary model of synchronistic phenomena, places this case history within section one, that is, within the framework of clock-time simultaneity.

The essential problem with Jung's discussion of the time element, I believe, can be traced to a general weakness in Jung's presentation of the synchronicity concept. The problem, as indicated at the beginning of this chapter, is that Jung did not develop a terminology that would unequivocally indicate whether synchronicity is being discussed in relation to the microphysical world of the archetype, that is, the world of space-time, or in relation to the world of space and time. Consequently, Jung was left without the means to differentiate in theory his position on time as it relates to the microphysical world of the psyche from his position on time as it relates to the macrophysical world of the psyche. This, of course, not only produced considerable confusion for Jung's reader, but this blending together of the conscious and unconscious levels seems to have complicated things for Jung himself, as his tendency to emphasize clock-time simultaneity in his case studies suggests. Understood within the framework of the new terminology introduced in this chapter, Jung does not separate his discussion of the time element in relation to the synchronicity principle from his discussion of the time element in relation to the synchronistic experience.

Given all of this, one is led to question how specifically the idea of simultaneity relates to the concept of synchronicity, if it does at all. Arthur Koestler himself was led to reflect about this same problem after having finally reached in his reading of Jung the point where he could recognize, in spite of all the above-described muddle, that synchronistic events are not always synchronous. "One wonders," Koestler writes, "why Jung created . . . unnecessary complications by coining a term which implies simultaneity, and then explaining that it does not mean what it means."[42]

Utilizing the new terminology introduced in this chapter to address this question, we see that the principle of synchronicity as such is associated with archetypal processes in nature, which constitute a psychophysical space-time continuum. In this continuum the time and space restrictions as we know them are nonexistent and accordingly there is no "before" or "after." In the archetypal world, Jung relates, "knowledge [meaning] finds itself in a space-time continuum in which space is no longer space, nor time time."[43] The synchronicity principle, then, as its etymology indicates, does relate to "a kind of simultaneity,"[44] for in the space-time continuum everything exists en bloc.

Whereas the synchronicity principle is a phenomenon of the space-time world of the archetype, the synchronistic experience takes place in the space- and time-bound world of ego-consciousness. In the case of a synchronistic event involving "absolute knowledge," such as our present example of the young woman and the golden scarab, a content from the archetypal unconscious maintains "a potential in the direction of consciousness."[45] Once this psychic content, as Jung explains, "crosses the threshold of consciousness . . . time and space resume their accustomed sway."[46] Therefore, even though this psychic content will manifest "a remarkable independence" of time and space,[47] it will be, in relation to the objective event, either synchronous according to clock time or distant in time and/or space. With a synchronistic experience of "absolute knowledge," then, information that is not space- and time-bound finds itself in the space- and time-bound world of ego-consciousness. This paradoxical situation is, it should be noted, exactly that which gives the synchronistic experience such an extraordinary character.

4) *The intrapsychic state and the objective event are not causally related to each other*

As with his treatment of the time element, the position Jung takes on the question of causality is obscured by the fact that he does not always differentiate his discussion of causality as it relates to the macrophysical world, that is, the space- and time-bound world of everyday experience, from his discussion of causality as it relates to the microphysical world, the space-time world of the archetype. Returning to Jung's summary of synchronistic phenomena, we find this tendency to blend these two levels at work. In section one of his descriptive model, the relevant lines of which I have italicized below, Jung writes:

The coincidence of a psychic state in the observer with a simultaneous, objective, external event that corresponds to the psychic state or content (e.g., the scarab), *where there is no evidence of a causal connection between the psychic state and the external event, and where, considering the psychic relativity of space and time, such a connection is not even conceivable.*

We can see from the above statement, even though Jung himself does not specifically delineate his argument in this way, that his position on the causality question is basically twofold. First, writing with reference to the macrophysical world of everyday experience, Jung establishes one of the criteria of the synchronistic event. Second, writing with reference to the microphysical world of the archetype, Jung provides an explanation of his concept of acausal connection.

With respect to the synchronistic event, we see that Jung indicates in the above passage that there can be "no evidence of a causal connection between the psychic state and the external event." Commenting further, Jung writes, "No reciprocal causal connection can be shown to obtain between parallel events, which is just what gives them their chance character."[48] Concerning the synchronistic experience, it is an essential criterion, therefore, that the events in question do not in any way appear to be related causally to each other. With this point established, we must now determine what specifically Jung means by the idea of causality.

If we are to identify two events as being causally related to each other, three factors, Jung argues, must be present. First, there must be a temporal succession in the form of the cause preceding the effect. "Causality," Jung writes, "is the way we explain the link between two successive events."[49] Second, there must be a transmission of energy from the cause to the effect. The " 'effect,' " Jung explains, "cannot be understood as anything except a phenomenon of energy."[50] Third, and this is perhaps the most important point, the cause must contain those conditions that are necessary for the occurrence of the effect, those conditions in the absence of which the effect would not have come into being. "The causality principle," Jung relates, "asserts that the connection between cause and effect is a necessary one."[51]

Returning to the case study of the young woman and the golden scarab, it is clear that there is no demonstrable causal connection between the events concerned. There is certainly no necessary connection between the woman's dream of the scarab and the appearance of the scarab the following day at Jung's office window. There is nothing to indicate that one of these events actually caused the other to occur, nothing to suggest any mutual dependency concerning the fact of their coming into being. The intrapsychic state and the objective event are, therefore, causally unrelated.

Here an important point should be made concerning the compensatory relationship that is understood to exist between the intrapsychic state and objective event. As we have just seen, the two events are not causally related. The point that must be borne in mind, then, is that even though the woman stands in a compensatory relationship to the scarab, it is certainly not the case, as some mistakenly conclude the synchronicity concept suggests, that the scarab appeared just for the woman. The idea is not that the world turns around one person, but rather, that the individual is a participant in, and meaningfully related to, the acausal patternings of events in nature.

Concerning Jung's explanation of acausality, we see that in contrast to the structure of time and space that dominates the macrophysical world of everyday experience, the synchronicity principle "relates to another order of things . . . in which neither 'here and there' nor 'earlier and later' are of importance."[52] This is the microphysical world of the archetype where the coordinates of space and time are nonexistent and where, moreover, as Jung explains, "a causality which presupposes space and time for its continuance can no longer be said to exist and becomes altogether unthinkable."[53] Here, we touch on that to which Jung was referring in the above passage when after having stated about the synchronistic experience that there can be no causal connection between the intrapsychic and objective events, he further remarked that "considering the psychic relativity of space and time, such a connection is not even conceivable." In the absence of space and time, causality, Jung is here asserting, cannot exist, for "causality is bound up with the existence of space and time and physical changes, and consists essentially in the succession of cause and effect."[54] With respect to the synchronicity principle, therefore, in that it is a phenomenon of the space-time world of the psychoid archetype, it is indeed rightfully characterized by Jung as an acausal connecting principle.

5) The synchronistic event is meaningful

Antony Flew has argued, with Jung's concept of meaningful coincidence in mind, that for a coincidence to be a coincidence it must be "both 'noncausal' and 'meaningful.' " Therefore, Flew concludes, "to say that all (or some) coincidences are 'pointed' or 'meaningful' is to utter a tautology (or a ludicrous understatement)." In support of his argument, Flew cites the Concise Oxford Dictionary, which defines coincidence as a " 'notable occurrence of events or circumstances without apparent causal connection' (my italics)."[55] In response to Flew, Jung would argue, I think, that to describe events without apparent causal connection as notable is not to say that they are meaningful, for as remarkable and as extraordinary as they are, coincidences are nevertheless regarded as products of mere chance and treated as such in that it is believed that nothing is to be learned from them. Following a similar line of reasoning, Rao, in support of Jung, states, that "by 'meaningful' Jung seems to imply more than what Flew grants him." To this, however,

Rao adds the criticism, "even though some examples of synchronicity given by Jung himself, devoid of their symbolism, appear to be no more than mere coincidence."[56] Here I think Rao puts his finger on a critical shortcoming in Jung's presentation—that Jung does not consistently demonstrate how the symbolical meaning of the synchronistic event specifically relates to the psychology of the individual. If these events are understood to have a special meaning for the subject, something that a chance coincidence by definition does not have, it is of the greatest importance, to paraphrase Fordham, to know in what exactly this meaningfulness consists, specific to the subject. This is something, however, which Jung does not consistently demonstrate.

Had Jung conducted his discussion of this subject more systematically there certainly would have been less confusion about how exactly these events are meaningful. Jung, we have already noted, refers to four different levels of meaning. What is particularly confusing for his reader is that he usually only touches on one of these levels of meaning at a time without connecting it to the other related levels. For instance, Jung may in one place indicate that a certain experience is a meaningful coincidence because the intrapsychic and objective events are similar in content. Then in another place he may say, in presenting a different example, that it is a meaningful coincidence because the two events are expressions of the same archetypal pattern. What is needed is an overview of Jung's notion of meaningfulness. As we now turn to examine the four interrelated levels of meaning in relationship to the scarab case history, such an overview of Jung's position will emerge.

a) *The intrapsychic state and the objective event as meaningful parallels*

Because the young woman's dream corresponded with the appearance and subsequent presentation of the scarab, the subjective and objective events are understood to constitute meaningful parallels. The assimilation of the first level of meaning relates then to the ability of the individual or individuals concerned to recognize these meaningful parallels. In this particular case study, there was an obvious recognition on the part of both Jung and the analysand. With respect to the latter, the fact of her recognition explains, in part, why "her natural being could burst through the armour of her animus possession" when she was presented with the scarab. Jung's own recognition is revealed through his action of catching the "golden scarab" and his subsequent statement " 'Here is your scarab.' "

In contrast to this, in some cases there may be no recognition of the meaningful parallels on the part of the subject. About such experiences von Franz writes: "When a synchronistic event takes place and *no* observer perceives its meaning, Jung speaks of *synchronous* (rather than of *synchronistic*) events."[57] In making this statement, an assertion, I should add, that I cannot support, von Franz has in mind, as she herself notes, Jung's following differentiation of synchronistic and synchronous events: "I am therefore using the general concept of synchronicity in the special sense of a coincidence in time [here again that misleading emphasis on simultaneity] of two or more causally unrelated events which have the same or similar meaning, in contrast to 'synchronism,' which simply means the simultaneous occurrence of two events."[58] What Jung is here saying is that synchronistic events, by definition, are events that form meaningful parallels, whereas synchronous events, by definition, are simply events happening at the same time. It is certainly not suggested here that a synchronistic event becomes a synchronous event simply because its meaningfulness is not recognized.

For Jung, a synchronistic event remains a synchronistic event whether or not its meaningfulness is recognized. Clearly the meaningfulness associated with these experiences is a highly personalized meaning, but it is a highly personalized meaning that is objectively present, not subjectively fabricated. Accordingly, it is no less present if it is not recognized by the subject—or anyone else, for that matter. When, therefore, the meaning of a synchronistic event is not recognized by the subject, or indeed anyone else, Jung simply speaks of an unconscious synchronistic experience. "Unconscious synchronicities," Jung explains, "are, as we know from experience, altogether possible, since in many cases we are unconscious of their happening, or have to have our attention drawn to the coincidence by an outsider."[59]

Provided that the intrapsychic content and the objective event literally correspond, recognition of the meaningful parallels is quite straightforward. However, if the correspondence of the two events is of a more figurative nature, as was Jung's vision of the bowing Chinese, which he rightfully understood to mean that Wilhelm was about to die, recognition becomes more problematic. Certainly Jung was able to reach this conclusion only because he was knowledgeable enough about the workings of such symbolical representations to interpret its cryptic message correctly.

Wilhelm, through his work as a sinologist, had allowed himself, Jung believed, to be gripped and shaped by old China "so that when he came back to Europe he brought us not only in his spirit but also, in his being, a true image of the East."[60] In the course of his "reassimilation to the West," however, which was carried out in a "somewhat unreflective" manner, Wilhelm placed himself in quite a vulnerable position. As Jung explains, "Since it was, so I thought, a passive assimilation, that is to say, a succumbing to the influence of the environment, there was the danger of a relatively unconscious conflict, a clash between his Western and Eastern psyche."[61]

The fatal turn of events for Wilhelm came in the midst of the psychic crisis, when he was stricken with a recurring case of amoebic dysentery.[62] As Jung relates, "A spiritual crisis of such dimensions often means death if it takes place in a body weakened by disease."[63] Wilhelm's dreams were now leading him back to "the endless stretches of desolate Asiatic steppes. . . . He was," as Jung explains, "groping his way back to the problem which China had set before him, the answer to which had been blocked for him by the West."[64] Passive assimilation had driven a wedge between his rich experiences in China and reality. Wilhelm thus could not get his China experience into consciousness even though, as Jung believed, his life, which in reality was now tied to the West, actually depended on his ability to do so. What Wilhelm required was the development of an integrated position that would take his Eastern and Western experiences into account. A strict regression to his experiences in China would in no way solve the problem. Indeed, in Jung's opinion, a strict regression to the past on the part of Wilhelm would not only constitute a form of psychic suicide but would also result in his physical death. In light of this, it is understandable why Jung, when confronted with the vision of "a Chinese in a dark blue gown, hands crossed in the sleeves" bowing low before him,[65] took it to mean that Wilhelm was, as it were, "bowing out." Through his ability to interpret the figurative nature of the hypnagogic vision, Jung was able to identify the corresponding objective event, in this case, Wilhelm's death. With respect, then, to those synchronistic experiences that are of a more figurative nature, it seems that recognition of the "meaningful parallels" ultimately depends on the interpretive skill of the individual concerned.

b) *The numinous charge associated with the synchronistic experience*

In that synchronistic experiences arise out of an archetypal ground, they have associated with them, like other archetypal manifestations, a numinous or spiritual charge that announces itself to the subject primarily on the feeling level. With archetypal content, there is, Jung explains, "a mystical aura about its numinosity, and it has a corresponding effect upon the emotions. It mobilizes philosophical and religious convictions in the very people who deemed themselves miles above any such fits of weakness." It implants in them, through the powerful activation of affect, a sense of "depth and fulness of meaning that was unthinkable before."[66] Accordingly, in acknowledgment of the power of the archetype to produce such numinous effects, and moreover, evincing his belief in the centrality of these feeling-level experiences to the development of religious conviction, Jung writes, "What counts in religious experience is not how explicitly an archetype can be formulated but how much I am gripped by it."[67]

The association of the feeling-level experience of the numinous with synchronistic type events is something, Jung suggests, that has long been recognized, although understood differently. For centuries it has been held that there exists a connection between the intensity of one's emotional state and the activation of special powers within, which in turn enable one magically to influence events taking place in the world. In illustration of this point, Jung cites a passage from the writings of Albertus Magnus (circa 1200–1280), the noted teacher of Thomas Aquinas. Drawing on the work of the Islamic philosopher and physician Avicenna (980–1037), Albertus Magnus writes:

> I discovered an instructive account [of magic] in Avicenna's *Liber sextus naturalium*, which says that a certain power to alter things indwells in the human soul and subordinates the other things to her, particularly when she is swept into a great excess of love or hate or the like. When therefore the soul of a man falls into a great excess of any passion, it can be proved by experiment that it [the excess] binds things [magically] and alters them in the way it wants, and for a long time I did not believe it, but after I had read the nigromantic books and others of the kind on signs and magic, I found that the emotionality of the human soul is the chief cause of all these things. . . . Whoever would learn the secret of doing and undoing these things must know that everyone can influence everything magically if he falls into a great excess . . . and he must do it at that hour when the excess befalls him, and operate with the things which the soul prescribes.[68]

In the above, Albertus Magnus identifies the existence of a direct connection between the powerful activation of affect, on the one hand, and the production of " 'magical' " (synchronistic) happenings, on the other. Impressive as this account was to Jung, he was not, however, led to agree completely with its interpretation of things, specifically with its claim that magical happenings are caused by affect. In contrast to this particular interpretation of the relationship between affect and the "magical" arrangement of outward events, Jung suggests that affect, rather than being the "arranger," is itself, so to speak, "arranged" by the constellated archetype that is present both inwardly and outwardly. "Naturally Albertus Magnus," Jung explains, "in accordance with the spirit of his age, explains this [the relationship between affect and the magical arrangement of events] by postulating a magical faculty in the soul, without considering that the psychic process itself is just as much 'arranged' as the coinciding image which anticipates the external physical process."[69] According to Jung, therefore, the intensely felt emotionality and sense of inner power described by Albertus Magnus refers in fact to a direct experience of the numinosity of the psychoid archetype.

Returning to our case history, we see, then, that with synchronistic experiences of "absolute knowledge," the affect-laden numinous charge is usually experienced first when the archetypal content enters consciousness, and second when the corresponding external event is observed. This pattern is evidenced in the following account given by Jung: "The dream alone was enough to disturb ever so slightly the rationalistic attitude of my patient. But when the 'scarab' came flying in through the window in actual fact, her natural being could burst through the armour of her animus possession." It should be recalled that prior to the unfoldment of these events the young woman had successfully sealed herself in an "intellectual retort." The dialectical aspect of the psychotherapeutic process had proven to be an innocuous weapon against the "armour of her animus possession." However, through the combined numinous charges of both the subjective and objective archetypal events, the desired result was achieved. "Evidently," Jung could retrospectively understand, "something quite irrational was needed which was beyond my powers to produce."[70]

Although the experience of the numinous charge of the archetype was quite dramatic in this case study, it should be noted that not all synchronistic experiences carry the same intensity of numinosity. Much as the intensity of one's experience of the numinous charge of the archetype varies in dreams, so also does it vary with synchronistic experiences. There are "little dreams" and "big dreams" and also some "very big dreams." Equally, this too is the case with synchronistic experiences. Not every synchronistic experience releases an earthshaking numinous charge.

In spite of this variability, the numinous charge of the archetype plays a very important role as an aspect of the meaningfulness of synchronistic events. The numinous charge, which is associated with the subjective and objective archetypal events, serves, it would seem, two very important purposes. First, it imparts, through the affect, a nonrational experience of transcendent meaning. Second, and subsequent to this, it infects the ego with a sense of wonder that in turn may lead the individual to investigate the two remaining levels of meaning.

c) *Import of the subjective-level interpretation*

With synchronistic experiences involving "absolute knowledge," it is often the case that the subject will interpret the internal content that has arisen from the unconscious only in terms of its relationship to the events of objective reality. This is to say that he will confine himself to an objective-level interpretation. In that the internal content has arisen in accordance with the principle of psychic compensation, it requires, however, in addition to this objective-level interpretation, interpretation on the subjective level. In the following, Jung describes precisely how these two levels of interpretation differ:

> I call every interpretation which equates the dream images with real objects an *interpretation on the objective level*. In contrast to this is the interpretation which refers every part of the dream and all the actors in it back to the dreamer himself. This I call *interpretation on the subjective level*.[71]

When the internal compensatory content associated with the synchronistic experience is interpreted on the subjective level, it must be determined exactly how this content relates to the subject's personality. In seeking to establish this fact, the following question might be addressed: What aspect of the individual's personality does this unconscious synchronistic content personify? It was mentioned above, for example, that Jung dreamt of Churchill during the war when he approached the Swiss border. If Jung was to interpret the internal compensatory content strictly on the objective level, he would simply think that this synchronistic dream is telling him about Churchill's presence near the Swiss border and he would leave it at that. On the other hand, an interpretation on the subjective level calls for Jung to understand exactly what aspect of his own personality Churchill personifies, so that he might know the specific compensatory import of this image. We saw that this particular experience related to the development of the extraverted side of Jung's personality.

Confining the interpretation to the objective level is, of course, something that many people do with these types of synchronistic experiences. They are fascinated with the paralleling of the inner and outer events and simply do not move beyond this to explore more directly their own subjective level of involvement with what has taken place. This type of attitude to these events certainly has its limitations, for when one consistently neglects the personal growth and self-knowledge that a subjective-level interpretation of these events introduces, when one never looks beyond the superficial, things become both sterile and monotonous, as often happens with groups studying psychical phenomena. For analytical psychology, and as we will see in the next chapter, for psychoanalysis as well, the analytical import of these events is always paramount.

In addition to the unconscious content standing in a compensatory relationship to consciousness, we have seen that the objective synchronistic event also is understood to stand in a compensatory relationship to consciousness. Both the inner image and the outer event are distinct aspects of the same compensatory pattern, and accordingly, are to be treated as parts of a unified whole, which as a total phenomenon requires interpretation on the subjective level. Along this line, Bender reports that Jung once explained to him that dreams and synchronistic experiences are to be examined in exactly the same way for their compensatory content. "He [Jung] told me," Bender writes, "if it was a dream or real life, it is all the same thing. It is an expression of the same cryptic acausal relationship between psyche and nature."[72] Similarly, Fordham writes, focusing more on the implications of all of this for parapsychological research in general, "the important element in Jung's thesis [about synchronicity] is . . . that it makes the whole subject of para-psychology accessible to analysis in terms of the [compensatory] relation between the ego and the archetypal objects."[73] Finally, we should note that Bolen, also seeking to draw attention to the compensatory relationship that exists between the ego and the inner and outer events of the synchronistic experience, has suggested that the synchronistic experience as a whole might very well be thought of as a type of "waking dream."[74]

In turning to the case study under investigation, it is clear that there are details that Jung has not included that would greatly aid the subjective-level interpretation. For instance, in developing a more complete understanding of this case, we would want to know who actually gave the golden scarab to the young woman in her dream. In other words, what specific aspect of her personality is working to facilitate the new development taking place, of which the scarab is the central symbol? In the absence of information like this, it is, nevertheless, possible to achieve a good sense of the import of the subjective level of meaning.

We do know that a standstill had been reached in the analytical process. As Jung's report indicates, the woman's animus problem, her neglect of her feelings in favor of the extreme onesidedness of a purely intellectual position, had proven to be a tremendous obstacle to progress. What, therefore, was required from a compensatory point of view was something to break this standstill—something to inject new life into the analysis. What was required was something to break the intellectual retort that had become, much to their mutual dismay, the inadequate container of the work. As we know, two events combined to do this. First, there was the intrapsychic event in which she was handed a golden scarab by a person who is not identified in Jung's report. Second, there was the synchronistic experience in which she was handed a real scarab by Jung. Clearly, the analysand's ego had reached its limits and, accordingly, it needed to be handed something, that is to say, dramatically compensated by the unconscious. It needed to be given something very specific and of great value that it did not possess in order for things to move more productively. In the first instance, this critical gift took the form of a golden scarab, a very expensive piece of jewelry. In the second instance, and this, I believe, is the important compensatory twist in this account, she was given an even more valuable scarab still, one that would be this time handed to her by Jung in the course of an analytical session. The scarab that she was presented with by Jung was not a costly piece of jewelry, but rather a priceless product of nature. It was a unique gift, whose acceptance, moreover, would require the utilization of her feeling. In handing his analysand the living scarab, Jung was symbolically handing the young woman her natural being.

d) *The archetypal level of meaning*

"Synchronicity," Jung writes, "postulates a meaning which is *a priori* in relation to human consciousness and apparently exists outside man."[73] The transcendental meaning to which Jung here refers is, of course, the psychophysical pattern of meaning of the psychoid archetype. The fourth layer of meaning is concerned, then, with the interpretation of those specific manifestations of the constellated psychophysical pattern of the archetype.

With synchronistic experiences involving "absolute knowledge," archetypal contents are present both within and outside of the individual. With respect to the inner experience, an unconscious content moves out of the space-time world of the archetype into the space- and time-bound world of ego-consciousness, bringing with it an element of the timelessness and spacelessness of that archetypal world. In this manner, the subject is provided with a non-sensory-based "absolute knowledge" of the corresponding external event, which, it should be emphasized, is an expression of the same psychophysical pattern of meaning. Forming the basis of the synchronistic experience of "absolute knowledge," there is, therefore, "in the unconscious something like an *a priori* knowledge or an 'immediacy' of events"[76] through the psychophysical continuum of the archetype, to which, furthermore, the individual has access in accordance with the principle of psychic compensation.

Returning to the case study of the golden scarab, we see the above-described intrapsychic compensatory activity at work in the young woman's dream. Writing with specific reference to this, Jung states: "The patient with the scarab found herself in an 'impossible' situation because the treatment had got stuck and there seemed to be no way out of the impasse. In such situations, if they are serious enough, archetypal dreams are likely to occur which point out a possible line of advance one would never have thought of oneself."[77] In response, then, to the psychic impasse that had been reached in the analysis, the image of the constellated archetype, the scarab, passed into consciousness, bringing with it some of the "absolute knowledge" characteristic of the archetypal world. Accordingly, the content of the young woman's dream was able to anticipate and form a meaningful parallel with the actual appearance and presentation of the scarab in Jung's office.

The question that now arises is, What is the specific compensatory significance of the scarab? What is the relevancy of this archetypal symbol to someone who has reached such an impasse in her analysis, someone who, moreover, desperately needs to develop a new feeling-based relationship to life? In answering this question,

Jung points to the important fact that the "scarab is a classic example of a rebirth symbol." Elaborating further on the scarab symbol and drawing on Egyptian mythology to do so, Jung writes, "The ancient Egyptian Book of What Is in the Netherworld describes how the dead sun-god changes himself at the tenth station into Khepri, the scarab, and then, at the twelfth station, mounts the barge which carries the rejuvenated sun-god into the morning sky."[78] Like the dead sun-god of the Egyptian myth, Jung's analysand too was in need of an experience of transformation and renewal. Accordingly, the scarab, as a symbol of the constellated archetypal pattern of rebirth and renewal, served to provide her with just such an experience. Appearing first in her dream, then in actual fact in the analytical session where Jung was able literally to hand her this living symbol of her emergent natural being, the scarab did indeed fulfil its archetypal role as a symbol of radical and dramatic rejuvenation.

In conclusion, four interrelated layers of meaning have been described in relation to the synchronistic experience. With respect to this, it should be borne in mind that the depth of one's experience of the synchronistic event will grow in proportion to the ability of the individual consciously to assimilate these various levels of meaning. Assimilation of these levels of meaning is not a task, however, that is easily achieved. Indeed, a considerable degree of self-knowledge is required in order for one to assimilate the full meaning associated with these synchronistic experiences.

In the case study that we have just examined, the compensatory images were experienced both inwardly and outwardly. There is, however, as has already been noted, a type of synchronistic experience in which the compensatory image is experienced outwardly only. This second type of synchronistic event is that with which we shall now be concerned.

Without distinguishing them as such, Jung does provide examples of both types of synchronistic experiences in his principal paper on synchronicity. As mentioned previously, one phenomenon Jung identifies as being based on the synchronicity principle that we would place in this second category is the casting of the *I Ching*. In addition to this, we find in the principal essay a case history that is also of this second type. Describing the case, Jung writes:

> The wife of one of my patients, a man in his fifties, once told me in conversation that, at the deaths of her mother and her grandmother, a number of birds gathered outside the windows

of the death-chamber. I had heard similar stories from other people. When her husband's treatment was nearing its end . . . he developed some apparently quite innocuous symptoms which seemed to me, however, to be those of heart-disease. I sent him along to a specialist, who after examining him told me in writing that he could find no cause for anxiety. On the way back from this consultation (with the medical report in his pocket) my patient collapsed in the street. As he was brought home dying, his wife was already in a great state of anxiety because, soon after her husband had gone to the doctor, a whole flock of birds alighted on their house. She naturally remembered the similar incidents that had happened at the death of her own relatives, and feared the worst.[79]

With this example, certainly no internal compensatory image provided the woman with information about her husband's serious condition. In fact prior to the arrival of the flock of birds, Jung notes, the woman was not at all concerned about her husband's health, "for the symtoms (pains in the throat) were not of a kind to make the layman suspect anything bad."[80] When, however, the "birds alighted on their house," much as they had done at the time of the deaths of her mother and grandmother, the woman became very alarmed and concerned for her husband. Her worst fears, which arose solely on the basis of this external synchronistic manifestation, proved, of course, to be well founded.

Although Jung does mention this experience in his principal essay, I do think that he tends to play down this type of synchronistic experience, perhaps because he was not able to express his thinking about both types of synchronistic events in a unified theory. This theoretical weakness is suggested by the fact that his summary of synchronistic phenomena really only addresses the first type of synchronistic event. We do know, however, in looking beyond this essay, that synchronistic experiences of this second type were highly regarded by Jung and considered no less meaningful than those of the first type. For example, when Jung analyzed in the " 'garden room', which was a small square room at the corner of his garden, directly on the lake," he would take, Hannah relates, based on an account given by von Franz, "every natural event, such as insects flying in, the lake lapping more audibly than usual, and so on, as belonging synchronistically to what was being said in the analysis."[81] This is to say, of course, that Jung would take the events taking place in the environment as a type of synchronistic commentary on the unfolding analytical session, the compensatory yea or nay of nature, as it were.

Given his belief in the synchronistic interrelatedness of the events of nature, and his remarkable familiarity with the symbolical language of the unconscious—the language of synchronistic phenomena—Jung, it is clear, had a highly refined sensitivity to those synchronistic events in which the compensatory image appears externally only. This sensitivity is well evidenced in the following account provided by Henry K. Fierz, based on a meeting he had with Jung in the 1950s.

Fierz, who had been "charged to publish a book of a scientist who had died just recently," had, at the request of the editors, forwarded a copy of the manuscript to Jung for his evaluation. After Jung had had time to examine it, an appointment for 5:00 p.m. was arranged to discuss publication. Describing the events of that meeting, Fierz writes:

> Jung had read the book and he thought that it should not be published, but I disagreed and was for publication. Our discussion finally got rather sharp, and Jung looked at his wristwatch, obviously thinking that he had spent enough time on the matter and that he could send me home. Looking at his watch he said: "When did you come?" I: "At five, as agreed." Jung: "But that's queer. My watch came back from the watchmaker this morning after a complete revision, and now I have 5:05. But you must have been here much longer. What time do you have?" I: "It's 5:35." Whereon Jung said: "So you have the right time, and I the wrong one. Let us discuss the thing again." This time I could convince Jung that the book should be published.[82]

1) *The specific intrapsychic state of the subject*
   b) *The conscious orientation of the subject around which the compensatory synchronistic activity centers*

Jung, we read, was against publication of the book and, moreover, not at all receptive to the arguments in support of publication being offered by Fierz. Jung's failure to give Fierz, and the manuscript for that matter, a sympathetic hearing was, therefore, the conscious orientation toward which the compensatory synchronistic event was addressed.

2) *An objective event corresponds with this intrapsychic state*
   b) *The objective event as the sole compensator of ego-consciousness*

The objective compensatory event that corresponded with Jung's conscious orientation was the stopping of his watch.

3) *Even though the intrapsychic state and the objective event may be synchronous according to clock time and spatially near to each other, the objective event may, contrary to this, be distant in time and/or space in relation to the intrapsychic state*

With this example, the subjective and objective events are spatially near to each other. Jung, it seems, was wearing his watch when it stopped. With respect to the time framework, we see that Fierz arrived at 5:00 p.m. and Jung's watch stopped at 5:05 p.m. Although we do not know the exact moment their discussion got underway, it is clearly the case that Jung's watch stopped very close to, if not exactly at the moment of, the beginning of what would be their failed attempt to exchange points of view.

4) *The intrapsychic state and the objective event are not causally related to each other*

With this case, there is no demonstrable causal connection between the intrapsychic event, Jung's intransigence, and the objective event, the stopping of Jung's watch. There is no necessary connection between these two events, no mutual dependency concerning their existence.

5) *The synchronistic event is meaningful*
   a) *The intrapsychic state and the objective event as meaningful parallels*

The fact that Jung was able to recognize so quickly the meaningful relationship between his conscious position and the stopping of his watch, and see in the latter a kind of compensatory statement about his discussion with Fierz, certainly evinces Jung's sensitivity to synchronistic events of this second type. Not everyone, of course, seeking to identify these types of events, could do so so readily. Accordingly, Progoff has introduced a technique simply termed "correlation," which is designed to heighten awareness of these events. The idea is for one to record the significant inner and outer events of one's life. We then, Progoff explains, "set the two side by side, and we let the correlations between them present themselves to us and speak to us." Through this technique, Progoff writes, one is able to perceive more fully the "unity of outer and inner in the continuity of life experience."[83]

b) *The numinous charge associated with the synchronistic experience*

The numinous charge associated with this synchronistic event is evidenced in Jung's experience of momentary shock when he noticed his watch has stopped. Having discovered that his watch was not showing the correct time, Jung, it seems, was immediately struck by the feeling that this event was of special significance to their discussion. Perhaps this is why he was led to ask himself: "What does this mean in terms of our discussion?" as opposed to the more expected question, "What did the watchmaker do to my wristwatch when he was working on it this morning?" One would think that a feeling-level sense of the numinous would have had to have been present for Jung to have so directly pursued the former question over the latter.

c) *Import of the subjective-level interpretation*

When Fierz arrived to discuss the possible publishing of the manuscript, Jung had already reached the conclusion that it should not be published. Jung, moreover, was confident he had reached the correct decision and, accordingly, was not interested in giving consideration to Fierz's ideas. However, as soon as Jung discovered that his watch had stopped and was able to reflect on the meaning of this synchronistic experience, Jung realized that it was Fierz, and not he, who was correct. Jung's acknowledgment of this compensatory synchronistic message is revealed in his statement to Fierz: " 'So you have the right time, and I the wrong one. Let us discuss the thing again.' "The second time around, we learn, Fierz was able to "convince Jung that the book should be published."

In order to interpret the compensatory meaning of synchronistic experiences such as this, one must really be able, as Jaffé puts it, to *think in the terms of the unconscious.* "It would be a mistake," Jaffé explains, "to harbor any illusion about the difficulty which the concept of synchronicity presents. In effect, it demands a way of thinking other than the thinking based on causality. . . . The concept of synchronicity . . . demands a sort of 'circular' or dream thinking."[84] With respect to our present case, it is clear that Jung was not genuinely listening to the arguments being put forward by Fierz. At a time when Jung should have allowed himself to be receptive to the points of view offered by Fierz, he was not. The stopping of Jung's watch, therefore, in terms of "dream thinking," corresponded with the stopping of Jung's mind as regards the ideas being presented in support of publication. The compensatory principle being followed here is thus the principle of "like curing like."

d) *The archetypal level of meaning*

The death theme is so strongly pronounced in this synchronistic case history that one is led to the conclusion that the active archetype is the archetype of death. Particularly salient are the following three features. First, we know that the manuscript that was brought by Fierz to Jung for his evaluation was the work of a scientist who had only recently died. Second, we know that Jung had been empowered by the editors to pass judgement on the work. The editors "wanted C. G. Jung's opinion." It seems that the fate of the manuscript was very much in Jung's hands. If Jung came out strongly against publication, as he was ready to do prior to the synchronistic manifestation, the editors would have most probably rejected the manuscript also. Jung, therefore, held in effect the power of life and death over this work, and he was initially very much partial to the latter. Third, the external compensatory event took the form of Jung's watch stopping, a synchronistic phenomenon commonly associated with death.[85]

Intrepidly carrying the light amidst all this darkness was Fierz. He was the one who had been "charged" to publish this work of the deceased scientist. He was the one who had had to deal with the obvious doubts of the publishers who, being unable to reach their own decision, sent him to Jung where he ran into an even greater resistance. Jung's opposition was a double blow, for not only did it threaten to kill the book itself, but it threatened also to kill the new life that the deceased author would be given through its publication. Fortunately for all concerned, however, when Jung saw that his watch had stopped and that Fierz had the correct time, he realized that he was the one standing in the darkness of the archetype of death, not Fierz. He, Jung realized, not Fierz, had made the error in judgement.

An interesting footnote to this synchronistic account is provided by Fierz. About the book's venture into the marketplace, Fierz reports, "It is now out of print, having made a profit for the heirs of the author, and for the editors; a new edition is planned."[86]

The Psyche as Microcosm

In the previous chapter, it was demonstrated that within Jung's synchronicity theory nature is understood to compensate consciousness not just intrapsychically, but rather both inwardly and outwardly. As also explained, however, it is the case that this synchronistic activity of nature is not always experienced by the subject on both of these levels in a given instance. We can, therefore, supported fully by Jung's examples, speak of two general types of synchronistic experiences. The first type concerns synchronistic events in which the compensatory activity of nature is experienced both inwardly and outwardly. The second type concerns synchronistic events in which the compensatory activity of nature is experienced outwardly only. In this chapter, we shall now turn to examine in greater detail the first type of synchronistic event. This will be followed by an equally comprehensive examination of the second type of synchronistic event in chapter 4.

The first synchronistic case history that we shall examine in this chapter is the much-discussed synchronistic experience that took place during Jung's visit with Freud in Vienna in 1909.[1] This synchronistic experience, it should be noted, is situated in time near the midpoint of the Freud-Jung collaboration, which extended from 1906 to 1913. This will be followed by a study of the development of Freud's thinking on telepathy—the most relevant area of Freud's work to the concerns of this chapter. Having compared and contrasted the thinking of Freud and Jung on the subject of telepathic-type phenomena, we shall turn to explore specifically the Jungian concept of the psyche as microcosm.

On the last evening that Jung spent with Freud during his visit to Vienna in 1909, Jung, it seems, seeking to learn what he could about Freud's position on parapsychological phenomena, took it upon himself to introduce this subject into their discussion. Freud, however, as Jung relates in his autobiography, "rejected this entire complex of questions as nonsensical, and did so in terms of so shallow a positivism that I had difficulty in checking the sharp retort on the tip of my tongue." Describing what then took place, Jung writes:

> While Freud was going on this way, I had a curious sensation. It was as if my diaphragm were made of iron and were becoming red-hot—a glowing vault. And at that moment there was such a loud report in the bookcase, which stood right next to us, that we both started up in alarm, fearing the thing was going to topple over on us. I said to Freud: "There, that is an example of a so-called catalytic exteriorization phenomenon." "Oh come," he exclaimed. "That is sheer bosh." "It is not," I replied. "You are mistaken, Herr Professor. And to prove my point I now predict that in a moment there will be another such loud report!" Sure enough, no sooner had I said the words than the same detonation went off in the bookcase. . . . Freud only stared aghast at me. I do not know what was in his mind, or what his look meant. In any case, This incident aroused his mistrust of me, and I had the feeling that I had done something against him.[2]

In the above description, we are presented with two instances of the synchronistic paralleling of inner and outer events. The first inner/outer parallel took the form, intrapsychically, of an actual physical sensation: "It was as if my diaphragm," Jung writes, "were made of iron and were becoming red-hot—a glowing vault." At that moment, the outer event, the first report, was heard. This was followed by a second and a different type of inner/outer paralleling, for the intrapsychic experience took the form of an intuition which prompted Jung to exclaim: " 'I now predict that in a moment there will be another such loud report!' " Confessing his own amazement with the accuracy of his prediction, Jung writes: "To this day I do not know what gave me this certainty. But I knew beyond all doubt that the report would come again."[3]

Even though Jung does not reflect in his autobiography on the compensatory significance of this synchronistic experience, there can be no question that both he and Freud sensed that the perplexing events of their last evening together in Vienna were of no small significance for their relationship. We should perhaps begin our investigation into the compensatory significance of this synchronistic experience, then, with a look at the Freud-Jung relationship at the time of Jung's trip to Vienna in 1909.

In 1909, Freud and Jung in both their personal relationship and, to a lesser degree, their scientific collaboration had become very much victims of their mutual projections. Freud, Jung recalls in his memoirs, "was the first man of real importance I had encountered. . . . There was nothing the least trivial in his attitude. I found him extremely intelligent, shrewd, and altogether remarkable."[4] Freud's feelings and expectations regarding Jung were no less intense and may in fact have been stronger still. Freud, for example, in a letter dated January 17, 1909, written roughly two months before their meeting in Vienna, states, "We are certainly getting ahead; if I am Moses, then you are Joshua and will take possession of the promised land of psychiatry, which I shall only be able to glimpse from afar."[5] It is clearly the case that in 1909 Freud and Jung, through their mutual projections, had trapped themselves in the psychological relationship of that of father and son, respectively. For Jung, however, who unlike Freud had not yet grasped the essence of that which would constitute his own scientific contribution, this arrangement was far more threatening. For Jung, who never would fully accept the scientific position put forward by Freud,[6] the weight of what he had come to describe in 1909 as "the oppressive sense of your [Freud's] paternal authority"[7] was beginning to make the younger man feel uncomfortable.

In his autobiography, Jung recalls how difficult he found it at the time to express to Freud certain reservations that he had about the sexual theory. Although he attempted on several occasions to challenge Freud, Jung simply found himself unable to gain any ground on this matter. Commenting on this problem, Jung writes:

> Above all, Freud's attitude toward the spirit seemed to me highly questionable. Wherever, in a person or in a work of art, an expression of spirituality (in the intellectual, not the supernatural sense) came to light, he suspected it, and insinuated that it was repressed sexuality. . . . I protested that . . . culture would then appear as a mere farce, the morbid consequence of repressed sexuality. "Yes," he assented, "so it is, and that is just a curse of fate against which we are powerless to contend." I was by no means disposed to agree, or let it go at that, but still I did not feel competent to argue it out with him.[8]

What is perhaps an even more striking example of not only the great differences in the points of view of these two men, but also of the extent of Jung's sense of intimidation, is another exchange that most probably also took place during Jung's visit to Vienna in 1909.[9] Jung relates in his autobiography how Freud in an emotional fatherly tone said to him: " 'My dear Jung, promise me never to abandon the sexual theory. That is the most essential thing of all. You see, we must make a dogma of it, an unshakable bulwark.' " Jung then inquired, " 'A bulwark—against what?' " To which, Jung relates, Freud replied, " 'Against the black tide of mud'—and here he hesitated for a moment, then added—'of occultism.' " This request, Jung recalls, seemed astonishing, for not only was Freud calling for an unscientific posture, but through his very broad definition of "occultism" he was in effect calling for the erection of a barrier against "virtually everything that philosophy and religion, including the rising contemporary science of parapsychology, had learned about the psyche." Remarkably enough, however, in the face of this assault on some of his most highly valued sources of information on the psyche, Jung, after "a few stammering attempts," simply abandoned his rebuttal and allowed the conversation to come to an end.[10]

We see from the above, then, that the "occult" had become the point around which Freud and Jung's personal and scientific differences were constellated. On one level, for Jung, the "occult" was a highly valued source of psychological data. In contrast to this, for Freud " 'the black tide of mud of occultism' " was a menacing element seeking to bury once again all that he had worked so hard to uncover. On yet another level, for Jung it was the ground upon which he could stand quite independent of Freud. In this way, it was somewhat of a symbol of Jung's individuality. For Freud, however, who had his own interests to protect, Jung's involvement with the "occult" was taken as a sign of potential rebellion. This analysis, as we shall now see, is further borne out in the exchange of letters that followed the Vienna visit.

In reading Jung's first letter to Freud after returning to Zurich—a letter begun on April 2, 1909 but not completed until April 12—one immediately experiences how the parapsychological events of the Vienna visit served to strengthen Jung's convictions about some of his own ideas. Indeed, seizing hold of the momentum of those events, Jung spoke freely not only about "a madly interesting case" involving "first-rate spiritualistic phenomena," but also about a subject that for Freud was, and would remain, an even greater anathema than the occult—the subject of "the prospective tendencies in man." Carried along by what he describes as "a flight of ideas," Jung writes "If there is a 'psychanalysis' [sic] there must also be a 'psychosynthesis' which creates future events according to the same laws." Even though in his letter Jung does not directly link his concept of psychosynthesis with his comments about spiritualistic phenomena, this idea could not have been far from his mind, as he had already linked the two in his dissertation for his medical degree. One of the central ideas of Jung's dissertation titled "On the Psychology and Pathology of So-called Occult Phenomena" (1902) is that there exists a relationship between the psychic states experienced by mediums and the emergence of new dimensions of personality in those same individuals. The mediumistic state, Jung argues in that work, may actually give expression to the "attempts of the future personality to break through."[11]

The parapsychological events of Freud and Jung's last evening in Vienna thus did a great deal to encourage Jung, in fact so much so that Jung felt he could even mention this to Freud. In the following excerpt from Jung's letter to Freud, it is interesting to see, first, how the compensatory synchronistic events of Freud and Jung's last evening together in Vienna served to remove the yoke of Freud's paternal control. Second, it is equally interesting to see how no sooner was this done than Jung himself placed it back on. "That last evening with you," Jung writes,

> has, most happily, freed me inwardly from the oppressive sense of your paternal authority. My unconscious celebrated this impression with a great dream which . . . I have just finished analysing. I hope I am now rid of all unnecessary encumbrances. Your cause must and will prosper, so my pregnancy fantasies tell me. . . . As soon as I get back from Italy, I shall begin some positive work, first of all for the *Jahrbuch*.[12]

Jung's above comments certainly reflect the degree of his own unconsciousness with respect to the subjective import of the synchronistic events in Vienna. Jung did correctly sense that he was being led toward an experience of greater freedom. Still, Jung's ultimate conclusion was that his energy was not being released for his own purposes, but rather to allow him to serve Freud more fully. Interestingly enough, Freud, however, was not satisfied with this statement of submission on the part of Jung. Freud, it seems, was more concerned with the inauspiciousness of the events of the last evening in Vienna. Freud was convinced that there was an element of rebellion in what had taken place. Jung's letter with its talk of

new feelings of freedom "from the oppressive sense of your paternal authority" served only to confirm this suspicion. Freud therefore wasted no time in writing back to Jung to exert his influence on
things. Using the full weight of his fatherly role to do this, Freud
chastised Jung for what he believed was an open attack on his authority. "It is strange," Freud writes in a letter dated April 16,

> that on the very same evening when I formally adopted you as
> eldest son and anointed you—*in partibus infidelium*—[in the
> land of the unbelievers]—as my successor and crown prince,
> you should have divested me of my paternal dignity, which
> divesting seems to have given you as much pleasure as I, on
> the contrary, derived from the investiture of your person. Now
> I am afraid of falling back into the father role with you if I tell
> you how I feel about this poltergeist business.[13]

From here, Freud proceeded to provide his own "explanation"
of the poltergeist[14] phenomena, which Freud frankly admitted he
could not believe in. "My willingness to believe," Freud writes,
"vanished with the magic of your personal presence; once again, for
some inward reasons that I can't put my finger on, it strikes me as
quite unlikely that such phenomena should exist; I confront the de-
spiritualized furniture as the poet confronted undeified Nature after
the gods of Greece had passed away." Freud then went on to ad-
monish Jung's general interest in both the occult and psychosynthesis, areas which Freud clearly associated with Jung's struggle for
greater personal and scientific freedom. "I put my fatherly horned-
rimmed spectacles on again," Freud writes about the occult,

> and warn my dear son to keep a cool head, for it is better not
> to understand something than make such great sacrifices to
> understanding. I also shake my wise head over psychosynthe-
> sis and think: Yes, that's how the young people are, the only
> places they really enjoy visiting are those they can visit with-
> out us, to which we with our short breath and weary legs can-
> not follow them.[15]

Having returned from Italy to find Freud's distressful letter
waiting for him, Jung wrote back to Freud on May 12, primarily
seeking, it seems, to stablize their relationship. "I am entirely of
your opinion," Jung writes, "that one must be careful not to be carried away by impressions or indulge in expectations and plans that

go too far. . . . I have not gone over to any system yet and shall also guard against putting my trust in those spooks [poltergeists]."[16]

Even though Jung does not identify a particular archetypal pattern as being associated with the synchronistic events in Vienna, one is led, nevertheless, by comments made by Jung himself about similar cases, to connect the "trickster" archetype with these events. The trickster archetypal symbols, Joseph Henderson explains, form part of a larger category referred to as " 'symbols of transcendence,' " which serve to guide the individual toward the realization of his highest level of being. The trickster symbols themselves, however, belong to "the most archaic level of this symbolism."[17] It is thus the case that the trickster manifests itself in a form that is notoriously unrefined. Accordingly, in the parapsychological area, Jung connects the trickster archetype with the poltergeist manifestations:

> certain phenomena in the field of parapsychology . . . remind us of the trickster. These are the phenomena connected with poltergeists, and they occur at all times and places in the ambience of pre-adolescent children. The malicious tricks played by the poltergeist are as well known as the low level of his intelligence and the fatuity of his "communications."[18]

Through its undifferentiated and often mischievous communications, the trickster initiates what will become a comprehensive movement of psychic energy. It is understandable, then, why with preadolescent children, who are unknowingly on the verge of a major psychic transition, the trickster-related poltergeist phenomena are not at all uncommon. Poltergeist phenomena, however, also tend to occur, as the Freud-Jung case study indicates, in the vicinity of individuals who may not be close in years to preadolescence, but are at a comparable point of psychic transition. Jung describes, for example, how he "had to overcome the greatest inner resistances" before he was able to write "Answer to Job." A major step was to be taken with this work and, therefore, when he was yet unaware of the "problem of Job in all its ramifications," Jung had a dream that contained, in one scene, poltergeist phenomena. Commenting on the meaning of these events, Jung writes: "Poltergeist phenomena usually take place in the vicinity of young people before puberty; that is to say, I am still immature and too unconscious."[19]

In 1909, Jung certainly was at a point of psychic transition comparable to that of the preadolescent. Like the preadolescent,

Jung was subjugated by the presence of seemingly unconquerable authority; specifically, in Jung's case, the authority of a seemingly unconquerable "father." Furthermore, like the preadolescent, Jung was unknowingly on the verge of a major psychic transition—in his case, a period of radical psychic transformation that would begin in 1913 and last for at least six years before providing Jung with those insights that would form the basis of his unique scientific contribution.[20] It would seem, then, that the trickster archetype was indeed the constellated archetypal pattern in this instance.

In conclusion, we have seen how in 1909 Jung was unknowingly on the verge of a major transitional period, comparable to the position of a preadolescent. Given the great degree of Jung's unconsciousness about his future, which would among other things involve parting ways with Freud in 1913, the situation was most certainly ripe for the activities of the trickster archetype which, so to speak, masterfully chose its time and place. The compensatory effect of the synchronistic events in Vienna was not such that an unmovable wedge was driven between the two men. The synchronistic events, however, did serve to support Jung in the development of his own point of view and to distance him somewhat from the oppressive side of Freud's paternalism. What Freud and Jung were presented with during their last evening in Vienna—significantly when Freud had just conferred on Jung the status of crown prince—was simply an inauspicious signal of what was to come. It was a signal whose meaning Freud, curiously enough, more so than Jung, was able to understand.

When "rebellion" comes to one as fate, which it seems was Jung's lot in his relationship with Freud, the task of rebellion itself is made all the more difficult to rationalize, both to oneself and others, when points of tension with the person against whom one is destined to rebel are lessened. Perhaps this is why amongst students of Jung, encouraged tacitly by Jung himself, it has remained a largely unacknowledged fact that shortly after the synchronistic events in Vienna, Freud's attitude toward telepathic-type events was to be considerably revised and, moreover, that Freud would go on to write, after Jung's departure, four rather favorable papers on this subject.

Some six months after the synchronistic events in Vienna, on September 29, 1909, Freud and Jung arrived back in Europe from what had been a very eventful trip to the United States, the highlights of which had been their lectures to a group of distinguished psychologists and psychiatrists at the Clark Conference, before being presented themselves with honorary doctorates of law by Clark University. From Bremen, Germany, where their ship had landed, Jung went on to his home in Zurich, while Freud and the Hungarian psychoanalyst Sandor Ferenczi, who had travelled with them to America, went on to Hamburg and Berlin.[21] While in Berlin, Ferenczi and Freud visited a medium, someone whom, Ernest Jones explains, "claimed to have the gift of reading letters while blindfolded." Although Freud did not believe that the woman medium had the skills she claimed to possess, he nevertheless concluded that the woman did appear to have certain telepathic powers. With this in mind, Freud wrote in a letter to Ferenczi on October 6, 1909, " 'I am afraid you have begun to discover something big, but there will be great difficulties in the way of making use of it.' "[22] On the seventeenth of that same month, Freud wrote to Jung to inform him of the "project" he and Ferenczi were working on, the results of which Freud would make known to Jung as they took shape.[23]

On August 17, 1910, with the telepathic "project" now underway, Ferenczi sent Freud a collection of notes he had put together describing the telepathic perceptions of one of his patients. On August 20, after having studied this material, Freud wrote back to Ferenczi, as Jones explains, stating in effect that this data "put an end to any possible remaining doubt about the reality of thought-transference. Henceforward the new knowledge was to be taken for granted." That December, when Freud met with Jung in Munich, he finally was able to inform Jung of Ferenczi's findings. Jones writes about this meeting that Freud "was not surprised to hear that Jung had long been fully convinced of the reality of telepathy and had carried out most convincing experiments himself."[24] Some five months later, Jung, now much inspired by the discussion that had taken place in Munich, suggested to Freud in a letter dated May 8, 1911, that "occultism is another field we shall have to conquer."[25] Responding favorably to what he would describe to Ferenczi as Jung's call for a "crusade,"[26] Freud, replying to Jung in a letter dated June 15, states: "In matters of occultism I have grown humble since the great lesson Ferenczi's experiences gave me. I promise to believe anything that can be made to look reasonable. I shall not do so gladly, that you know. But my [hubris] has been shattered. I should be glad to know that you are in harmony with F. [Ferenczi] when one of you decides to take the dangerous step into publication."[27]

Nothing did, of course, come of the "crusade" that Jung and Ferenczi were to set out on with Freud's blessing. For Freud's own part, on the other hand, it would be a few years before he would himself "take the dangerous step into publication." No doubt his interest in this area was dampened for a few years by the upheaval created with Jung's departure in 1913. In the summer of 1921, however, new life was to be breathed into Freud's own interest in the subject of telepathy. Perhaps, as Jones suggests, it had something to do with the fact that during that summer, Freud received invitations from three periodicals devoted to the study of psychical research to serve as coeditor. Freud, whom we might note had been made a Corresponding Member of the Society for Psychical Research in London in 1911 and an Honorary Fellow of the American Society for Psychical Research in 1915, however, declined all three offers,[28] most certainly very much to Jones's great relief.

Of the three invitations, one came from Hereward Carrington of New York.[29] In his reply to Carrington, Freud revealed a great deal about his position on the subject of psychical research at that particular time. Indeed it was in this letter that Freud tellingly remarked, "If I were at the beginning rather than at the end of a scientific career, as I am today, I might possibly choose just this field of research, in spite of all difficulties." Freud went on, however, to ask that Carrington not associate him with their work, providing three reasons for his request. First, Freud rightly pointed out that he did not have the training to judge the wide variety of work taking place in that field. Freud's interest in psychical research was, and would remain, confined to its application to psychoanalytical practice. Second, reflecting a position toward the "occult" that had hardened as a result of both Jung's departure and the greater influence wielded now by Jones, Freud wrote, "I have good reason to be interested in sharply demarcating psychoanalysis (which has nothing occult about it) from this as yet unexplored sphere of knowledge." Finally, Freud confessed that "certain sceptical-materialistic prejudices" that he held provided a considerable obstacle to his study of such phenomena.[30]

Although Freud did in fact decline in the summer of 1921 three invitations to participate, in an editorial capacity, in psychical research being conducted by others, that summer was nevertheless a turning point with respect to his own investigations into psychical phenomena, specifically into the subject of telepathy. Just weeks after he wrote to Carrington, Freud began his first full paper on the subject of telepathy, which he read the following month, in September, before a small group of his most trusted followers who had gathered for a meeting in the Harz mountains. It had been Freud's intention to put before this group three relevant case studies. When he arrived at Gastein and examined his notes, he discovered, however, that he had inadvertently left what was to be the third case behind in Vienna. Characteristic of the meticulous analysis to which Freud was not reluctant to subject himself publicly, he later attributed this oversight to "resistance." In spite of this, Freud still managed to put together three cases for the Harz meeting. Several years later, the missing "third case" was utilized by Freud in his paper "Dreams and Occultism" (1933).[31]

The Harz paper, "Psycho-analysis and Telepathy," was not published during Freud's lifetime, something for which Jones claims partial credit.[32] It was, however, eventually published in 1941. In "Psycho-analysis and Telepathy," Freud argues that serious attention needs to be given to the study of occult phenomena, as it is only a matter of time before investigations into these events confirm "the occurrence of a number of them."[33] The real difficulty, though, Freud adds, is to know how to further this type of study without precipitating "the fearful collapse of critical thought, of deterministic standards and of mechanistic science." To this end, Freud suggests, psychoanalysis may have something rather special to offer, even though it may very well attract the hostilities of both the "occultists" and "official science" for its efforts.[34] To demonstrate exactly what the special contribution of psychoanalysis might be, Freud introduces his case material, which he notes has two distinguishing characteristics. First, making a rather moot point, Freud asserts that his material "is exempt from the uncertainties and doubts to which most of the observations of the occultists are prone." Second, and this is a much more important point as it identifies the specific contribution depth psychology makes to this area, he notes that the case material being presented for consideration "only develops its convincing force after it has been worked over analytically."[35] In other words, in the absence of psychoanalytical decoding, the exchange of information that is in fact taking place telepathically would go unnoticed.

It is certainly not possible, as interesting as it would be to do so, to examine all the cases Freud presents in this paper and in his other essays on telepathy. Accordingly, we shall confine our examination of the case material to three examples, which will provide us with a good sense of the type of work carried out by Freud in his case studies on telepathy. With respect to the essays themselves, we shall move through Freud's papers on telepathy in chronological order, noting as we proceed their outstanding features.

Several of Freud's case studies on the subject of telepathy appear in more than one essay, and the case we are about to examine is not an exception.[36] The following case is characteristic of a type Freud found particularly attractive. It involves a situation in which information provided by a professional fortune-teller, which at first glance appears not to be accurate, is ultimately shown to relate directly to the life of the subject. Its relevancy, however, is something that can only be established through the utilization of psychoanalytical technique, for the information that the professional fortune-teller has unknowingly produced relates not to the conscious life of the subject, but rather to the unconscious life of the subject. One thing that we should note about the case to follow is that it had been in Freud's possession for some time. Freud actually sent this case as an example of telepathy to Ferenczi in January of 1911.[37]

The case involves a woman who had grown up as the eldest child in "a family of five, all girls." As the eldest child, she had been thrust into the position of serving as a type of "repository" for the family worries: her father, to whom she was very close, had never been able to support them financially, and her parent's relationship was not a happy one. For a period of time, after she had become an elementary school teacher, she remained indifferent to the men with whom she had become acquainted. It was not until a very rich cousin entered the scene that marriage became a possibility. "She calculated," Freud explains, "that her cousin would give her father financial support . . . [and] provide her sisters with dowries and *trousseaux* so that they could get married. And she fell in love with him, married him soon afterwards and followed him to Russia." For the most part, the marriage went well. The one problem, however, was that she had remained childless. Then, to make things worse, when she was twenty-seven and in the eighth year of her marriage, all remaining hope was suddenly shattered when she learned that her husband suffered from a fertility problem. Knowing that she now would not be able to have children, and that her husband would never become the "father," more specifically, the substitute father for her own, that she had always wanted him to be, she fell into a serious depression.[38]

Several years later, when she was in her early forties, she recalled, as she described the events of her life to Freud, an unusual experience she had had shortly after her depression began. During a visit to Paris with her husband, the arrival at their hotel of a highly regarded fortune-teller had provided her with the opportunity to listen to his predictions about her own future. Removing her wedding ring, she presented herself to the fortune-teller, who in turn asked her simply to give an imprint of her hand by placing it in a sand filled dish. This she did, and after studying her imprint the fortune-teller explained: " 'In the near future you will have to go through some severe struggles, but all will turn out well. You will get married and have two children by the time you are 32.' "[39]

In listening to this woman's story, Freud was perplexed by the pleasure this prediction seemed to have given his patient, especially because she had no real sense as to how the prediction related to her life, if it did at all. "My comment," Freud relates, "that it was nevertheless unfortunate that the date laid down by the prophecy had already gone by some eight years made no impression on her. . . . What, then, were the source and meaning of these numbers? The patient herself had no notion." Describing how his further investigation provided an answer to this question and thus served to create the occult fact itself, Freud continues:

> The obvious thing would be to dismiss the question entirely and to consign it to the rubbish heap among so many other meaningless and ostensibly occult messages. That would be delightful. . . . But unluckily I must add that it was possible— and precisely by the help of analysis—to find an explanation of the two numbers and one which . . . was completely satisfactory and arose, almost as a matter of course, out of the actual situation.
>
> For the two numbers fitted in perfectly with the life-story of—our patient's *mother.*[40]

The patient's mother had married late, at thirty, and to make up for this situation she had managed to give birth to two children by the time she was thirty-two. What, therefore, the fortune-teller had in fact given voice to, Freud was able to conclude, was the patient's longtime, yet still very much active wish to be like her mother, specifically, her wish to take her mother's place with her father.[41] The wish that the fortune-teller had telepathically picked up while in the presence of Freud's analysand was, Freud explains, that which had been "the strongest wish of her youth, the wish on account of whose non-fulfilment she was just beginning to fall ill."[42]

. We should note once again, then, as Freud himself does, that it is only through the employment of psychoanalytical technique that the occult fact, that is to say, the telepathic transmission of information that would have otherwise gone unnoticed, is established. This important point, as we shall now see, is taken up again by Freud in his essay "Dreams and Telepathy."

"Dreams and Telepathy" (1922), Freud's first published work on this subject, is, as Jones explains, a "more cautiously worded" paper than "Psycho-Analysis and Telepathy."[43] Accordingly, from its outset, Freud attempts to impress the following upon his reader: First, that his own views on this subject will remain hidden. As Freud relates, "You will not even gather whether I believe in the existence of 'telepathy' or not." Second, seeking to check at the earliest stage any thoughts his reader might have about the broader implications of his reflections on telepathy for psychoanalysis, Freud argues the point "that if the existence of telepathic dreams were to be established there would be no need to alter our conception of dreams in any way."[44] Very cautiously indeed, therefore, Freud begins his first paper to be published on this subject.

In spite of his declared neutrality, Freud does make some rather interesting observations about telepathy, which we should note. As he had suggested in his presentation in the Harz mountains, Freud returns in this paper to the important point that "psycho-analysis may do something to advance the study of telepathy," especially because it has the means to identify and decode telepathic communications that would otherwise go unrecognized.[45] A second observation made by Freud is that even though sleep is not a necessary condition for "the occurrence of telepathic processes," it is nevertheless the case that sleep "creates favourable conditions for telepathy."[46] Finally, we should note that Freud makes the very significant assertion, especially as regards our study of the synchronicity concept, "that no one has a right to take exception to telepathic occurrences if the event and the intimation (or message) do not exactly coincide in astronomical time." Although Freud understandably provides a different explanation than the one given by Jung to account for the lack of simultaneity between the two events—Freud suggests the "telepathic message might arrive contemporaneously with the event and yet only penetrate to consciousness the following night during sleep"[47]—the observation itself is nonetheless an important one.

Turning now to our second example of Freud's case work on telepathy, we should note that Freud gives an account of this particular case study in both the paper we are presently considering and later in his "Dreams and Occultism." The case itself is actually based on a letter that Freud received from a man in Germany. Freud claims that in 1922, after having worked for twenty-seven years as an analyst, he had not yet "been in a position to observe a truly telepathic dream in any of [his] patients."[48] It is for this reason, then, that Freud turns to the case provided to him by his German correspondent. Briefly stated, the story develops as follows. The subject's daughter, with whom the subject had a particularly close relationship, was pregnant and expecting her child in the middle of December. On the night of November 16–17, however, something striking occurred. That night the subject dreamt, "with a vividness and clearness [he had] never before experienced," his "wife [his second wife and his daughter's step-mother] had given birth to twins." Describing what then took place following the dream, Freud's correspondent continues:

> At breakfast I told my wife the dream, which much amused her. She said, "Surely Ilse (my daughter) won't have twins?" I answered, "I should hardly think so, as twins are not the usual thing either in my family or in G's" (her husband). On November 18, at ten o'clock in the morning, I received a telegram from my son-in-law, handed in the afternoon before, telling me of the birth of twins, a boy and a girl. The birth thus took place at the time when I was dreaming that my wife had twins.[49]

In keeping with the cautious tone of the essay as a whole, Freud cleverly avoids taking a definite stand on the question of whether or not this case constitutes a genuine telepathic communication. Freud does this, however, in such a manner that he is not kept from expressing his own views about how such a dream might be understood if the telepathy hypothesis were to be accepted. If psychoanalysis were to accept the existence of a telepathic communication in this case, Freud thus relates, it would certainly not have the problem that others have with the divergence that exists between the dream content (the dreamer's wife having twins) and the actual occurrence (the dreamer's daughter, who was living in another city, giving birth to twins). "The psycho-analytic interpretation of dreams," Freud writes," . . . does away with this difference between the dream and the event, and gives both the same content."[50] Describing more precisely how he is led to this conclusion, Freud continues:

The father knew that his daughter clung to him. . . . In his heart I think he grudged her to his son-in-law, to whom in one letter he makes a few disparaging references. On the occasion of her confinement (whether expected or communicated by telepathy) the unconscious wish became active in the repressed part of his mind: "she ought to be my (second) wife instead"; it was this wish that had distorted the dream-thoughts and was the cause of the difference between the manifest content of the dream and the event.[51]

Freud's essential argument with this case is, then, that the telepathic communication came to the subject from without, much as the banging of a door plays on an individual during sleep, and like the banging door and similar stimuli, it was simply incorporated into the dream through the process Freud refers to as the "dream-work." More specifically, the message that the dreamer's daughter was giving birth to twins was telepathically communicated to the dreamer from without, yet as this message was being raised to consciousness, through the dream, it became contaminated, so to speak, with the very powerful unconscious wish of the dreamer to have his daughter for his own wife. The intervention of the unconscious wish, therefore, is that which accounts for the divergence between the inner and outer events.[52]

The highly refined equivocation that characterized Freud's first published essay on telepathy was suddenly, in 1925, to give way to a more honest and direct presentation of Freud's position. At the end of that year, Freud published a paper entitled "The Occult Significance of Dreams," in which, as Jones himself admits, Freud "pretty plainly indicated his acceptance of telepathy."[53] In this paper, Freud identifies two types of dreams that tend to be regarded as occult phenomena, as he puts it himself. The first type are the prophetic dreams; the second type are telepathic in character. With respect to the former, it is clearly the case that Freud's worldview prevented him from even entertaining the possibility of their existence. About prophetic dreams, Freud thus writes, "The notion that there is any mental power, apart from acute calculation, which can foresee future events in detail is on the one hand too much in contradiction to all the expectations and presumptions of science [that is to say, the deterministic standards of mechanistic science] and on the other hand corresponds too closely to certain ancient and familiar human desires which criticism must reject as unjustifiable pretensions."[54]

Concerning telepathic dreams and other telepathic phenomena, however, Freud's position is quite different, as Jones's above comment reveals. This time clearly arguing in support of the existence of telepathy, Freud again makes use of that class of examples that he suggests "is exempt from the doubts which are otherwise justified—namely, unfulfilled prophecies made by professional fortune-tellers."[55] His specific example is the case study we have already examined: the account of the woman about whom it was wrongly predicted she would have two children by the time she was thirty-two. Beyond the presentation of this case, an additional point of considerable import to our study is Freud's identification of the critical role played by the emotional factor in the telepathic transference of thoughts. Concerning this observation, we know from Jones that in March of 1925, Freud, Ferenczi, and Freud's daughter, Anna, conducted a number of experiments with telepathy, the results of which Freud described in a letter as " 'remarkably good, particularly those in which I played the medium and then analysed my associations.' "[56] There can be no doubt that it is with reference to these same experiments that Freud would assert in 1925 in "The Occult Significance of Dreams" that the emotional factor seems to play a central role in thought transference. "I have often had an impression," Freud writes in his essay, "in the course of experiments in my private circle, that strongly emotionally colored recollections can be successfully transferred without much difficulty. If one has the courage to subject to an analytic examination the associations of the person to whom the thoughts are supposed to be transferred, correspondences often come to light which would otherwise have remained undiscovered."[57] Freud ends this paper, we should point out, on the progressive note of urging his fellow psychoanalysts to seek out further information that might serve to shed more light on the subject of telepathy.

Before making his decision in 1925 to speak out publicly in support of the existence of telepathy, Freud gave careful consideration to the possible damage that his actions might do to the psychoanalytical movement. Jones had argued, and Freud had adhered to this position himself prior to 1925, that publicly acknowledged interest in telepathy would only serve to block further the acceptance of psychoanalysis. Accordingly, when criticism stemming from Freud's writings on telepathy began in 1925, Jones wrote in a circular letter: " 'So once more my predictions have unfortunately been verified and we have one more resistance to face.' "[58] In contrast to the fears expressed by Jones, for Freud the inevitable conflict that was to follow his publications on telepathy was something with which he had come to terms. In 1925, Freud no longer regarded telepathy as an issue that could be put to the side and ignored simply to avoid further conflict. For Freud, in 1925, public disclosure of his position on telepathy had become a type of moral issue, comparable to the moral challenge that he had faced with the publication of *The Interpretation of Dreams*. It was as if, Freud would relate in a letter, " 'I had to repeat the great experiment of my life: namely, to proclaim a conviction without taking into account any echo from the outer world. So then it was unavoidable.' "[59]

It was, then, out of this background that Freud's fourth and final paper on telepathy, "Dreams and Occultism" (1933), emerged. In this essay, we find a freedom and openness in Freud's treatment of the subject of telepathy. We also find a genuine sense of purpose that is not to be found in Freud's other papers on this subject. It is as if Freud sensed that in presenting his observations on telepathy he would be making a very special contribution to the collective search for knowledge about the psyche. "The history of science itself," Freud explains toward the beginning of his paper, seeking to activate at once his reader's sympathies and a sense of the weightiness of the subject under consideration, "abounds in instances which are a warning against premature condemnation."[60] And concerning such premature condemnation, Freud frankly admits, he himself is not blameless. "When they [occult phenomena] first came into my range of vision more than ten years ago," Freud writes,

> I too felt a dread of a threat against our scientific *Weltan-schauung*, which, I feared, was bound to give place to spiritualism or mysticism if portions of occultism were proved true. To-day I think otherwise. In my opinion it shows no great confidence in science if one does not think it capable of assimilating and working over whatever may perhaps turn out to be true in the assertions of occultists.[61]

In "Dreams and Occultism," Freud essentially calls for a type of new beginning wherein psychoanalysts will undertake the study of parapsychological phenomena in a spirit of open-mindedness and honesty. Concerning the question of the objective reality of telepathy, Freud does not make the claim that it has been conclusively demonstrated. He does note, however, that his own work in this area has already served to reveal a body of material that "is at all events favourable" to the establishment of its objective reality.[62]

Freud presents five carefully organized case studies in "Dreams and Occultism," amongst which we find the "third case" that Freud left behind in Vienna when he presented his first paper on telepathy to the group of psychoanalysts meeting in the Harz mountains. We shall examine this case in some detail, but because it describes an experience that leads us into the concerns of our next chapter, we shall do so at the end of this chapter rather than here.

In his closing remarks, Freud, in keeping with the more open-minded character of the work as a whole, takes the time to reflect about the relevancy of telepathy to questions outside the range of the more limited concerns of psychoanalysis. It is not understood, Freud writes, "how the common purpose comes about in the great insect communities: possibly it is done by means of a direct psychical transference of this kind." Perhaps, Freud further muses, this was the exclusive means by which humans themselves communicated originally, and only under certain conditions, such as with the singlemindedness characteristic of mob activities, is this alternative method now put to use. "One is led to a suspicion," Freud writes, "that this [telepathy] is the original, archaic method of communication between individuals and that in the course of phylogenetic evolution it has been replaced by the better method of giving information with the help of signals which are picked up by the sense organs." Perhaps this is also why, Freud seems to suggest next, children whose language skills are yet largely undeveloped demonstrate a definite propensity to communicate telepathically with their own parents.[63]

Having traced in the above section the development of Freud's thinking on the question of telepathy, we should perhaps now pause to reflect, in summary, on the points of agreement and disagreement that exist between the positions taken up by Freud and Jung on this subject.

In contrast to Jung, Freud's scientific worldview, by his own admission, conformed to the deterministic standards of a mechanistic science. This, of course, was to influence greatly Freud's theorizing about telepathic-type experiences. For Freud all psychic content followed from psychic antecedents; psychic content did not emerge under the direction of teleological influences. Accordingly, Freud never could give serious consideration to the possibility of there being extrasensory perceptions of the precognitive type, since for him there were simply no such "goals" to be anticipated. We shall give special attention to this point in Freud's case study that is presented at the end of this chapter.

The differences that we find in the positions of Freud and Jung regarding the interpretation of the content of telepathic experiences are, in the main, the same type of differences that we find with their respective approaches to the interpretation of dreams themselves. These idiosyncratic differences notwithstanding, Freud and Jung certainly stand in agreement on a number of key points. First, both acknowledged that the subjective and objective events in a telepathic experience need not fall within a clock-time simultaneity in order to be regarded as being meaningfully related. Both men did, of course, give different explanations as to why this is the case. The observation itself, however, I believe, is no less an important one. Second, both had no problem accepting the fact that the subjective and objective events may not literally correspond, but that their correspondence may be more symbolical in nature. Third, and related to this, both Freud and Jung acknowledged that the element that we can refer to as the core content of the telepathic message becomes intermixed with other psychic contents. For Freud, this core content is subjected to the "dream-work"; for Jung, the core content is subjected to the "compensatory activities" of the unconscious. Both, therefore, saw the telepathic message as ultimately carrying, beyond its core content, a highly subjective message which, like dream material itself, must be analyzed and integrated by the subject. Here we should note that Freud's cases are excellently presented, for whether one agrees with Freud's analyses of the case material or not, there is never any doubt about how exactly Freud relates the telepathic event to the psychology of the individual concerned. This is certainly not true of Jung's own examples. Finally, we should note that both Freud and Jung recognized that a powerful emotional element often plays a pivotal role in these events. Highly charged emotion, both men acknowledged, seems to favor the occurrence of telepathic experiences.

Returning our focus to the synchronicity theory, we should recall that Jung in his characterization of the specific type of synchronistic experience that we are examining in this chapter—synchronistic experiences in which the compensatory activity of nature is experienced both inwardly and outwardly—speaks of the individual as having, through the unconscious, access to an "absolute knowledge." The knowledge to which one is given access inwardly with these synchronistic events, especially with cases of foreknowledge, "is certainly not a knowledge," Jung writes, "that could be connected with the ego, and hence not a conscious knowledge as we know it, but rather a self-subsistent 'unconscious' knowledge which I would prefer to call 'absolute knowledge.' "[64] Clearly the knowledge that is associated with synchronistic experiences of the type under consideration is not a knowledge that is space- and time-bound, nor is it a knowledge that is mediated by the sense organs, nor is it a knowledge, as Jung also points out, that is connected with the ego. Rather, it is a knowledge that is associated with a "self-subsistent meaning," that is to say, it is a knowledge associated with the "irrepresentable spacetime continuum"[65] of the psychoid archetype. This, therefore, is for Jung the "absolute knowledge" to which each individual potentially has access through the compensatory activities of the unconscious.

It is the case, then, that either by consciously looking within, as in active imagination, or simply through the spontaneous emergence of archetypal contents into consciousness, as with dreams, one is able to acquire a nonsensory-based knowledge of events taking place in the outer world, a knowledge that is not conditioned, moreover, by spatial and temporal limitations. For Jung, therefore, analogous to the ancient depictions of the psyche as microcosm, there is to be found in the unconscious the presence of macrocosmic events. The following passage, which is taken from the sixth century B.C. Chinese text the *Tao Te Ching*, gives expression to this ancient idea:

> Without going outside, you may know the whole
> world.
> Without looking through the window, you may see
> the ways of heaven.
> The farther you go, the less you know.[66]

For Jung the individual is, through the unconscious, coextensive with the totality. Thus we find in the deepest levels of the psyche the presence of an "absolute knowledge" which, moving into consciousness, provides the astute observer with insights into the events of outer reality, past, present, and future. Utilizing the writings of the ancient Chinese philosopher Chuang-tzu to illustrate this point, Jung writes: "If you have insight, says Chuang-tzu, 'you use your inner eye, your inner ear, to pierce to the heart of things, and have no need of intellectual knowledge.' This is obviously an allusion," Jung continues, "to the absolute knowledge of the unconscious, and to the presence in the microcosm of macrocosmic events."[67]

That the individual is conjoined with the totality through the unconscious is indeed one of the fundamental concepts of the synchronicity theory. This being the case, it does not follow, however, with synchronistic experiences involving "absolute knowledge," that the inner and outer events will mirror each other in the strict sense of that idea. Indeed it is often the case that the inner image and outer event vary significantly. Why, we should then ask, is this so? To answer this question, we must first reevaluate Jung's understanding of the nature of the relationship between the psyche and the macrocosm.

In the previous chapter, it was explained that with synchronistic experiences involving "absolute knowledge" the inner and outer synchronistic events constitute compensatory equivalents. By this it was meant that the two events, as expressions of the same psychophysical pattern of meaning, work together, so to speak, to produce the needed compensatory result. With the scarab case history, for example, both the scarab of the analysand's dream, the inner "golden scarab," and the living scarab that appeared at the window during the analytical session were equally significant compensatory expressions of the constellated archetypal pattern, in this instance, the archetypal pattern of rebirth and renewal. Both events, it is clear, played special compensatory roles in helping to put life back into an analysis that had come to a standstill. They did this, moreover, not simply as general compensatory expressions of the constellated archetypal pattern, but rather as very precise and highly differentiated expressions of the compensatory pattern.

With synchronistic experiences of "absolute knowledge," then, both the inner and outer synchronistic events perform very precise and specific roles in what we might characterize as the compensatory strategy of the constellated archetypal pattern. Indeed, much as an archetypal image in a dream takes on, in the higher, more refined stages of the compensatory process, a very personalized coloring, it is the case that they too carry a very specific message. Perhaps in the case of the outer synchronistic event it is more accurate to say that the highly personalistic compensatory twist with which the subject is synchronistically confronted is simply an intrinsic characteristic, simply a distinguishing feature of the animate or inanimate object itself. In this way, the fact that the subject is synchronistically confronted with one type of person or object as opposed to another type is in itself the compensatory twist that requires very special study.

The challenge, therefore, with synchronistic experiences involving "absolute knowledge" is to determine exactly what type of unique compensatory message the two events are, so to speak, working together to produce. To do this, it seems, one must not only study and evaluate the two events separately, but one must also evaluate the two events in relationship to each other, that is to say, in terms of their dynamic interplay as aspects of the same compensatory pattern. Utilizing again the dream analogy, we might imagine the relationship that exists between the inner and outer events to be comparable to the relationship that exists between the separate but related dreams in a dream series. As with such a dream series in which each dream expresses a different aspect of the more comprehensive compensatory theme and, accordingly, must be analyzed in terms of the compensatory whole, so too is it the case with synchronistic events of "absolute knowledge" that the separate manifestations of the archetypal ground, the inner and outer synchronistic events, must be analyzed in terms of their dynamic interplay if we are able to disclose their full compensatory import. Why, for instance, was it the case that the inner scarab was an expensive piece of jewelry—a golden scarab, while the outer scarab was a living, flying insect? Is there a compensatory message in this difference? Why, to use another example, did Freud's German correspondent dream that his second wife and not his daughter had given birth to twins? What is the significance of this intrapsychic twist? These are the types of questions that must be addressed in synchronistic experiences involving "absolute knowledge" if we are to understand fully the nature of the subject's relationship to the constellated, synchronistic pattern.

Returning to our original question, perhaps it is the case, then, that nature, in the form of the psychoid archetype, is not concerned so much with presenting one with mirrorlike correspondences between the inner and outer synchronistic events as it is with the more important task of furthering the development of one's consciousness through its compensatory activities. If it serves nature's compensatory purposes, we might say in conclusion, to present such mirrorlike correspondences, it will certainly do so, but only for that reason.

Clearly some of the most dramatic examples of synchronistic experiences of "absolute knowledge" occur in connection with the powerful constellation of the archetype of the self. And indeed one very critical situation in which we often find the self powerfully constellated is with experiences of near-death. We shall now examine two such cases.

The first case involves a woman who was a patient of Jung's, someone, Jung points out, "whose reliability and truthfulness I have no reason to doubt." When this woman was giving birth to her first child, complications developed that resulted in a loss of a considerable amount of blood. At first it seemed like she was not in any danger. After a period of time had passed, however, and her doctor and family had left, her condition suddenly worsened; she had a "heart collapse" and immediately slipped into a coma. At that very moment, Jung relates "she had the feeling that she was sinking through the bed into a bottomless void. She saw the nurse hurry to her bedside and seize her hand in order to take her pulse." At this point a gap in her consciousness occurred. Then, something quite incredible followed. She had the very strange sense of looking down on the room, and being able to see all that was going on inside it, as if her eyes were in the ceiling. Below she could see herself lying on the bed, "deadly pale, with closed eyes," yet she knew she would not die, and thus was not alarmed by her situation. She could see, though, that her husband and doctor, who were now again by her bedside, certainly were. In fact, it seemed like the doctor "had lost his head and didn't know what to do."

Throughout all of this, she knew that there was behind her a world of indescribable beauty and peacefulness. She knew also, however, that as much as she was supported by this knowledge, she could not turn to view this world directly, for if she did, and was tempted to enter it, she would certainly die. Approximately half an hour from the time she had slipped into the coma, she awoke to find her nurse leaning over her. The next day, Jung relates, after having regained some of her strength, the woman commented to her nurse "about the incompetent and 'hysterical' behaviour of the doctor during her coma." The nurse, of course, acting in support of the doctor, and thinking that the patient could not have known what had taken place, simply denied all that she said. "Only," Jung relates "when she described in full detail what had happened during the coma was the nurse obliged to admit that the patient had perceived the events exactly as they happened in reality."[68]

With this case history, as Jung himself maintains, we certainly do not have a situation in which a sensory-based perception occurs. What we do have, however, Jung argues, is an example of an inner synchronistic vision,[69] that is to say, an experience of the "absolute knowledge" of the unconscious. Curiously enough, even though there is with this experience of the "absolute knowledge" of the unconscious a remarkably high degree of correspondence between the inner and outer events, we still find in the interplay of these events a notable compensatory twist to which we shall now give some consideration.

It was stated in the previous chapter that death-related experiences, perhaps like no other experiences, make one aware of the great differences that exist between the points of view of the ego and the self. It was also pointed out that in such experiences of crisis the individual is very much in need of the compensatory intervention of the self. Confronted with what from the ego's perspective is the brutal reality of death, the individual is very much in need of the wholeness of the self's perspective. In the above example, we see both perspectives come into play. The panic that had overtaken the doctor and the others in the hospital room clearly is the chaos and panic that the ego's fear of death releases. The wholeness, in contrast to this, that the woman experienced in knowing she had just behind her a world of great beauty and peace, the vision of wholeness, moreover, that she was most fully identified with when viewing the chaotic events "below," is, from the Jungian perspective, most definitely a compensatory experience of the wholeness and peace that the self alone transmits.

With the above case history, we see, then, how the self specifically intervened to compensate the ego in a time of crisis. We know, however, that the compensatory activities of the self are not confined to such moments of extreme crisis. Indeed, for Jung, the self is all the time working to facilitate the "assimilation of the ego to a wider personality."[70] This, moreover, the self does at considerable cost to itself. The self, Jung was previously quoted as saying, "demands sacrifice by sacrificing itself to us." That the self, and not just the ego, undergoes sacrifice in the individuation process when it willingly submits itself to the limitations of incarnation in this world is a point of no small importance to Jung. Something valuable is being offered at considerable cost to the *Giver* and it is necessary that the ego learns to receive it with genuine humility.

The realization that the self is voluntarily submitting itself to the limitations of a more human existence for the sake of the ego is a realization that comes, in different ways and in varying degrees of intensity, to individuals who are walking the path of individuation. For Jung's own part, perhaps his most intense experience of the reality of the self's sacrifice took place in 1944, during a time in which

he lay close to death following a heart attack. "In a state of unconsciousness," Jung writes in his autobiography,

> I experienced deliriums and visions which must have begun
> when I hung on the edge of death. . . . My nurse afterward
> told me, "It was as if you were surrounded by a bright glow."
> That was a phenomenon she had sometimes observed in the
> dying, she added. I had reached the outermost limit, and do
> not know whether I was in a dream or an ecstasy. . . . It
> seemed to me that I was high up in space. Far below I saw the
> globe of the earth, bathed in gloriously blue light. I saw the
> deep blue sea and the continents.[71]

Plunged into a deep state of unconsciousness, Jung moved toward an experience of his existence that ever-increasingly was being
derived not from the familiar point of view of the ego, but rather
from the point of view of the self. As he floated in space, Jung saw
at a distance "a tremendous dark block of stone" that too was floating in space. He approached this massive rock and immediately noticed that a temple had been created by hollowing out the stone in a
manner similar to what he had previously seen along the coast of
the Gulf of Bengal. Jung drew closer still to the temple, and just as
he was about to climb the steps at its entrance, he was suddenly
struck by the strange experience of having everything that he had
"aimed at or wished for or thought, the whole phantasmagoria of
earthly existence" being stripped away. This experience was, Jung
relates, "an extremely painful process."[72] Remarkably enough, however, just as his earthly perspectives were being ripped away from
him, he started to feel on another level a fullness that he had not
known previously. "There was no longer," Jung explains, "anything
I wanted or desired. I existed in an objective form; I was what I had
been and lived. At first the sense of annihilation predominated, of
having been stripped or pillaged; but suddenly that became of no
consequence. . . . I had everything that I was, and that was
everything."[73]

At that very moment, Jung had the fascinating insight that if
he were to enter the temple he would know the full meaning of his
existence. "There I would at last understand," Jung relates, " . . .
what had been before me, why I had come into being, and where
my life was flowing."[74] As Jung contemplated this, something happened, though, that served both to prevent Jung from entering the

temple and to direct him back to the world of ego-consciousness. At a great distance, Jung caught sight of the figure of a man floating up toward him from Europe. As the figure drew closer, Jung could see that it was in fact his own doctor, Dr. H., the heart specialist.[75] Now, however, he had assumed a form quite different from the one he had had on earth, for Dr. H. stood before Jung "in his primal form, as a *basileus* of Kos."[76] With his appearance, Jung became immediately aware of the fact that he too was in his primal form. As Hannah learned from Jung following his illness, Jung's primal form was also that of a *basileus* of Kos.[77] Describing what then followed, Jung writes: "As he stood before me, a mute exchange of thought took place between us. Dr. H. had been delegated by the earth to deliver a message to me, to tell me that there was a protest against my going away. I had no right to leave the earth and must return. The moment I heard that, the vision ceased."[78]

Jung's journey back to what he would experience as the painfully limiting world of the ego was now underway. The fall which he now had to endure from the world of the self to the world of the ego was experienced as a devastating loss of freedom. Jung felt like a condemned man whose life would be lived out in the confinement of a small four-walled cell. " 'Now I must return' ", Jung thought to himself, " 'to the "box system" again.' For it seemed to me as if behind the horizon of the cosmos a three-dimensional world had been artificially built up, in which each person sat by himself in a little box."[79] In comparison to the expansive world of the self, the world in which Jung now had to find meaning seemed oppressive and colorless. Accordingly, for Jung, a sense of relationship to this earthly life did not come quickly. Indeed, after his "return," Jung struggled with a serious depression for three weeks before he could, as he relates, "truly make up my mind to live again."[80]

Through both his ecstatic elevation to, and painful fall from, the archetypal world of the self, Jung thus came to experience first-hand the very great sacrifice that the self makes in working to further the development of the ego. This aspect of Jung's near-death experience had alone, therefore, revealed a great deal. Something else, however, was yet to occur that would serve to make the idea of the self's sacrifice even more real to Jung.

Jung recalls how from the time that he regained consciousness he was troubled by very ambivalent feelings toward his doctor, Dr. H. On the one hand, Jung was angry with him for having saved his life. After all, was it not his fault that Jung was brought back into

the " 'box system' "? On the other hand, Jung felt deeply concerned for his doctor's safety, for Dr. H. had appeared to him in his
primal form and this suggested to Jung that his doctor's life was in
danger. "Suddenly," Jung writes, "the terrifying thought came to
me that Dr. H. would have to die in my stead."[81] Jung, for his part,
did what he could to talk to his doctor about his vision. Not surprisingly, though, Jung did not get far with his attempts to convince Dr.
H. that he too was a *basileus* of Kos, nor could he convince him that
because he had appeared in his primal form his life was now threatened. Sadly enough, as fate was to have it, on April 4, 1944, the
very day in which Jung sat up for the first time on the edge of his
bed, Dr. H. "took to his bed and did not leave it again." Stricken
initially with bouts of fever, Dr. H. died shortly afterward of
septicemia.[82] With reference to the death of his doctor, Jung later
commented to Hannah "that Zeus himself was said to have killed
Aesculapius [God of medicine and healing] by a thunderbolt because he had brought back patients from death."[83]

In connection with Jung's near-death experience, we see,
therefore, that the idea of there having to be a sacrifice carried out
on Jung's behalf, if he were to be empowered to fulfil his destiny on
this earth, was an idea that was conveyed on two levels. First, Jung
directly experienced the sacrifice that the self willingly undergoes to
bring about its incarnation in this space- and time-bound world,
that is to say, more specifically, to bring about its incarnation in the
life of an individual. Through its sacrifice, the self empowers the
personal and transpersonal meanings that make up one's destiny to
intersect and flow into reality. Second, and notably in the context of
the above, Jung, through his experience of the "absolute knowledge" of the archetypal world, witnessed yet another sacrifice on
his behalf. This time, though, it was one that would affect him on
an even more personal level. From both sides of life, so to speak,
Jung witnessed the synchronistic "sacrifice" of the man who had
literally saved his life. Dr. H. was the specialist who had saved
Jung's life following his heart attack, yet would himself take to his
bed at the turning point of Jung's own recovery. Dr. H. was also the
one who appeared to Jung in his primal form in the archetypal
world, where he forced Jung to return to the earth without, apparently, returning with him.

Clearly, when one individual's life is given to save the life of
another, the one whose life has been extended through this sacrifice
is invariably left with the feeling that his life is no longer strictly his
own. Often, such an individual is led to a less egocentric way of

life. For Jung, this seems to have been especially the case. "After the illness," Jung writes in his autobiography,

> a fruitful period of work began for me. A good many of my principal works were written only then. The insight I had had, or the vision of the end of all things, gave me the courage to undertake new formulations. I no longer attempted to put across my own opinion, but surrendered myself to the current of my thoughts. Thus one problem after the other revealed itself to me and took shape.[84]

Moving now outside the Jungian literature for our next example of a synchronistic experience of "absolute knowledge," we find a very interesting case of this type in the "bowing journals"[85] of the American-born, Buddhist monks Heng Sure and Heng Ch'au of the Gold Mountain Monastery, San Francisco. From May 1977 to October 1979, Heng Sure and Heng Ch'au undertook a traditional, Chinese Buddhist bowing pilgrimage which took them along a 600-mile stretch of the Californian coast of the United States. In fulfilment of his vow, every three steps along the route Heng Sure made a full prostration to the ground. Heng Ch'au, in fulfilment of his vow, accompanied Heng Sure as his assistant and protector.

From the very outset of their journey, which began along a row of bars in one of the roughest neighborhoods in Los Angeles, the two monks became immediately aware of the link between their inner orientations and the events taking place in their environment. The establishment of a proper inner orientation was, they recognized, absolutely necessary if they were to have any hope of surviving in such a hostile environment. Repeatedly, they were confronted with the seething aggression of the masculine power principle, especially so when they found themselves literally bowing through gatherings of the local street gangs. Success, and indeed their survival, they came to see, depended not on their abilities to defend themselves outwardly, verbally or physically, but rather, on their abilities to hold themselves in balance inwardly.[86] In a great number of situations, this specifically entailed, putting it in Jungian terms, keeping their own masculine shadows from sabotaging their work. In short, Heng Sure and Heng Ch'au were learning to confront the threat coming from without, first and foremost, within themselves by coming to terms with their own shadows. At the heart of their inner work was a verse composed by their teacher, Hsuan Hua. The verse reads:

Truly recognize your own faults and don't discuss the faults of others. Other's faults are just my own. Being of one substance with everything is called Great Compassion.[87]

One synchronistic experience that I believe is particularly indicative of the progress made by Heng Ch'au in coming to terms with his shadow took place in connection with an actual attempt made by two men to steal some of their gear. Each day, Heng Ch'au would drive a car in which they slept and kept their supplies and equipment between the starting and stopping points of that day's bowing. Being unguarded for a good deal of the day, the car was, of course, quite an easy target for thieves. In fact, during the month previous to the account we are about to examine, their sleeping bags had been stolen.

One morning just after Heng Ch'au awoke, he reported the following to Heng Sure: "I just dreamed that some more thieves came to rip us off. I got there in time to tell them, 'We got your license and the police are our good friends. They said they would help us out. So you've got two choices. Either you put all of the stuff back right now and split or else you go to jail.' They started putting our gear back in the car like mad."[88] After having evaluated the significance of Heng Ch'au's dream, both monks agreed that caution and inner focus were especially called for that day, and indeed the events that followed were to bear this judgement out. That afternoon as the monks bowed along an isolated stretch of road, Heng Sure suddenly intuitively felt that he should speed up the bowing pace to move them ahead more quickly. Shortly after this, without any verbal communication taking place between them, Heng Ch'au himself walked past Heng Sure and on down the road, "something," Heng Sure notes, "he [Heng Ch'au] never does."[89] Reaching the top of a hill, Heng Ch'au could see their car in the distance; he could now also see that at their car were "two men pulling at the doors and trying the windows. . . . When they saw me coming," Heng Ch'au writes, "they ran back across the freeway. What blew my mind was that they were the *same* men in the dream—clothes, hair, and all."[90]

With this synchronistic experience of "absolute knowledge," we have a good example of the compensatory paralleling of inner and outer events. Both Heng Sure and Heng Ch'au were, it is clear, working hard to come to terms with their respective shadows, and progress, moreover, was being made. This was certainly reflected in both the dream and outer synchronistic event. In Heng Ch'au's dream, when he was confronted with the shadow figures trying to steal their gear, the way in which he dealt with these figures evidenced a progressive, conciliatory attitude toward the shadow. This is not to say, however, that he let these figures have their way, for he certainly did not allow them to walk off with the equipment. Rather, he resisted them, but this he did not with violence but by trying to win them over by reasoning with them. The shadow figures clearly were out to disrupt the bowing pilgrimage by stealing the gear that was essential to the work. What Heng Ch'au in effect did was to prevent them from doing this by bringing these shadow figures into the service of the pilgrimage. Curiously enough, a rather similar outcome would be experienced outwardly that same day when Heng Ch'au, freed inwardly from the dark activities of his own shadow, would, through his "presence" alone, save their gear from theft.

Something of importance that Heng Ch'au notes elsewhere about his dream is that in it he and Heng Sure were strictly following the specific rules and work schedule they had laid down for themselves. This, moreover, Heng Ch'au notes, was not only the case in the dream itself, but it was also the case in real life. That very afternoon instead of taking extra time to shave and wash, they decided to stick to their bowing schedule.[91] The shadow figures that would have had them delay the more important work of bowing to attend to their personal needs were, therefore, being kept in check. In contrast to this vigilance, when their sleeping bags were actually stolen the month before, they were taking a very casual, even careless approach to their work. At that time, their carelessness, which would be synchronistically compensated outwardly through the experience of having their sleeping bags stolen, was also being compensated inwardly in Heng Ch'au's dreams. Indeed, seeking to demonstrate just how far off the mark they had gone with their work, the unconscious, following the compensatory tactic of like curing like, had identified the monks with the thieves. Describing this compensatory activity in his dreams at that time, Heng Ch'au relates: "Back . . . north of Ventura, there were similar dreams about our sleeping bags being stolen. In those dreams, we were breaking rules and practically giving the equipment to the thieves like they were old friends. As it turned out, a few days later, we did break our rules (being late and rapping) and that day our bags were stolen."[92]

In summary, we have seen, then, with this synchronistic experience of "absolute knowledge," how the inner and outer events constitute compensatory equivalents. We have also seen how for the individual to perform an active and productive role in this synchronistic interplay of inner and outer events, one must first understand exactly what the nature of one's compensatory relationship is to these events. In this particular case that required knowledge of the shadow. Here the degree of one's self-knowledge is put to the test, for with such synchronistic experiences one must be able to understand them from, so to speak, the inside out.

The final case, with which we shall now close this chapter is, as previously indicated, that very special "third case" of Freud's. It should be recalled that Freud had intended to present this case to the small group of psychoanalysts gathering in the Harz mountains in the late summer of 1921, but was unable to do so as, "owing to resistance," the case had been left behind in Vienna. The case, which was to be later utilized by Freud in his "Dreams and Occultism" in the New Introductory Lectures (1933), is notably introduced by Freud in that paper as "the one [example of telepathy] which has left the strongest impression behind on me."[93] The case unfolds as follows.

On an autumn day in 1919, Dr. David Forsyth arrived from London at 10:45 a.m. and immediately had his card passed to Freud, who was with a patient. Pressed by his other appointments, Freud was only able to speak with Forsyth very briefly and then make an appointment to see him later. About Forsyth, Freud notes that he had come to Vienna to be initiated into the methods of psychoanalysis. Furthermore, because he was the first foreigner to arrive after the war, he represented to Freud something of a "promise of better times,"[94] both in the sense of the spread of psychoanalytical thought, as Forsyth was regarded by Freud as an excellent ambassador in that respect, and in the more immediate financial sense, since the war years had left Freud impoverished.[95] Forsyth's arrival, therefore, was not surprisingly likened by Freud to the experience of the "first dove after the Deluge."[96]

At 11:00 a.m., Freud's next patient, Herr P., arrived. This particular analysand, Freud explains, had "originally come to him because of difficulties with women." Analysis, however, had not helped to resolve these problems. In spite of this, they had mutually decided to continue their work together. Herr P., who had developed a "well-tempered father-transference" to Freud, seemed to benefit from their talks, while Freud himself found them to be "stimulating and refreshing."[97] All of this was, though, continued with one qualification. Freud had made it clear to Herr P. that once the "foreign pupils and patients returned to Vienna" their sessions would end.[98]

During their session on the day in question, Herr P. spoke again to Freud of his attempt to have an erotic relationship with a young woman with whom he had been acquainted for some time. Freud relates this was certainly not the first time that his patient had mentioned her, but it was the first time that he mentioned the name that she called him. To Freud's great surprise, Herr P. explained that she called him " 'Herr von Vorsicht' [Mr. Foresight]." As Freud relates, "I was struck by this information; Dr. Forsyth's visiting card lay beside me, and I showed it to him."[99]

Curiously enough, Freud continues, all of this had taken place against the background of another seemingly related event. Herr P., who had spent several years in England and as a result developed a lasting interest in English literature, had lent Freud a number of English books. What Freud found particularly odd was that Herr P. had recently introduced him to the series *The Forsyte Saga*, and just days before had given him a fresh volume from that series. Developing this point further, Freud writes:

> Now the name "Forsyte" in these novels differs little from that of my visitor "Forsyth" and, as pronounced by a German, the two can scarcely be distinguished; and there is an English word with a meaning—"foresight"—which we should also pronounce in the same way and which would be translated "*Voraussicht*" or "*Vorsicht*." Thus P. had in fact selected from his personal concerns the very name with which I was occupied at the same time as a result of an occurrence of which he was unaware.[100]

This was not the end of it, however. During the previous week Freud had visited Dr. Anton von Freund in his *pension*, and while at his home had learned, much to his surprise, that Herr P. actually lived in the same building on another floor. Following this, Freud did mention to P. that he had "in a sense paid him a visit in his house," but he certainly did not mention exactly whom he had visited in the building. "And now," Freud writes, "shortly after mentioning 'Herr von Vorsicht' he asked me whether perhaps the Freud-Ottorego who was giving a course of lectures on English at the *Volksuniversität* was my daughter. And for the first time during our long period of intercourse he gave my name the distorted form to which I have indeed become habituated by functionaries, officials and compositors: instead of 'Freud' he said 'Freund'."[101]

Finally, near the end of the session, Herr P. mentioned a dream that had been particularly frightening, "a regular '*Alptraum*.' " To this P. added that he had recently forgotten the English word for *Alptraum*, and when asked by someone had said "that the English for '*Alptraum*' was 'a mare's nest'. This was nonsense, of course, he went on; 'a mare's nest' meant something incredible, a cock-and-bull story: the translation of '*Alptraum*' was 'nightmare'. The only element in common," Freud continues, "between this association and the previous one seemed to be the element 'English'." Freud did recall, however, something further. The month earlier Ernest Jones had arrived, "unexpectedly . . . after a long separation," during Freud's session with Herr P. Recognizing Jones from a photograph hanging in Freud's waiting room, P. had asked at the time to be introduced to Freud's English colleague. "Now Jones," Freud explains, "is the author of a monograph on the *Alptraum*—the nightmare. I did not know whether P. was acquainted with it; he avoided reading analytic literature."[102]

We have, then, the key features of Freud's case—a case in which there are three possible instances of telepathy. Not surprisingly, in his evaluation of this case Freud initially sets to one side the question as to whether these events are or are not genuinely telepathic in character and first undertakes a psychoanalytical analysis of the three associations themselves. This approach is, of course, very much in keeping with Freud's position that all associations, even those with telepathic content, are to be psychoanalytically evaluated.

Central to all three associations, Freud notes, is the common thread 'English.' Beyond this, though, and on a more personal level, we also find, Freud explains, "the mixture of jealous demand and melancholy self-depreciation." Why, Freud asks, did his patient decide to bring the name that his girlfriend had given him long ago, Herr von Vorsicht, into the analysis at that particular time? The answer, Freud suggests is that he was simply jealous of Dr. Forsyth's presence and wanted to attract Freud's attention back to him. As Freud explains, Herr P. was simply trying to say: " 'It's mortifying to me that your thoughts should be so intensely occupied with this new arrival. Do come back to me; after all I'm a Forsyth too— though it's true I'm only a Herr von Vorsicht [gentleman of foresight], as the girl says.' " This last twist represents, of course, for Freud, the depreciatory element. Jealous demand, Freud continues, was likewise connected with the substitution of the name "Freund" for "Freud." With this, Freud argues, Herr P. was in effect trying to ask, why did you visit Freund and not me when you were at my house? Finally, concerning the *Alptraum* association, Herr P., it is suggested, was once again giving expression to both jealous demand and melancholic self-depreciation, for in the person of Jones, P. was up against someone "of whom he was no doubt equally jealous, but for whom he also felt he was no match." Whereas Jones, Freud explains, could write a monograph on the nightmare, P. could only have them. Furthermore, Freud writes, P.'s "mention of his mistake about the meaning of 'a mare's nest' comes into this connection, for it can only mean to say: 'After all I'm not a genuine Englishman any more than I'm a genuine Forsyth.'"[103]

Next, taking up the question as to whether "these associations could or could not have been made without thought-transference," Freud expresses the opinion that two of them indeed could have. With the Forsyth association, however, Freud concludes, "the scales weigh in favour of thought-transference."[104] Concerning the von Freund association, it is possible, Freud suggests, that he told Herr P. he had "visited a friend" [literally "Freund" in the German] in his building, and that P. had simply picked this word up. With regard to the *Alptraum* association, it is equally possible, Freud explains, that P. saw the title of Jones's monograph at some point.[105] As Freud himself admits, all of this is speculation. Interestingly enough, though, whereas Freud is quite willing with the von Freund and *Alptraum* associations to accept these alternative explanations to the telepathic one, the equally credible alternative explanation he comes up with for the Forsyth association is given far less weight. Concerning that association, it could be true, Freud offers, that he had mentioned to P. during the previous summer that he was expecting a doctor from England. Perhaps, Freud suggests, "I may have even mentioned his name, though that seems to me most improbable." If this were so, however, P. may then have crossed paths with Forsyth on the street on the way to his appointment and "recognized him by his characteristically English appearance."[106] Of the different alternative explanations provided by Freud for the three associations, this one is, to my mind, the most reasonable. Freud, however, inclines to dismiss it. The reason for this, I would suggest, is that the Forsyth example fits more straightforwardly into Freud's notion of thought transference.

For Freud, as was indicated above in our examination of his other cases, thought transference seems to involve the direct transference from one person to another of a powerfully constellated thought, that is to say, a thought that is highly emotionally charged. This thought, furthermore, passing from the source to the recipient usually undergoes a type of "dream-work" in which it becomes personalized in conformity with the wish-fulfilment bent of the recipient. Accordingly, with the Forsyth example, there can be no doubt that when the thought transference in question took place Freud was in a state of emotional arousal due to the appearance, just minutes before, of his "first dove after the Deluge," Dr. Forsyth. The name Forsyth was thus, as Freud would have it, telepathically transmitted from Freud to P., who in turn introduced it into the analytical session in the converted form of Herr von Vorsicht [Mr. Foresight].

Given its very complex character, with this particular case we are confronted, I believe, in a way we were not with the other two cases of Freud's that we looked at above, with the very real limitations of Freud's theoretical position concerning the operation of telepathy. Indeed, looking at the case from the perspective of the synchronicity theory, we are led to conclude that Freud's theoretical assumptions greatly limited his access to the material in question. With regard to this, I shall here make just two general points. First, by approaching these events from a theoretical position that focused primarily on a type of mechanistic, telepathic exchange of information between two individuals as opposed to Jung's notion of psychophysical continuum, Freud was kept from acknowledging the meaningful interplay of the separate events of the case in terms of their roles in the larger pattern. Second, as previously mentioned, just as Freud's scientific worldview prevented him from being able to conceive of prospective tendencies in the psyche, it equally was a barrier to his recognition òf prophetic-type extrasensory perceptions. This position, I believe, kept Freud from coming to terms with the key word of the case and its implications. The word, of course, is *foresight*. What we shall now undertake, therefore, is a reexamination of the facts of this very important case to see what different perspective on things the synchronicity theory offers.

With this case, we essentially have a situation in which the analysand is functioning as "oracle" for the analyst, much as the fortune-teller in Freud's above-described case brought to light the childless woman's desire to be like her mother and have two children by the time she was thirty-two. Unlike Freud's interpretation of that case, however, where it was suggested that the fortune-teller as oracle tuned in, so to speak, to the thoughts of the woman, with this case it shall be argued that the analysand tuned in to the constellated psychophysical pattern, thus attaining an "absolute knowledge" of certain key events in that pattern—events that had already taken place and events that would unfold in time in both the near and distant future.

About the psychophysical pattern itself, we know, as Freud observed, that the unifying theme involves things "English." Furthermore, within this pattern we find a type of swing between, or interplay of, the experiences of happiness/pleasure and hardship/suffering. Indeed, the interplay of these opposites is present at the very beginning of the case, where the situation was such that Freud and Herr P. would evaluate very differently the arrival of the Englishman, Dr. Forsyth. Prior to Forsyth's arrival, Freud's loss, in the sense of being cut off from the world by the war, had been P.'s gain; following Forsyth's arrival, however, the situation reversed, and Freud's gain was now P.'s loss. What for Freud was cause for happiness, "promise of better times," was for P. cause for sadness, or as we might also put it, "promise of less interesting and meaningful times." From the outset, therefore, the unifying theme of things English, within which there is also this interplay between pleasure and suffering, was clearly established.

Because there are in this case so many interconnecting events, what we shall have to do in our analysis is simply describe how the pattern was to unfold in time. This is the best way, I believe, to convey clearly what the meaning of the associations identified by Herr P. was, and would be, for Freud, in both the short and long term. As we shall see, we have in this case a very complex interplay between the figures and events of the pattern not only in the symbolical sense, but in actual reality as well. Something to again bear in mind as we examine this case is a point made in chapter 2. There it was stated that the idea of the synchronicity theory is not that the world turns around one individual. Rather, the idea is that each individual is a participant in, and in the compensatory sense, meaningfully related to, the acausal patternings of events in nature. Accordingly, even though the destinies of several individuals intersect in such a psychophysical pattern, the compensatory import of their participation in the pattern is usually quite different for each individual. For example, with Herr P. and Freud, even though they were related to each other in a complementary way within the same pattern, the compensatory meaning of their participation in it was not the same for each man. Thus we could say that even though each player performs a role that is complementary to the psychophysical drama as a whole, the compensatory import of the drama is nevertheless unique to each separate player.

In 1919, from Freud's perspective of things, and that is the perspective from which we are evaluating this case, the psychophysical pattern in question was so to speak, in its positive phase. Under Herr P.'s guidance, Freud, still at leisure to pursue such interests, was investigating English literature, most recently the series *The Forsyte Saga*. In October of that year, Dr. Forsyth arrived from England, thus marking the opening up of communication once again with the outside world and the reappearance of all its attendant benefits. Very much at the center of the positive turn that events were taking in 1919 was the Hungarian psychoanalyst Anton von Freund. In his own analysis of the associations presented by Herr P., Freud himself describes von Freund as the individual "whose donation had made the foundation of our publishing house possible."[107] In January 1919, the *Internationaler Psychoanalytischer Verlag*[108] had indeed been established, much to Freud's very great pleasure, with funds provided by von Freund. With the establishment of the *Verlag*, Freud and the psychoanalytical movement as a whole were given a literary freedom that they had not previously enjoyed. Not surprisingly, in a letter to Ferenczi, Freud referred to von Freund as "the man whom Providence has sent us at the right moment."[109] In the autumn of 1919, Jones, as we know, also visited Vienna. Freud had mentioned that Jones had been in Vienna "about a month earlier"[110] than Forsyth; actually it was, as Jones relates, "the same week, for I dined with Forsyth in Zurich when I was returning from Vienna and he on his way there."[111] In 1919 Jones, it is interesting to learn, was encouraging Freud to move to England.[112] Something further about Jones's visit that directly links him to von Freund, and the latter in turn to England, is the very significant piece of information that Jones was in Vienna at that time to smuggle some of the funds of von Freund's donation to England to save it from the damaging effects resulting from the collapse of Austria-Hungary.[113] Finally, we should point out that Freud, who had been concerned about a tumor that von Freund had developed, was very much "cheered," as Jones reports, "by Forsyth, who was then in Vienna, expressing the opinion that the tumor in question was not malignant."[114]

Reviewing again, then, the associations given by Herr P. to Freud and the latter's interpretation of their meanings, we have seen that Freud did link the name Mr. Foresight to both *The Forsyte Saga* and the arrival of Dr. Forsyth from England. Further, Freud also linked the association Freund with Anton von Freund, the one "whose donation had made the foundation of our publishing house possible." Freud said nothing though, about the connection between Forsyth and Freund, that is, how he was greatly "cheered" by Forsyth's opinion that von Freund's tumor was not malignant. With the *Alptraum* association, Freud brings Jones into the picture without, however, linking him to Forsyth in the way that Jones later did himself. Nothing, moreover, is said about the important connection between Jones and von Freund and their promising scheme to smuggle some of the funds of the latter's donation to England. Finally, we should note that the word *foresight*, in its proper sense, is left undeveloped, as is the word *Alptraum*, and nothing further is said about Herr P.'s linking of Freud's daughter with von Freund. It is in this latter group of associations that we find, I would suggest, intimations of the radical turn downward that the generally upbeat events of the autumn of 1919 were about to take.

"In the first month of 1920," Jones relates, "fate dealt Freud two grievous blows: one for which he was prepared, though not resigned, the other a startingly unexpected blow." Near the end of November 1919, the great hope that Freud had had for von Freund's health was suddenly shattered when a "further exploratory operation" revealed the presence of cancer.[115] From that time onward, von Freund's condition deteriorated rapidly. Each day, Freud visited him, and daily he was witness to the suffering of "poor Freund" being "devoured piecemeal by his cancer".[116] "The end," Jones writes,

> came on January 20, 1920, and Freud remarked that von Freund had died heroically without disgracing psycho-analysis. Freud had been specially fond of him, and his death was a severe personal blow; he said it was an important factor in his ageing.
>
> Then only three days later, on the very evening of the day von Freund was buried, came news announcing the serious illness of Freud's beautiful daughter Sophie, the one they called their "Sunday child," at her home in Hamburg; it was the influenzal pneumonia so rife in that year. . . . Two days later, on January 25, a telegram announced her death. She was only twenty-six, had been in perfect health and happiness, and left behind her two children, one of whom was only thirteen months old. The news was a thunderbolt from a clear sky. On the day after receiving it Freud wrote to me: "Poor or

happy Toni Freund was buried last Thursday. . . . Sorry to hear your father is on the list now, but we all must and I wonder when my turn will come. Yesterday I lived through an experience which makes me wish it should not last a long time."[117]

Had those two tragic deaths in 1920 represented the full unfoldment of the pattern that Herr P.'s associations had given voice to, they alone would have been all that one could imagine a waking "nightmare" to be. Fate, however, had something even more difficult to bear awaiting Freud. Indeed, a waking nightmare of even greater magnitude was to begin in 1923 with the discovery of what Jones describes as "the mortal disease that was to cause untold suffering,"[118] Freud's cancer, and not end until Freud, after having been driven out of his own country by the Nazis in 1938, died in England on September 23, 1939. Just as Freud had watched von Freund be "devoured piecemeal by cancer," Freud himself was now to undergo an incredibly arduous struggle with the same disease, and like the example of courage he had been witness to in the person of von Freund, Freud too would stoically bear his suffering and die "heroically without disgracing psycho-analysis." Just as von Freund's money had been smuggled by Jones to England in 1919, Freud, in 1938, would himself be spirited to England by Jones, this time, however, under the diplomatic "cover" of world powers.[119] Sixteen years from the time his cancer was first discovered, thirty-three operations later,[120] Freud would die in England at 20 Maresfield Gardens,[121] a name which makes one think again about "Herr Foresight's" rendering of the German word *Alptraum* [nightmare] into the English as "mare's nest."

Curiously enough, though, in its final form the psychophysical pattern that in 1919 was in its highly optimistic phase and then suddenly, shortly afterward, tragically took an exclusively downward turn, had become in England a very striking blend of the two currents of happiness/pleasure and hardship/suffering. In England, Freud's personal physical suffering was, of course, enormous. As his condition worsened it seemed at times that his world had simply become, as Freud in a letter to Marie Bonaparte would relate, nothing but "a little island of pain floating on a sea of indifference."[122] On the other hand, it was also in England that Freud was finally to be released from the suffering of an illness that had lasted sixteen years. Similarly, concerning his feelings about leaving the city that had been his home for seventy-nine years,[123]

Freud, writing to Max Eitingon on the very day of his arrival in London, explained, " 'The feeling of triumph at being freed is too strongly mingled with grief, since I always greatly loved the prison from which I have been released.' "[124] Leaving Vienna was for Freud a very sorrowful experience, yet on the other hand, there can be no question that he was greatly pleased with the knowledge that in England he and his immediate family would now be free from further torment at the hands of the Nazis—the most trying experience of which being the day his daughter Anna was detained by the Gestapo.[125] In the same manner, Freud, who had lived through the horrifying sight in Vienna of the Nazi destruction of his life's work, including "his beloved *Verlag*," now in England was to witness its full resurrection, not only in the founding of the Imago Publishing Company,[126] but in the form of the firmly established British Psycho-Analytical Society which now had made London "the principal site and centre of the psychoanalytical movement."

The pattern, therefore, that had been first identified in the prophetic words of "Mr. Foresight" in 1919 was now for Freud in 1939 reaching its completion. Quite remarkably, in his last letter to Jones, dated March 7, 1939, on the occasion of the twenty-fifth anniversary of the founding of the British Psycho-Analytical Society,[127] Freud wrote as if he were seeking to raise this very pattern to consciousness:

> 20, Maresfield Gardens, London, N.W.3
> Dear Jones
> It still remains surprising to me how little we human beings can foresee the future. When, shortly before the war, you told me about founding a Psychoanalytical Society in London, I could not foresee that a quarter of a century later I would be living so near to it and to you; even less would I have thought it possible that I, in spite of living so near, would not be taking part in your celebration.
> But in our helplessness we have to accept everything as fate brings it to us. Thus I have to content myself with sending your celebrating Society a cordial greeting and hearty good wishes from afar and yet so near. The events of recent years have made London the principal site and centre of the psychoanalytical movement. May the Society carry out the functions thus falling to it in the most brilliant manner.[128]

In conclusion, I would like to offer one final thought. Concerning the Forsyth case, something that Jones had always found particularly puzzling was Freud's reference to this case as "the one which has left the strongest impression behind on me." For Jones, by contrast, of all of Freud's examples of telepathy, the Forsyth case was "the most tenuous."[129] If in our examination of this case history we too, like Jones, were to have confined our interpretation of it to the one offered by Freud, I think we also would have questioned the great importance that Freud assigned to it. What I would suggest, however, is that the reason Freud found this case so impressive was not for the reasons he provided himself. It has been suggested in our analysis that what Herr P. gave voice to in 1919 was something more than a jealous protest arising out of his sudden telepathically based awareness of the arrival of Dr. Forsyth. Indeed it has been argued that Herr P., acting as "oracle," identified some of the key elements of the psychophysical pattern that was to be at the heart of Freud's destiny as he entered the last twenty years of his life. I would like now to suggest that Freud also experienced this meaning, on some level, though not necessarily consciously. Accordingly, what attracted Freud to this case and led him to so highly value it was not his experience of his analysand's telepathically based jealous protest, but rather his experience of hearing in the words of Herr P. a statement about his own destiny.

The Synchronistic Patterning of Events ❧

As indicated in chapter 2, Jung held that microphysics and depth psychology, quite independently of each other and following their respective methodologies, have reached the frontier of the unitary world, the *unus mundus.* Through the discoveries of modern physics, the veil of phenomenal reality, Jung recognized, has been pulled back, revealing a world that constitutes a dynamic inseparable whole in which the traditional notions of isolated objects, space and time, cause and effect are rendered meaningless. Through his own investigations of synchronistic phenomena, Jung himself, we have seen, reached a similar understanding about the nature of reality, and consequently was led to revise radically his theoretical model of the archetype. The *unus mundus,* Jung explains, "is founded on the assumption that the multiplicity of the empirical world rests on an underlying unity, and that not two or more fundamentally different worlds exist side by side. . . . Rather, everything divided and different belongs to one and the same world."[1] For Jung the *unus mundus* is not, to be sure, a mere metaphor; it is a very real world which subsumes the world of our everyday experience. For Jung the *unus mundus* is specifically the world of the psychoid archetype—the unitary world whose tangible presence is the synchronistic patterning of events in nature.

Through his study of the synchronistic patterning of events, the *unus mundus* thus became a living reality for Jung. What before were incommensurable opposites now linked. Opposites such as inner/ outer, psychic/physical, symbolical/actual, and spiritual/worldly were now conjoined in psychophysical patterns of meaning. For Jung, nature assumed a more unified appearance, and not surprisingly, Jung found himself experiencing an ever-deepening affinity for that ancient worldview that exemplifies this unitary perspective—I refer here to the unitary worldview of traditional Chinese philosophy.

There can be little doubt that the traditional Chinese world-view does considerable justice to the ideas associated with the synchronistic perspective. Like the latter, the Chinese worldview is not concerned strictly with "this-worldliness," nor is it concerned strictly with "other-worldliness." It is not concerned strictly with "realism," nor is it concerned strictly with "idealism." Similarly, the "actual" is not placed over the "symbolical" or vice versa, for to do so would be to go against the unified view of nature characteristic of the Chinese worldview. Above all else, the emphasis in Chinese philosophy is on "synthesis." "This-worldliness and other-worldliness," Fung writes, "stand in contrast to each other as do realism and idealism. The task of Chinese philosophy is to accomplish a synthesis out of these antitheses. That does not mean that they are to be abolished. They are still there, but they have been made into a synthetic whole."[2] Accordingly, the Chinese concept of the individuated man, to put it in Jungian terms, is a person who has brought these opposites together, not just intellectually, but more importantly, in actual practice. Such an individual would be both "this-worldly" and "other-worldly." He would be fully involved with the activities of everyday life, yet he would conduct himself in a manner that was in harmony with his inner world. He would, in other words, allow the unconscious to give direction to his everyday activities so to bring his actions into harmony with the synchronistic patterning of events in nature. Essentially, his would be the type of personality development that in Chinese philosophy is described with the expression " 'sageliness within and kingliness without.' "[3]

At the very heart of the traditional Chinese worldview is the belief that the activity of nature as a whole, visible and invisible, is governed by a single principle.[4] This principle is, of course, the Tao. The word *Tao* literally translates as the path or way.[5] The original Chinese character for the word *Tao* presents an image "of a 'track which, though fixed itself, leads from a beginning directly to the goal'. The fundamental idea," Wilhelm explains, "is that the Tao, though itself motionless, is the means of all movement and gives it law."[6] The Tao, then, is perhaps best characterized as the path along which all things in nature travel. It is that which, though unchanging itself, gives rise to all things in nature.

Out of the Tao, the two principles of the phenomenal world arise: the active, light principle termed *yang* and the passive, dark principle termed *yin*. Through the interaction of these polar opposites, all the elements of phenomenal reality, referred to in Chinese philosophy as the "ten thousand things," come into being. In that the "ten thousand things" arise out of Tao and their activities are "governed by the one primal law" of Tao,[7] all of the activity of nature is regarded by the Chinese as unified. Accordingly, in the Chinese worldview, the life of the individual is understood to entwine with the activity of nature as a whole. Chinese philosophy, Wilhelm writes, emphasizing this point,

> is built on the premise that the cosmos and man, in the last analysis, obey the same law; that man is a microcosm and is not separated from the macrocosm by any fixed barriers. The very same laws rule for the one as for the other, and from the one a way leads into the other. The psyche and the cosmos are to each other like the inner world and the outer world. Therefore man participates by nature in all cosmic events, and is inwardly as well as outwardly interwoven with them.[8]

In the traditional Chinese worldview, nature does indeed constitute a dynamic, organic whole. The individual is clearly not understood to be an isolated figure in an indifferent environment, rather he is understood to participate in, and be subject to, the laws that govern nature in its entirety in accordance with the more comprehensive unitary pattern of Tao. With respect to the Chinese description of the unfoldment of events in nature, we find, therefore, that the Western notion of mechanistic causation gives way to a description in terms of interdependence. About Chinese physics, Nathan Sivan writes, it "is perfectly unitary. It is build upon none of our classical conceptions of causality, but rather on the idea of simultaneous resonance between categorically related physical entities. The causality of Newtonian mechanics occurs only as an insignificant degenerate case, and action at a distance is in no way anomalistic."[9] Similarly, Joseph Needham writes about the Chinese worldview in his major work *Science and Civilisation in China*:

> The key-word in Chinese thought is *Order* and above all *Pattern*. . . . The symbolic correlations or correspondences all formed part of one colossal pattern. Things behaved in particular ways not necessarily because of prior actions or impulsions of other things, but because their position in the ever-moving cyclical universe was such that they were endowed with intrinsic natures which made that behaviour inevitable for them. If they did not behave in those particular ways they

would lose their relational positions in the whole (which made them what they were), and turn into something other than themselves. They were thus parts in existential dependence upon the whole world-organism.[10]

In that the mechanistic-causal principle could play no significant role in the unitary worldview of the Chinese, "the idea of succession was always subordinated to that of interdependence."[11] Accordingly, when the Chinese looked out into the world they did not look to study " 'successions of phenomena,' " but rather sought to identify the relatedness or orderedness of events through the observation of their qualities.[12] The tendency of the Chinese, therefore, was to classify the activity of nature in terms of patterns. These patterns were not based on mechanistic causation, but rather on an equivalency of meaning with respect to the phenomena contained therein. This approach is, of course, the synchronistic way of seeing. It is the study and classification of events wherein meaningful interdependence supersedes space, time, and causality as the determining factor. In the following, Jung, drawing on his own experience, provides us with a case example of such a synchronistic patterning of events. Prefacing his comments with a reference to the role played by the archetypal continuum in such cases, Jung writes:

> As it is not limited to the person, it is also not limited to the body. It manifests itself therefore not only in human beings but also at the same time in animals and even physical circumstances. . . . I call these latter phenomena the synchronicity of archetypal events. For instance, I walk with a woman patient in a wood. She tells me about the first dream in her life that had made an everlasting impression upon her. She had seen a spectral fox coming down the stairs in her parental home. At this moment a real fox comes out of the trees not 40 yards away and walks quietly on the path ahead of us for several minutes. The animal behaves as if it were a partner in the human situation.[13]

With this example, there are three meaningfully related events appearing in the psychophysical, synchronistic pattern. They are (1) the woman's dream of the spectral fox, (2) the woman's description of this dream to Jung as they walked through a wooded area, and (3) the appearance of a real fox as this description was being given. Here, then, we have a synchronistic patterning of events—events which are not linked collectively by space, time, or causality—events whose import can only be properly established through an investigation of their roles in relationship to the psychophysical pattern as a whole.

The first event concerns a dream that Jung's analysand identifies as the first dream of real significance in her life: "She had seen a spectral fox coming down the stairs in her parental home." That this dream is identified by Jung's analysand as the first dream of real significance in her life suggests that this is a dream which contains an important key to her individuation. About such dreams Jung writes "Significant dreams . . . are often remembered for a lifetime, and not infrequently prove to be the richest jewel in the treasure-house of psychic experience."[14] A dream like Jung's analysand's dream of the spectral fox is indeed often the "richest jewel" because in it one will invariably discover—once the individuation process has progressed sufficiently to interpret it contextually—the essential goal of one's individuation. With such dreams, one is given a first glimpse of the archetypal pattern that will be at the heart of one's unique journey toward wholeness. As Erich Neumann would put it, one is given a first glimpse of the *absolute field knowledge of the central archetypal pattern of one's individuation.*[15] Commenting on the emergence into consciousness of such an archetypal pattern at the earliest stages of the individuation process, Neumann, drawing on Jung, writes:

> We encounter the problem of foresight not only in many childhood dreams, in the initial dreams of analysis, and in prospective dreams in general, and in the *I Ching*, but especially in the process of individuation, of which Jung writes: "Over the whole procedure there seems to reign a dim foreknowledge—not only of the pattern, but of the meaning." Jung also speaks of the archetype which determines the course of the *Gestaltung* "with seeming foreknowledge, or as though it were already in possession of the goal to be circumscribed by the centering process."[16]

The dream of the spectral fox was, it seems, such an initiatory dream depicting the central archetypal pattern of the analysand's individuation. This being so, the importance of this particular archetypal pattern, whose central symbol was the fox, cannot be overstated. No doubt as Jung and his analysand walked through the woods discussing the dream in question, the import of this archetypal pattern was moving closer to consciousness. Then, as if to add even more momentum to the process underway, as the woman was telling Jung about her dream of the fox coming down the stairs of her parental home, "a real fox," Jung explains, "comes out of the trees not 40 yards away and walks quietly on the path ahead of us for several minutes." Describing his impression of this sudden objectification of the archetypal pattern under examination, Jung writes with reference to the fox: "The animal behaves as if it were a partner in the human situation."

Jung's description of the activity of the fox is certainly apt, for its timely appearance and subsequent behavior suggest that indeed it was there to contribute something to their discussion. As Jung and his analysand examined her dream of the spectral fox descending the stairs in her parental home, the real fox entered the path on which Jung and the woman were travelling. Quietly it walked ahead, leading them, on a symbolical level, in their investigation of this very important archetypal pattern—the psychophysical pattern in which they were now in fact all contained. The fox, therefore, clearly was a partner in the human situation, for it was a compensatory, synchronistic partner in the struggle to bring the central archetypal pattern of the woman's individuation into consciousness.

Jung, as we know, took considerable interest in the study of psychophysical patterns such as the one described above. As mentioned in chapter 2, when Jung analyzed in his "garden room" he would often indicate to his analysands how certain natural events taking place in the immediate environment, such as the lapping of the lake, synchronistically related to what was taking place in the analytical session. In accordance with the traditional Chinese way of thinking—which Jung in keeping with Granet characterizes as a propensity toward *"thinking in terms of the whole"*[17]—Jung was here seeking to raise to consciousness the psychophysical pattern in which the analytical session was contained. This he was doing, moreover, not only for his own benefit, but for the benefit of his analysand as well.

Concerning the tendency of the Chinese to view and evaluate events in terms of such psychophysical patterns, Needham explains that certain sinologists regarded this to be such a fundamental feature of the Chinese worldview that they adopted the terms " 'coordinative thinking' [and] 'associative thinking' " to describe this traditional Chinese way of thinking. With coordinative thinking, as with "synchronistic thinking," the idea is that the meaning of a particular event cannot be revealed through the examination of its mechanistic-causal relationship to other events, but rather that its real meaning can only be uncovered by understanding the role that the event in question plays as a part in a whole group of events that exist "side by side in a *pattern*."[18] Another term that is used to describe essentially the same thing is the term "field thinking." Neumann, as we saw above, uses this expression, as does von Franz, to describe both the Chinese and synchronistic ways of thinking. "Synchronistic thinking," von Franz writes, "the classic way of thinking in China, is thinking in fields."[19]

In his work as an analyst, one type of synchronistic "field" patterning of particular concern to Jung was "the 'strange recurrences' that happen in the lives of certain individuals" giving rise to considerable suffering. Jung, for example, describes a woman who was attacked by birds whenever she was in the country. In fact, when Jung was once walking with this patient, he actually saw this happen. Curiously enough, although Jung was right at her side at the time, the birds did nothing to Jung himself.[20] In his autobiography, Jung recalls a similar, yet more tragic case. It involved a woman who had come to Jung seeking only one consultation, as her sole objective was to lay before him a confession. Some twenty years previous, the woman, who identified herself to Jung as a doctor, had committed a murder. Thinking herself at the time to be above any moral considerations, she "had poisoned her best friend because she wanted to marry the friend's husband." Much to her alarm, however, she found herself increasingly at odds with nature as the years passed. In all its aspects, her life had become completely dominated by the negative aspect of the archetype of death. Accordingly, the constellated pattern was one of death and alienation only; there was no transformation, no rebirth. Describing the events that followed her act of murder, Jung writes:

> She had in fact married the man, but he died soon afterward, relatively young. During the following years a number of strange things happened. The daughter of this marriage endeavored to get away from her as soon as she was grown up. She married young and vanished from view, drew farther and farther away, and ultimately the mother lost all contact with her.
>
> This lady was a passionate horsewoman and owned several riding horses of which she was extremely fond. One day she discovered that the horses were beginning to grow nervous under her. Even her favorite shied and threw her. Finally

she had to give up riding. Thereafter she clung to her dogs. She owned an unusually beautiful wolfhound to which she was greatly attached. As chance would have it, this very dog was stricken with paralysis. With that, her cup was full; she felt that she was morally done for. She had to confess, and for this purpose she came to me.[21]

With her act of murder, the woman, Jung believed, had committed a crime not only against an individual, but also against nature itself. Accordingly, even though she had failed herself to acknowledge the immorality of her action, nature had not. Everywhere she turned she was thus confronted with the reality of her crime. About such situations, Jung writes with reference to the compensatory psychophysical pattern, "Sometimes it seems as if even animals and plants 'know' it."[22]

In studying the above example, one thing we should not conclude is that all synchronistic experiences of suffering arise as a result of some "crime" against nature, for just as it is the case on the intrapsychic level that the experience of suffering serves as a tempering factor with respect to the development of personality, so too is it the case with the synchronistic patterning of events. Perhaps the image of Christ on the cross is a fitting symbol of the point being made here. For Christ, the cross was not an instrument of punishment, but rather the means by which Christ's unique destiny was to be fulfilled. The cross was the means by which those qualities unique to the personality of Jesus were to unfold and be realized fully. Similarly, with the process of individuation the unfoldment of personality cannot be achieved without hardship. Accordingly, each individual will, subject to the unique demands of that person's individuation, be called upon to endure suffering. Giving expression to this same idea, Edward Edinger writes: "The favorites of God receive the severest ordeals, i.e., it is one's potential for individuation that causes the test."[23]

In the autobiography of the eminent Chinese Ch'an (Zen) Master Hsu Yun (1840–1959),[24] we certainly find numerous examples of growth through hardship. Hsu Yun was the most highly regarded Ch'an Master of the modern period in China. He was a man of exceptional spiritual skill who, for example, could walk, even when he was over 100 years of age, thirty miles " 'in a day with less fatigue than most of the young men who [would] follow him.' "[25] We perhaps should note that when Jung was very near the end of his life, he read a collection of Hsu Yun's Ch'an lectures and was very impressed with them.[26] The following autobiographical account, which is viewed by many as a description of Hsu Yun's enlightenment even though he does not himself describe it in that way, provides us with special insight into the two problems with which we are presently concerned. First, it provides us with a good example of the psychophysical patterning of events, which in this case centers around the symbol of water. Second, it indicates how the hardship and suffering associated with the unfoldment of such a psychophysical pattern functions as a necessary catalyst in the journey toward spiritual wholeness.

In 1895, while journeying to Kao-min Monastery, where he was to participate in a Ch'an session, Hsu Yun accidently fell into a river and nearly drowned as a result. Seriously ill from his accident, he nevertheless continued on to the monastery where he entered the Ch'an hall. There he sat in meditation day and night simply " 'awaiting death,' " as he put it. Describing the remarkable experiences that then followed, Hsu Yun writes:

"My concentration became so pure that I did not know I had a body. After a little over twenty days, all my ailments were suddenly cured. . . . My work began to progress (*kung-fu lo-t'ang*). . . . One night during the rest from meditation, I opened my eyes and suddenly there was a great radiance like broad daylight. I could see through everything, inside and out. Through the walls that separated us I could see the verger urinating. I could also see a monk from the Western ranks who was in the latrine. Further off I could see boats going up and down the river, and trees on its banks of every kind and color. At this point three boards were struck [about 2:30 a.m.]. The next day I asked the verger and the monk from the Western ranks, and it was just as I had seen it. . . . In the last month of the year, on the third night of the eighth week, during the recess after the sixth period, the attendants poured hot water according to the rule. It splashed on my hand. The tea cup fell to the ground and broke to bits with loud noise. Suddenly the roots of doubt were cut. In my whole life I had never felt such joy. It was like waking from a dream. I thought of the many decades of wandering since I became a monk. I thought of the hut by the Yellow River and how when that fellow asked me, I did not know what water was. . . . And now if I had not fallen into the water and gotten very ill, if I had not been through easy times and hard times that taught me lessons and changed my understanding, I might have almost missed my chance in this life and then how could this day have ever come?"[27]

With the above account, there are several instances in which the water symbol appears. Placing the events in their proper chronological order, we see, first, that when Hsu Yun was once at the Yellow River, someone questioned him about the true nature of water. He was not able, however, to answer this question as he then " 'did not know what water was.' " Hsu Yun was here being challenged to look into the real meaning of the water symbol—the symbol that was to constitute the central symbol of the psychophysical pattern at the heart of his enlightenment. Much as the woman in the above example involving the fox symbol had been presented, through her first significant dream, with what was to be the central problem of her individuation, Hsu Yun was here presented with the problem whose proper resolution would be the key to his enlightenment. Second, it is the case that Hsu Yun almost met his end in water when he fell into the river. Although he survived this near-drowning, he did become very ill and was close to death when he arrived at Kao-min. Certainly the physical and mental shock of such an experience would be more than enough to stop most, yet Hsu Yun was not forced from his path. He went to the Ch'an hall and there applied himself completely to the work at hand. Consequently, after approximately three weeks, his physical " 'ailments were suddenly cured.' " Third, following his physical recovery, Hsu Yun had an inner vision of events taking place at a distance—events once again involving the water symbol. He saw " 'the verger urinating' " and " 'boats going up and down the river.' " Fourth, and finally, we see that Hsu Yun's enlightenment experience came when " 'the attendants poured hot water,' " spilling some of it on his hand. With this, as Hsu Yun relates: " 'The tea cup fell to the ground and broke to bits with loud noise. Suddenly the roots of doubt were cut.' " These, then, are the key events of the psychophysical pattern.

With this particular example of the psychophysical patterning of events, we are given a very clear indication of how the self, utilizing the water symbol to do so, relentlessly exerted its authority over the ego as it reached out to destroy completely the latter's false sense of control. With Hsu Yun's near-drowning, the self exerted its authority with absolute violence. For most people, this alone would come as such a devastating blow that they would simply collapse beneath it. This, however, was not the case with Hsu Yun, who had the strength of character to continue in the face of such seemingly insurmountable adversity. Hsu Yun had lived a life dedicated to the realization of the self's wholeness—the Buddha- or self-nature. Accordingly, when in fact he was confronted with death, he did not lose sight of this objective. Indeed, faced with death, he had the spiritual skill to focus himself in such a manner that he could surrender to this objective even more fully. Stated more specifically in Jungian terms, he had the ego strength to relinquish total control to the self. Without attempting to control his situation, particularly his physical illness and suffering, he simply continued with the work as best he could. In this way, his physical ailments were suddenly cured after a period of about twenty days. Subsequent to this physical healing, we see that a new relationship to the archetypal pattern emerged. The violent experience of the near-drowning now was replaced with more harmonious water images. Inwardly, he had an extrasensory knowledge, an "absolute knowledge," it should be noted, of events in his environment. He saw boats travelling up and down the river, the banks of which were covered with trees " 'of every kind and colour.' " He witnessed natural instinctive activities. A man was in the latrine, and in yet another location he saw the verger urinating, both being perhaps simple representations, following the water theme, of the ego's inability to control the forces of nature.

It is clearly the case that only when the ego gives up its ambition to control the forces of nature will it be able to be in harmony with them. Hsu Yun's life was consciously dedicated to the achievement of this goal. Therefore, when he was pressured through suffering to release, in actual practice, the self-nature from the grip of the ego's false sense of control, he did so fully. As he himself pointed out, without the pressure of hardship, he would never have achieved such a realization. With the process of individuation, the self thus seeks, in degrees unique to each individual, to be freed from its imprisonment in the limiting cup of the ego. The controlling ego is, to be sure, a mere teacup, and not at all an adequate container of the self. When the hot water was poured, Hsu Yun was "ripe" to let that cup go completely. When the hot water splashed on his hand, he did just that. In the following *gatha*, Hsu Yun describes his experience:

> 'A cup crashed to the floor
> The sound was clear and sharp

The emptiness was shattered
And the turbulent mind fell suddenly to rest.'[28]

To the individual whose worldview is rigidly grounded in the mechanistic-causal framework characteristic of the Western way of thinking, the "field" or "coordinative" approach of traditional Chinese thought appears to be the road to certain chaos. The coordinative approach produced, however, quite the opposite for the Chinese. "Chinese coordinative thinking," Needham explains, "was *not* . . . an alogical or pre-logical chaos. . . . It was a picture of an extremely and precisely ordered universe, in which things 'fitted', 'so exactly that you could not insert a hair between them'."[29] Utilizing the coordinative approach in their study of phenomenal reality, the Chinese clearly did produce a highly systematized understanding of nature. Indeed, as Jung saw it, what the Chinese were able to achieve with the coordinative approach was, in effect, a " 'science' " quite different from, but comparable to, the science of the West. More specifically, the Chinese, Jung believed, developed a " 'science' " based on the principle of synchronicity. In the passage that follows, which is an excerpt from a memorial address given by Jung in honor of Richard Wilhelm, Jung identifies the synchronicity principle as forming the basis of traditional Chinese " 'science.' " The following, which was delivered in Munich on May 10, 1930, is particularly noteworthy because it was in this address that Jung for the first time publicly introduced his synchronicity concept. "Some years ago," Jung told his Munich audience,

> the then president of the British Anthropological Society asked me how I could explain the fact that so highly intellectual a people as the Chinese had produced no science. I replied that this must really be an optical illusion, because the Chinese did have a "science" whose "standard work" was the *I Ching*, but that the principle of this science, like so much else in China, was altogether different from our scientific principle.
>
>   The science of the *I Ching*, indeed, is not based on the causality principle, but on a principle (hitherto unnamed because not met with among us) which I have tentatively called the synchronistic principle.[30]

In the *I Ching* (Book of Changes),[31] which is itself something of a foundational text for the whole of Chinese culture, the synchronistic " 'science' " of the Chinese, Jung believed, reached its highest point.[32] The *I Ching,* according to tradition, has its origins in the twelfth century B.C.,[33] and, as Wilhelm explains, "Nearly all that is greatest and most significant in the three thousand years of Chinese cultural history has either taken its inspiration from this book, or has exerted an influence on the interpretation of its text." Accordingly, the two central schools of Chinese philosophy, "Confucianism and Taoism, have their common roots here."[34] Consistent with what we have noted above about the Chinese worldview, fundamental to the text is a unitary concept of nature. Nature is understood to constitute a dynamic, highly ordered whole. All phenomena, in this way, are understood to be constantly undergoing transformation—transformation that proceeds in a very ordered manner. "Change," Wilhelm writes, "is not meaningless—if it were, there could be no knowledge of it—but subject to the universal law, tao."[35] In a world, therefore, that is as ever-changing and as highly ordered as that of the Chinese, a world, moreover, in which the individual is subject to the same laws that govern nature as a whole, it is clearly of the greatest importance for the individual to establish the "right" relationship to the psychophysical patternings of events. The question, therefore, that then arises is, How is the individual to go about establishing the right relationship to events? This is the question that the *I Ching* is designed to answer.

The following discussion of the *I Ching* will, for the sake of greater clarity, be presented in two parts. First, the concept of synchronicity will be examined in relationship to the actual casting of the oracle. Second, we shall look at the synchronistic character of the wisdom of the text itself.

For centuries the *I Ching* has been used as a book of divination. In the text, the various possibilities of change in nature are represented by the sixty-four hexagrams. "The hexagrams and lines in their movements and changes," Wilhelm explains, "[reproduce] the movements and changes of the macrocosm."[36] Expressed in the framework of analytical psychology, the hexagrams in their various stages of movement symbolize the different forms that the archetypal patterning of events in nature take. Through the prescribed method, employing the yarrow stalks or three coins,[37] the individual thus draws a hexagram which enables him "to survey the condition of things" and determine, utilizing the commentary accompanying the hexagram, his most profitable course of action.[38]

As early as 1919,[39] even before he had come in contact with Richard Wilhelm, Jung was working with the text on his own, using at the time Legge's translation. In his memoirs, Jung describes how he spent a good deal of his time one summer around 1920 engaged in what he characterizes as "an all-out attack on the riddle of this book." In the early twenties Jung met Wilhelm, and shortly afterward asked him to deliver a lecture at the Psychological Club in Zurich. In 1923 Wilhelm came to Zurich, where he spoke to that exclusive audience of Jung's followers on the subject of the *I Ching*. Following this lecture, a close relationship developed between the two men. In the person of Wilhelm, Jung was not only given the opportunity to learn a very great deal about Chinese philosophy and culture, but he was able to do this, moreover, with the assistance of a preeminent sinologist whose understanding of the Chinese worldview was compatible with his own. Accordingly, when Wilhelm's German translation of the text appeared in 1924, Jung was greatly encouraged now to have a translation of the *I Ching* "that . . . took," as he states, "much the same view of the meaningful connections as I had."[40]

Jung, we can be sure, was quite convinced of the reliability of the *I Ching* as a method of divination. We are told, for example, that during Jung's above mentioned "all-out attack" on the text in the early twenties, he observed numerous instances of highly significant psychophysical parallels. Later, he was to regret not having taken notes on these impressive results.[41] One thing that Jung came to believe about the *I Ching* during this period was that it essentially follows the principle expressed in the statement " 'the master speaks but once.' "[42] One does not find, therefore, in its answers, the type of repetition that one is looking for with experimental work. In the late fifties, when Fordham was himself testing the oracle in connection with his paper "Reflections on the Archetypes and Synchronicity," he too was to discover much the same thing. Having received, Fordham explains, "a good answer to an acute problem to which I could get no other solution, I decided to throw the coins again on the same problem with a view to seeing what would happen." On this second throw, Fordham drew the hexagram "Meng—Youthful Folly" whose Judgement reads in part: "The young fool seeks me. At the first oracle I inform him. If he asks two or three times, it is importunity. If he importunes, I give him no information."[43] Writing to Fordham about this result, Jung in a letter dated January 3, 1957, comments: "The experience you had with the *I Ching*, calling you to order when trying to tempt it a second time, also happened to me in 1920 when I first experimented with it. It also gave me a wholesome shock and at the same time it opened wholly new vistas to me."[44]

Following his investigations into the *I Ching* in the early twenties, Jung started "experimenting" with the oracle in actual analytical sessions. "Later," Jung writes, " . . . when I often used to carry
out the experiment with my patients, it became quite clear that a
significant number of answers did indeed hit the mark." One such
case concerned a young man with a pronounced mother complex
who was having trouble deciding whether or not a young woman
he had met would be a suitable match for him. Jung describes how
they cast the *I Ching* and significantly were given a hexagram which
read: " 'The maiden is powerful. One should not marry such a
maiden.' "[45] Jung does not tell us, however, whether the oracle's
advice was taken. Concerning Jung's personal use of the *I Ching*, it
seems that Jung consulted it primarily on very special occasions.
One such occasion was prior to his trip to Africa in 1925. Jung, Hannah explains, was concerned about the great difficulties that were
clearly going to be connected with the trip and, therefore, turned to
the *I Ching* to learn what he could from it about this journey. Essentially, what he was after in doing this, Hannah relates, was "a direct message from the unconscious, to assure him that his plans
were in accordance with its present constellation."[46] Progoff, we
might note finally, in describing his personal experience of being
initiated into the use of the *I Ching* by Jung in the summer of 1953,
provides a good indication of how Jung actually worked with the
oracle. The outstanding impression that Progoff gives us of Jung in
this regard is that of an old man who is very familiar indeed with
the divinatory method of the *I Ching*.[47] This too is the impression
that Jung himself was to convey in his 1949 foreword to the Wilhelm
translation of the *I Ching*. "Since I am not a sinologue," Jung writes,
"a foreword to the Book of Changes from my hand must be a testi-
monial of my individual experience with this great and singular
book."[48]

It was, of course, in Jung's highly regarded foreword to the *I
Ching* that he was to describe the casting of the oracle as a phenomenon of the synchronicity principle, a position with which, Fordham notably states, "I take it that most analytical psychologists can
agree."[49] "The ancient Chinese mind," Jung writes about the principle underlying the casting of the *I Ching*, here with special reference to the field approach to thinking,

> contemplates the cosmos in a way comparable to that of the
> modern physicist, who cannot deny that his model of the
> world is a decidedly psychophysical structure. The microphys-

ical event includes the observer just as much as the reality underlying the *I Ching* comprises subjective, i.e., psychic conditions in the totality of the momentary situation. Just as causality describes the sequence of events, so synchronicity to the Chinese mind deals with the coincidence of events. The causal point of view tells us a dramatic story about how *D* came into existence: it took its origin from *C*, which existed before *D*, and *C* in its turn had a father, *B*, etc. The synchronistic view on the other hand tries to produce an equally meaningful picture of coincidence. How does it happen that *A*, *B*, *C*, *D*, etc., appear all in the same moment and in the same place? It happens in the first place because the physical events *A* and *B* are of the same quality as the psychic events *C* and *D*, and further because all are exponents of one and the same momentary situation.[50]

With regard to the casting of the *I Ching*, then, Jung is here suggesting that in the throwing of the coins or the division of the yarrow stalks expression necessarily will be given to the constellated psychophysical pattern, that is to say, to the archetypal field in which the psychological situation of the subject is also contained. "It is assumed," Jung writes, "that the fall of the coins or the result of the division of the bundle of yarrow stalks is what it necessarily must be in a given 'situation,' inasmuch as anything happening in that moment belongs to it as an indispensable part of the picture. If a handful of matches is thrown on the floor, they form the pattern characteristic of that moment."[51]

Having given careful consideration to Jung's above-described theorizing about the *I Ching*, I am led to conclude that once again Jung's discussion of the time factor in relationship to synchronistic phenomena, here specifically the casting of the *I Ching*, is both inaccurate and very misleading. What Jung is saying in the above is that time, specifically a "moment" in time, is one of the central factors uniting the events of the archetypal field; this is certainly not the case.

Before I explain why, I should point out that von Franz, following Jung, says essentially the same thing. Her position, however, is even more radical than Jung's, in that she identifies time alone as the central unifying element of the psychophysical field. Jung, it should be recalled, spoke in the above passage not just of time as the factor common to all the events of the field, but he emphasized also that they were similar in quality, that is, meaning. In contrast to this, von Franz's position is diagrammatically illustrated as follows. The archetypal field is represented by a circle whose perimeter is marked with seven equally distanced points—these are the synchronistic events associated with the field. Each point or synchronistic event is marked with a letter, A to G, and from each a line converges on the center of the circle. This center point of the field is identified as "a time moment." Commenting further on this idea, von Franz writes, "Though causal thinking also poses the problem of time in some form because of the before and after, the problem of time is much more central in the synchronistic way of thinking because there it is the key moment—a certain moment in time—which is the uniting fact, the focal point for the observation of this complex of events."[52]

As was explained in some detail in chapter 2, Jung never did come to terms with the shortcomings of his discussion of the time factor with regard to synchronistic phenomena. Accordingly, what we have here, I believe, is simply another sampling of this problem. Specifically, here it is a case of Jung's fascination with the idea of clock-time simultaneity—a personal fascination that is not supported by the synchronistic case material itself.

When we are talking about the idea of "a moment in time" we are describing something taking place in the world of ego-consciousness, that is to say, in the world of clock time, for by Jung's own definition the idea of "moment" simply does not exist in the psychophysical continuum of the archetype. Concerning such clock time, then, it has been repeatedly evidenced by the examples given throughout this work that time is not the unifying factor of the psychophysical archetypal field; the unifying factor is simply meaning. Certainly key events in the psychophysical pattern may appear simultaneously within the clock-time framework, but this is not to say that events that do not appear simultaneously are regarded as not belonging to the pattern. Let us return again to an important point made in chapter 2, using one of our earliest examples. With the scarab case history there were three significant events associated with the pattern: first, the woman's dream about being presented with the golden scarab; second, her discussion with Jung about the dream during her analytical session; and third, the appearance of the scarab at the window during that session. In his discussion of this case, as we saw, what Jung likes to emphasize, in keeping with his fascination with clock-time simultaneity, is the paralleling of the discussion he had with his analysand about the dream with the appearance of the actual scarab. This is the synchronistic paralleling to which he draws his reader's attention. It is the case, however, that the dream is equally part of the psychophysical pattern in question, and if, for example, their discussion about the scarab dream had not taken place, the paralleling of the analysand's dream with the actual appearance of the scarab would have been no less significant a synchronistic experience. Clock-time simultaneity, therefore, is not a unifying factor of the psychophysical pattern. Similarly, the other above-described psychophysical patterns, such as the case involving the fox symbol, the case of the woman whom Jung spoke of as being attacked by birds whenever she was in the country, and Hsu Yun's experience of the water symbol pattern, are all examples of the patterning of events joined not by time but by meaning alone. Indeed, with the example involving Freud and "Mr. Foresight" the pattern in question extended over a great many years.

Turning, then, specifically to the problem of the casting of the *I Ching*, it is certainly one thing to say that the casting of the oracle is actually carried out in a particular moment in time, which it is, yet it is quite another thing to take this to mean that that particular moment in time is the unifying element of the psychophysical pattern to which one is given access. Certainly the casting of the *I Ching* takes place in a particular moment in time, yet the psychophysical pattern to which one is given access through the hexagram is not bound by the "moment in time" at which the oracle was cast, for the constellated psychophysical pattern that is depicted in the hexagram relates to events past, present, and future. The proper analogy here is a synchronistic dream. A synchronistic dream certainly does take place in a moment in time, yet the psychophysical pattern and the resultant information to which one is given access are not space- and time-bound. Accordingly, the moment at which the dream occurred is clearly not the unifying factor of the psychophysical field in question; the unifying element of the psychophysical pattern is meaning. It should be emphasized, therefore, that even though the casting of the *I Ching*, like the dream, does in fact take place in a moment in time, the moment in time is certainly not the unifying element of the psychophysical field.

Interestingly enough, several years after he wrote his foreword to the *I Ching*, Jung was asked by a correspondent, Reverend W. P. Witcutt, to comment on the hexagram/dream analogy. Jung's reply is particularly noteworthy because it supports three of the key points made above, which I shall again review. First, the hexagram and dream are both representative of the constellated archetypal field. Second, both fulfil a compensatory role in relationship to consciousness. Third, even though both manifest themselves at a particular moment in time, they both, as expressions of the space-time archetypal continuum, transcend the moment and thus contain elements of the past, present, and future in their compensatory messages. In keeping with these three points, Jung, in a letter dated August 24, 1960, thus writes:

> As you have found out for yourself, the *I Ching* consists of readable archetypes, and it very often presents not only a picture of the actual situation but also of the future, exactly like dreams. One could even define the *I Ching* oracle as an experimental dream, just as one can define a dream as an experiment of a four-dimensional nature. I have never tried even to describe this aspect of dreams, not to speak of the hexagrams, because I have found that our public today is incapable of understanding. I considered it therefore my first duty to talk and write of things that might be understandable and would thus prepare the ground upon which one could later on explain the more complicated things. I quite agree that the *I Ching* symbolism can be interpreted like that of dreams.[53]

Before proceeding to investigate the synchronistic character of the actual text of the *I Ching*, I would like to present another example of how the above-described synchronistic principle was put to use by Chinese Buddhist monks. The following is a slight variation of the above in that here the outward compensatory activity of nature is being employed to meet the needs of a group—a collective consciousness—as opposed to that of one individual.

Just as it is assumed with the casting of the *I Ching* that the relevant psychophysical pattern will manifest itself in the falling of the coins or the division of the yarrow stalks, the same assumption lay behind the unique method employed at the Kuei-yuan Monastery in China for selecting that monastery's abbot. At Kuei-yuan, the process of selecting the abbot was based entirely on the drawing of lots.[54] Certainly the utilization of lots to select an abbot was not completely foreign to other monasteries. However, when it was carried out in these monasteries it was generally only done so using a small list of names that had been developed through consultation and/or balloting. In contrast to this, at Kuei-yuan there was no such practice of limiting the number of candidates, and thus it was the case that many hundreds of names were involved in the process. To really appreciate why this was particularly problematic, we have to know something about the complexity of the procedure itself. Holmes Welch describes it as follows:

> all the names would be written on slips of paper and placed in a metal tube before the image of Wei-t'o, the guardian of monasteries. Incense would be lit and all present would recite "Homage to the bodhisattva Wei-t'o, who protects the dharma." Then, as they looked on, ready to detect any sign of fraud, a senior officer appointed by the abbot would shake the metal tube and pick out one slip with a pair of chopsticks. It would be recorded and replaced and then he would shake the tube again and make a second drawing. This was repeated until the same name was drawn out three times in a row. That was the name of the abbot to be.[55]

At Kuei-yuan, the abbot himself, not an appointee, was the one who actually drew the names from the metal tube. Certainly it is of some significance, Welch suggests, that the person selected through this process was not always an individual who had been generally regarded as suitable for the position of abbot. In the 1930s, for instance, a monk who was serving as a stoker at the Ling-yin Monastery was selected. "He was so stupid," Welch relates, "that he had the nickname 'Big Stoop,' but as soon as he took office, people found that he was able to preach the dharma and do everything else expected of an abbot."[56] The case of "Big Stoop," and that of the selection of other monks who were generally regarded as unfit for the office of abbot, is significant, Welch points out, because it suggests that the process of selection by lot was carried out in a completely legitimate manner. Commenting on this point and speaking further about its implications, Welch writes: "If the elections at the Kuei-yuan Ssu were rigged, why would anyone like 'Big Stoop' have been elected? But if they were honest, how could anyone at all have been elected? With hundreds of slips in the tube, if all were properly shuffled each time, how could the same slip be drawn three times in a row? Mathematically speaking, the chances were infinitesimal. Yet this is what always happened according to all the monks I have talked to about it."[57]

Beyond Kuei-yuan, other Chinese monasteries did occasionally use lot drawing to appoint their abbots. In 1952, for example, an abbot was selected by lot at the Yun-men Monastery in Kwangtung to replace the venerable Hsu Yun, who was retiring. In keeping with the directions of the Master, "each of the seventy to eighty permanent residents" were assigned a lot. For two days, without result, the drawing continued under the watchful eyes of the resident monks. Finally, on the third day, at approximately 3:00 p.m., a name was drawn three times in a row. Appropriately, it was the name of the individual to whom Hsu Yun, the previous year, "had transmitted the dharma," that is to say, had certified as having the correct understanding of the teaching. The selection of Fo-yuan, who among the various candidates was unquestionably the most qualified, was certainly timely. As Welch relates, "Indeed, if he had not been chosen, 'things would never have worked.' "[58]

A final example concerns the selection of an abbot at P'u-chi Monastery in Hunan. At this monastery, unlike the two described above, not only was the position of abbot filled by drawing lots, but so too were the positions of all the senior officers. The selection process worked as follows. The name of each position that was to be filled was recorded on a slip of paper. Each individual would then in turn draw a slip. The individual who drew the slip with the title abbot written on it would be given that position and so on. It was not necessary to draw the slip for the position concerned more than once.[59] Clearly the method used at P'u-chi Monastery was not outwardly as impressive as the methods used in the two above-described examples; still, we should bear in mind that it was believed to follow the same principle. Perhaps the specific appointment with which we are here concerned is something of a vindication of the method. In 1930, Welch tells us, a monk was chosen by lot for the position of abbot from a group of fifty-four. However, because he had been ordained only three months prior to this, he felt completely unworthy and declined. Respecting his wishes, the monks held a second drawing, only "this time among seventy-eight candidates." Amazingly enough, he drew the abbot's slip again. This time he felt obligated to accept. Following the completion of his term in 1935, names were drawn once again for the position of abbot. As Welch relates, "In 1935 . . . he drew the abbot's slip a third time. Truly a remarkable coincidence!"[60]

In summary, the above-described examples of how lot drawing was employed by Chinese Buddhist monks to select their abbots has provided us with additional insight into the way in which the Chinese, in practice, followed the synchronistic principle that nature will present one outwardly with the relevant compensatory pattern. This, it has been argued, is the very principle that Jung believed to underlie the casting of the *I Ching*. Having thus examined the concept of synchronicity in relationship to the actual casting of the *I Ching*, our investigation will now turn to the problem of the synchronistic character of the text itself.

Apart from its divinatory role, the *I Ching* also has the distinction of being acknowledged as a book of wisdom of unparalleled stature. "Of far greater significance than the use of the Book of Changes as an oracle," Wilhelm relates, "is its other use, namely, as a book of wisdom."[61] In keeping with this, Jung, in his foreword to the *I Ching*, writes about the very unique and enduring wisdom of the text: "I know that previously I would not have dared to express myself so explicitly about so uncertain a matter. I can take this risk because I am now in my eighth decade, and the changing opinions of men scarcely impress me any more; the thoughts of the old masters are of greater value to me than the philosophical prejudices of the Western mind."[62] Clearly the wisdom of the *I Ching* is of a unique sort, for in that it has arisen out of the unitary worldview of the Chinese, the wisdom of the text is itself unmistakably synchronistic in character. Accordingly, even though Jung does not directly make this point in his foreword, there is no doubt in my mind that what Jung found particularly impressive about the wisdom of the *I Ching* is its synchronistic character. Regarding this point, von Franz is more forthright. "In the final analysis," she writes about the *I Ching*, "this book is based entirely on the observation of synchronistic coincidences."[63]

In examining the synchronistic wisdom of the *I Ching*, two salient features emerge. First, it is the case that in the text, events are not evaluated from the perspective of the egocentric concerns of the individual; rather, they are viewed in terms of the larger pattern within which these events are contained. The emphasis of the text, therefore, is always on balance, that is to say, how one is to maintain, and restore if necessary, a balanced relationship to the events of the constellated psychophysical pattern, and by extension of this the all-encompassing synchronistic pattern of the Tao. "The judgments make it possible," Wilhelm explains,

> for a man to make a decision to desist from a course of action indicated by the situation of the moment but harmful in the long run. In this way he makes himself independent of the tyranny of events. In its judgments, and in the interpretations attached to it from the time of Confucius on, the Book of Changes opens to the reader the richest treasure of Chinese wisdom; at the same time it affords him a comprehensive view

of the varieties of human experience, enabling him thereby to shape his life of his own sovereign will into an organic whole and so to direct it that it comes into accord with the ultimate tao lying at the root of all that exists.[64]

The idea that one should act with an eye to the course of events in nature as a whole and not simply from an egocentric position is central to the synchronistic wisdom of the *I Ching*. The following excerpt, which is taken from the Judgement of the hexagram titled *Sung* (Conflict), gives us a sense of just how the text directs the individual toward such balanced action. The text reads:

Conflict. You are sincere
And are being obstructed.
A cautious halt halfway brings good fortune.
Going through to the end brings misfortune.[65]

Commenting on the meaning of this particular passage, Wilhelm writes: "If a man is entangled in a conflict, his only salvation lies in being so clear-headed and inwardly strong that he is always ready to come to terms by meeting the opponent halfway. To carry on the conflict to the bitter end has evil effects even when one is in the right, because the enmity is then perpetuated."[66] Clearly, it is the case that people often think because they are "in the right" on a particular issue they are entitled to exploit their "rightness" to the fullest. This, however, is not what the text would have one do, for to push beyond the halfway point brings misfortune.

Perhaps the case described in the previous chapter involving the American Buddhist monks Heng Sure and Heng Ch'au provides us with a practical example of the idea being presented here. Heng Sure and Heng Ch'au, it should be recalled, on one occasion during their bowing pilgrimage lost their gear to thieves, yet the second time around were able to play a considerable part in preventing the theft of their gear. The key to their success on this second occasion rested in their abilities to "halt halfway," that is to say, to recognize that that with which they were in conflict was not something that was strictly outside themselves, for much as the thieves were outwardly working to undermine their pilgrimage, so too were their shadows inwardly engaged in some of their own thieving. Essentially, what Heng Sure and Heng Ch'au were able to achieve was a recognition that in the larger perspective of the constellated psychophysical pattern, they too were, so to speak, the thieves. For the individual, on the other hand, unable to perceive consciously his relationship to the pattern, it would most probably be the case that he would not "halt halfway," but would vigorously and relentlessly persecute the outward thieves. Thus, the "thief" that the compensatory pattern was seeking to raise to consciousness would go unrecognized, and as a consequence of this the individual "in the right" would find himself in ever-darkening circumstances, a situation characterized by misfortune. To "halt halfway" one must, as Wilhelm explained above, be "clear-headed and inwardly strong." Heng Sure and Heng Ch'au demonstrated both of these qualities. Accordingly, they were able to achieve the type of balanced perspective that the synchronistic wisdom of the *I Ching* counsels—a balanced perspective that sees events not from the limited point of view of the ego, but in the context of the psychophysical pattern as a whole.

Concerning the second salient feature of the synchronistic wisdom of the *I Ching*, it should be recalled that looked at from the Jungian perspective each of the sixty-four hexagrams along with its interpretations is understood to depict the interplay of the events in a specific archetypal field—a psychophysical pattern that functions in conformity with the more comprehensive pattern of nature, the Tao. Accordingly, in that the psychic and physical events being depicted are themselves acausally ordered events, the analysis of these events that the text gives one when a hexagram is drawn is an analysis that is itself synchronistic in character. Essentially, what one is given is an analysis of the synchronistic interplay of these events in the psychophysical pattern in question. We thus find throughout the text that subjective and objective events, which are not causally related to each other, appear side by side in the psychophysical patterns associated with the hexagrams. Indeed, in the *I Ching*, this type of synchronistic interlinking of the events of inner and outer reality is such a given that it is represented in the very structure of the hexagram, which we should note is actually made up of two distinct trigrams. "The upper trigram," Cary Baynes explains, "is considered to be 'outside,' the lower 'inside.' This distinction underlies the constant juxtaposition, to be observed throughout . . . [the *I Ching*], of inner, mental states and external actions or events, of subjective and objective experiences."[67]

As a book of synchronistic wisdom, then, the *I Ching* objectifies and analyzes for its reader the synchronistic interplay of inner and outer events, thus enabling one to perceive the most beneficial course of action. In illustration of this type of synchronistic analysis that the text provides, we can use the following, which appears under the hexagram titled *Pi* (Holding Together). The text reads:

> Hold to him in truth and loyalty;
> This is without blame.
> Truth, like a full earthen bowl:
> Thus in the end
> Good fortune comes from without.[68]

In the above there is clearly a paralleling of one's subjective orientation with that which one encounters outwardly. Specifically, it is the case that good fortune is indicated to arise outwardly when one, "like a full earthen bowl," is filled inwardly with truthfulness.

As with the above, we see throughout the *I Ching* that the subjective position, that is, the way in which one both thinks and acts, is regarded as something of a pivotal factor that, so to speak, defines the role one will assume in the synchronistically ordered pattern. For example, again under the hexagram *Pi* (Holding Together), the idea is expressed that when one develops oneself inwardly and attains a certain degree of wholeness of personality, those who will benefit from this wholeness will be synchronistically brought into relationship with the person concerned. "If a man," Wilhelm writes about this particular idea, "cultivates within himself the purity and the strength that are necessary for one who is the centre of a fellowship, those who are meant for him come of their own accord."[69] Clearly this idea represents a radical departure from the hype-oriented commercialism characteristic of modern society, which utilizes every conceivable form of manipulation to push its message. Here, the individual does absolutely nothing to entice others; one's concern is with self-cultivation only. Once, however, one has developed the essential subjective qualities necessary to fulfil the leadership role in the pattern in question, "those who are meant for him come of their own accord." "Neither propaganda," Jung writes in a letter dated September 14, 1960, with direct reference to this same synchronistic idea, "nor exhibitionist confessions are needed. . . . Thus an old alchemist gave the following consolation to one of his disciples: 'No matter how isolated you are and how lonely you feel, if you do your work truly and conscientiously, unknown friends will come and seek you.' "[70]

To ensure that the reader does not wrongly conclude, as one could easily do looking just at the above examples, that in the *I Ching* favorable outward events necessarily arise in association with "correct" subjective attitudes, and unfavorable events in association with "incorrect" ones, I would like to present one further example of subjective/objective paralleling in the text. As was explained previously using Hsu Yun's enlightenment experience to demonstrate the point, adversity fulfils an important compensatory role in the tempering of personality. Accordingly, just as we find with synchronistic case histories, we too find in the *I Ching* that favorable outward events do not necessarily arise in association with "correct" inner attitudes. In the following, which is taken from the hexagram titled *Chen* (The Arousing), we have an example of this. The text reads:

> Shock comes bringing danger.
> A hundred thousand times
> You lose your treasures
> And must climb the nine hills.
> Do not go in pursuit of them.
> After seven days you will get them back again.[71]

What we have in the above is a situation in which considerable losses are experienced. "Resistance," Wilhelm explains, however, "would be contrary to the movement of the time and for this reason unsuccessful." All that one can do is "climb the nine hills," that is to say, "retreat to heights inaccessible to the threatening forces of danger."[72] The idea is that one must maintain a sense of inner balance and not allow oneself to be turned inwardly by the outward events of sudden misfortune. Furthermore, the compensatory patterning is such that in the face of this extreme suffering one must not seek to alter the course of events outwardly. Indeed, as the text points out, only by holding the center inwardly and not outwardly chasing after the things that have been taken away will all that has been lost be recovered.

In summary, we have come to see in our above investigation why Jung regarded the *I Ching* to be the " 'standard work' " of the synchronistic " 'science' " of the Chinese. As the foundational text of Chinese philosophy, the *I Ching* addresses the principal concerns of what Jung would describe as the synchronistically oriented mind of the Chinese. With respect to the casting of the oracle, from the Jungian perspective it is understood to be the case that in the falling coins or the division of the yarrow stalks expression is given to the constellated psychophysical pattern. Likewise, when a hexagram and its accompanying interpretations is drawn subsequent to this, it is also believed to be the case that the counsel offered by the text is itself synchronistic in nature. The wisdom of the text, in other words, is understood to constitute a highly refined study of the acausal patterning of events in nature.

Jung, we know, used the *I Ching* both as an oracle and book of synchronistic wisdom, and in this way, complemented by his own study of synchronistic phenomena in his life and work, acquired a very deep sense of relationship to the Chinese worldview. For Jung, however, the *I Ching* was certainly not a type of synchronistic panacea, for to use it effectively, Jung maintained, one must possess considerable psychological insight, just as such insight must also be possessed to interpret accurately the full meaning of any synchronistic pattern. "One must have a far-reaching psychological understanding," Jung writes in a letter dated January 29, 1934, "in order to enjoy the *I Ching* with advantage. Too much Oriental knowledge, however, takes the place of immediate experience and thus blocks the way to psychology."[73] When, for example, Jung would here have us recognize, the text speaks of "inner truth" one must be sufficiently in touch with oneself to identify that to which the text is referring. One must be able to identify what exactly one's unique truth is in a given situation. Similarly, when the text counsels one to "halt halfway" one must know what this means in the psychological sense, and in order to know what this means considerable self-knowledge is required. "If I understand anything of the *I Ching*," Jung explains in a letter dated October 25, 1935, "then I should say it is *the* book that teaches you your way and the all-importance of it."[74] This Jung believed is the spirit of the text; the great difficulty though, Jung also believed, is to have sufficient psychological insight to seize hold of that spirit.

The synchronistic patterning of events revealed by the *I Ching* was for Jung, of course, no less evident in the environment, and perhaps it was for this reason that Jung felt at times he should not rely on the *I Ching*, but put his own observational skills in this regard to the test. In a letter to Liliane Frey-Rohn dated February 27, 1945, Jung writes about the *I Ching*: "You know, I have not used it for more than two years now, feeling that one must learn to walk in the dark, or try to discover (as when one is learning to swim) whether the water will carry one."[75]

The conscious individual looking out into his environment, Jung held, will discover in the synchronistic patterning of events valuable insights into the problems with which he is concerned. Hannah, for example, relates how during the summer of 1936 Jung came upon a dead snake with a dead fish sticking out of its mouth. This particular synchronistic image, Hannah tells us, so fascinated Jung because in it he saw a very precise statement of the problem with which he was then preoccupied, that he carved the image into a wall at Bollingen. From Jung's point of view, the image was a depiction of how the new emerging pagan spirit, symbolized by the snake, was seeking to devour the Christian spirit, symbolized by the fish. The interplay of these two opposites, it should be pointed out, was full of import for Jung because he believed that through the clash of the pagan and Christian spirits a uniting symbol would arise that would be of particular healing significance to our present age.[76]

For Jung, a scarab hitting the window, a flock of birds settling on a house, a watch stopping, a loud report in a bookcase, the lapping of the lake, red sap running over a family crest from a vine above, the violence of a near-drowning, a fox entering the path along which two people walk through a wood—all were seen as guideposts of the synchronistic patterning of events, and, as such, were compensatory sources from which considerable insight into the problems of one's individuation could be derived. It was, therefore, through his own observation of synchronistic representations such as these that Jung was provided not only with key compensatory insights into the problems with which he was having considerable difficulties, but also, in some instances, with insights into problems of which he was not yet even conscious. We shall look at such a case shortly.

Here, however, it should be again emphasized that for Jung the key to benefiting from this type of outward synchronistic patterning rests in the degree of one's psychological insight. This is not only true because one might otherwise entirely overlook or misinterpret these outward compensatory representations, but it is also true because it is the case that in certain situations if one is able to penetrate a synchronistic pattern in its earliest stages of unfoldment, one will be able to play a more active role in bringing about the most beneficial outcome. This idea is very much in keeping with Wilhelm's following statement, in which he describes how in the *I Ching* there too is an emphasis on perceiving and acting on things while they are still in their beginnings: "The germinal phase is the crux. As long as things are in their beginnings they can be controlled, but once they have grown to their full consequences they acquire a power so overwhelming that man stands impotent before them."[77]

The ability, for example, to recognize at the earliest possible point when one has drifted, either consciously or unconsciously, from the more comprehensive pattern of one's individuation is particularly important, because it is not uncommon when one is so floundering for the synchronistic compensatory response of nature to become increasingly aggressive until the situation is satisfactorily corrected. It is, therefore, very much in one's interests to catch such developments in their beginnings and to take the appropriate action as quickly as possible. Jung refers to such a situation in a letter to Philip Metman dated March 27, 1954. Metman and his wife, apparently, had just narrowly escaped serious injury in a car accident. In writing to Metman, Jung very notably, as we shall see in the following, drew Metman's attention to the possible synchronistic relationship between their narrow escape from injury and some writing Metman was engaged in at that time. Jung's essential point was that Metman may not have been giving his creative energy sufficient freedom in his writing, and consequently he found himself at odds with the synchronistic flow of outward nature. "I gather with great concern," Jung writes,

> that you have had a hair-breadth escape from a car accident. The accident has affected only the outer shell, but evidently you and your wife were not affected physically by this broad hint. Naturally this may have an inner connection with what you are writing, for experience shows that accidents of this sort are very often connected with creative energy which turns against us because somehow it is not given due heed. This may easily happen, for we always judge by what we already know and very seldom listen to what we don't yet know. Therefore we can easily take a step in the wrong direction or continue too long on the right path until it becomes the wrong one. Then it may happen that in this rather ungentle way we are forced to change our attitude.[78]

Much as is the case with dreams, synchronistic experiences, such as the above, tend to repeat themselves, as Bolen explains, "until the inner psychological conflict or the conflicting external situation changes," that is to say, until the desired compensatory effect is realized. Bolen, interestingly enough, presents a case that is rather similar to the above, only with her example, not one but three car accidents took place before things were put back on course. Bolen relates how a woman with a perfect driving record found herself in the very awkward position of having to make two "it's me again"-type calls to her claims adjustor. Particularly troubling about these accidents was the fact that in each case the woman herself was blameless. In the first collision, she was hit from behind while stopped at a traffic light by a woman who failed to brake quickly enough on a rain-wetted street. On the second occasion she was hit again by a woman who was changing lanes. The third accident was similar to the first, only more serious still. She was again struck from behind while stopped at a traffic light, but in this instance by a woman whose brakes had failed. This time the impact of the accident was so great that her gasoline tank ruptured, fortunately without igniting, and her vehicle was dangerously pushed forward into the intersection. After this third collision, the analysand, we are told, finally began to give serious thought to a possible synchronistic connection.[79] Commenting on the specific compensatory meaning of this particular synchronistic pattern, Bolen writes:

> The first accident had seemed to be a metaphor for what was deeply troubling her: A woman co-worker had recently made an emotional impact, and the intense feelings had been jarring (a situation that might have been caused by not putting the brakes on feelings soon enough). The possibility of synchronicity in the second accident was also considered and ignored. The third accident was, however, absolutely convincing: On the same day as the last accident (in which she was hit by a woman whose brakes had failed), her co-worker's car brakes also failed. After that, it was clearly time to accept the accidents as synchronistic events that were commenting on the situation. The accidents were like a series of dreams in which the same theme repeated itself in different settings until the dreamer got the message, and acknowledged that the relationship was mutually damaging.[80]

We see from the above examples, therefore, that when one is at odds with the compensatory flow of one's individuation, it is very much to one's advantage to discover as quickly as possible how the subjective position is not right, and then to make the needed adjustments immediately, lest the compensatory synchronistic pattern take an even more sinister turn. This synchronistic maxim is one with which Jung, as we shall now see, became well acquainted at a relatively early, yet very critical point in his career.

In 1916, during the period described above as the time of Jung's confrontation with the unconscious, Jung had a very curious fantasy that he recorded. In his fantasy, the figure Jung refers to as his anima had flown away. She had disappeared, Jung would later understand, into the collective unconscious—"the mythic land of the dead, the land of the ancestors." About this motif, Jung writes: "If . . . one has a fantasy of the soul [anima] vanishing, this means that it has withdrawn into the unconscious or into the land of the dead. There it produces a mysterious animation and gives visible form to the . . . collective contents. Like a medium, it gives the dead a chance to manifest themselves."[81] Jung's anima had indeed withdrawn far into the world of the psyche where it was to form a mediumistic-type bridge between the "spirits of the dead" and the ego. More specifically, as Jung ultimately was to discover, it had withdrawn to enable the "dead" to present themselves to Jung and petition him with their unresolved spiritual problems—spiritual problems which, significantly, Jung was himself destined to take up in his own work.

At the time of Jung's fantasy, however, Jung did not comprehend its real meaning, nor did he sense how powerfully the archetypal forces were constellated. Jung, to be sure, was unaware of the magnitude of the compensatory movement that was underway and thus could not know, in keeping with the compensatory principle outlined above, that his failure to descend with his anima to meet the "dead" closer to their own world would result in the powerful, relentless compensatory ascent of these same figures into his own. Accordingly, Jung was completely unprepared for the compensatory synchronistic events that were about to take place in his environment. So it was that shortly after the time of Jung's fantasy of his anima having flown away, the Jung household was struck by a full-scale haunting. "It began with a restlessness," Jung writes in his autobiography,

> but I did not know what it meant or what "they" wanted of me. There was an ominous atmosphere all around me. I had the strange feeling that the air was filled with ghostly entities. Then it was as if my house began to be haunted. My eldest daughter saw a white figure passing through the room. My second daughter, independently of her elder sister, related that twice in the night her blanket had been snatched away; and that same night my nine-year-old son had an anxiety dream.[82]

Something, Jung correctly sensed, was being demanded of him, yet he did not know exactly what it was " 'they' wanted." The response of nature therefore was to increase the intensity of this compensatory synchronistic flow of energy. The situation in the Jung household thus worsened as the haunting continued. "Around five o'clock in the afternoon on Sunday," Jung writes,

> the front doorbell began ringing frantically. It was a bright summer day; the two maids were in the kitchen, from which the open square outside the front door could be seen. Everyone immediately looked to see who was there, but there was no one in sight. I was sitting near the doorbell, and not only heard it but saw it moving. We all simply stared at one another. . . . Then I knew that something had to happen. The whole house was filled as if there were a crowd present, crammed full of spirits. They were packed deep right up to the door, and the air was so thick it was scarcely possible to breathe. As for myself, I was all a-quiver with the question: "For God's sake, what in the world is this?" Then they cried out in chorus, "We have come back from Jerusalem where we found not what we sought."[83]

Now finally recognizing the need to come immediately to terms with the compensatory import of this increasingly threatening situation, Jung sat down, took pen and paper in hand, and simply allowed the unconscious to express itself without restriction. With this action, Jung thus descended into the unconscious in pursuit of his anima. The response was immediate. "As soon as I took up the pen," Jung relates, "the whole ghostly assemblage evaporated."[84] For three evenings Jung continued to write and completed in that period of time a work which he titled *Septem Sermones ad Mortuos (Seven Sermons to the Dead)*[85]—a work that Jung would in retrospect acknowledge as "a kind of prelude to what I had to communicate to the world about the unconscious."[86] Describing the lasting impact this experience was to have on Jung's thinking about synchronistic phenomena, Hannah relates: "The fact that the whole uncanny phenomena and thick atmosphere in the house vanished the moment he took up his pen made an enormous impression on Jung. It was a great encouragement in continuing the work on the unconscious, for he saw that any neglect of this affected his whole environment adversely."[87]

With the above examples, we have seen, then, how one comes into conflict with nature—specifically the synchronistic patterning of events in nature—when the development of personality is neglected. For Jung, the call to individuate arises from the deepest sources of life and is supported inwardly and outwardly by the compensatory activities of nature. It is a call, therefore, that is not to be taken lightly. Both inwardly and outwardly nature strives unceasingly to bring about the realization, in the life of the individual, of a unique pattern of meaning. "The fact is," Jung relates about the individuation process, "that what happens to a person is characteristic of him. He represents a pattern and all the pieces fit."[88] Similarly, Jung writes with specific reference to the synchronistic patterning of events in the individuation process: "It is perfectly possible, psychologically, for the unconscious or an archetype to take complete possession of a man and to determine his fate down to the smallest detail. At the same time objective, nonpsychic parallel phenomena can occur which also represent the archetype. It not only seems so, it simply is so, that the archetype fulfils itself not only psychically in the individual, but objectively outside the individual. My own conjecture is that Christ was such a personality."[89] We are reminded here of Neumann's above-mentioned concept of the central archetypal pattern of one's individuation, three examples of which were the case involving the fox symbol, the psychophysical patterning associated with Hsu Yun's enlightenment, and the psychophysical pattern of Freud's case history involving "Mr. Foresight"—the pattern that ultimately proved to be so central to Freud's own life.

For Jung, as evidenced by his own writings on synchronicity and, perhaps more importantly, by the way he lived his own life, the individuation process extends beyond the psychological realm and assumes the character of a drama that takes the whole of nature for its stage. What we normally regard as the discontinuous inner and outer worlds become enclosed within the same circle of wholeness. Inwardly and outwardly nature works, through the compensatory patterning of events, to further the movement of the individual toward wholeness. Accordingly, the conscious individual is led, much as the traditional worldview of the Chinese would carry one, into a new experience of life wherein one is able to perceive with ever-increasing clarity how events in the outer world relate to the events of one's inner world. Now one is challenged to achieve a full understanding of the meaning that conjoins one, not only to the unconscious, but to nature in its entirety. This is the new spiritual challenge of individuation. It is the task of experiencing within the sacred circle of nature as a whole the meaning of an individual existence.

Jung's Psychology of Religion: The Synchronistic Model 🍎

Ritual Dimension

In 1937 when Jung exhorted his Yale audience to move beyond the confines of established religion and accept the challenge of "immediate religious experience," what Jung had in mind was for them to enter consciously into a direct encounter with the unconscious. For those for whom the rituals of conventional religion had lost their efficacy, what Jung offered as an alternative was an intrapsychic ritual which, properly followed, would lead to the emergence of a highly personalized spiritual wholeness. What Jung had in mind in 1937, then, was a ritual to be enacted within the sacred circle of the psyche. As we have seen in the preceding chapters, however, this earlier Jungian notion of religious ritual has been dramatically transformed by the synchronicity concept, indeed, so much so that we can now say that Jung's notion of "immediate religious experience" may be taken to refer not simply to an intrapsychic encounter, but to a direct encounter with nature in its entirety. The Jungian ritual, to put it simply, is now a ritual which is to be enacted within the sacred circle of nature as a whole.

In our study of the synchronicity concept, we have seen how for Jung the "holy" is encountered as much outwardly, in the synchronistic patterning of events, as it is inwardly. Accordingly, the individual in search of "immediate religious experience" is now required to attend to the compensatory images with which nature presents one outwardly with the same religious seriousness with which one attends to the "images of wholeness offered by the unconscious." With regard to the former, we are reminded of Jaffé's description of one having to "think in terms of the unconscious" in interpreting synchronistic phenomena, Bolen's similar notion of treating synchronistic events as "waking dreams," and Progoff's "correlation method" designed to heighten one's experience of the interplay of inner and outer events. The religious need, as Jung puts it, longs for wholeness, and here the wholeness to which one must open oneself is a wholeness that is not only transmitted intrapsychically, but transmitted to the individual through the synchronistic patterning of events in one's environment. Describing what she regards as the specifically religious character of attending to the compensatory activities of nature as experienced both inwardly and outwardly—a practice which she likens to the traditional Chinese idea of acting in harmony with Tao—von Franz writes:

> Religion means never acting only in accordance with conscious reasoning, but with constant attention . . . [to] the unknown participating factors. For instance, if someone says: "Let us have coffee together after the lecture," if I think only that I have time since I don't have lunch until 12:30, that would be conscious reasoning, which of course is also correct, but if I am a religious person, I will stop for a minute and try to get a feeling as to whether it is right to do that, and if I have an instinctive feeling against it, or at that moment a window bangs shut, or I stumble, then I might not go. . . . [A]ll the time one should concentrate and try to get some sign from the Self. . . . In Chinese philosophy, it is tantamount to paying constant attention to Tao, whether what I am now doing is right, in Tao.[1]

What von Franz describes above as the "participating factors," that is to say, the compensatory manifestations of nature as experienced both inwardly and outwardly, are the stuff of Jung's "immediate religious experience." Jung, we know, could take such raw material and masterfully draw out its compensatory import. This he did, moreover, as we have seen, not only with the inner and outer events of his own life, but with the events of the lives of his analysands as well. Here Jung reached out to complete consciously the sacred circles enclosing the lives of individuals, including his own. Here he performed what we now acknowledge to be the distinctive ritual of the Jungian worldview.

In chapter 1, in seeking to extend our understanding of the Jungian notion of religious ritual, we touched on some of the parallels that exist between practices and concepts in shamanism and the analytical process. I would now like to continue this theme, giving special consideration to the further ideas and questions raised by the synchronicity concept.

The most obvious yet nonetheless important point to be made is that the link between shamanism and the analytical process is fundamentally strengthened by the fact that analytical psychology acknowledges, as does shamanism, that that which is the subject of their concern is not something confined to the intrapsychic level. The "forces" with which one must struggle and come to terms are for both as much outside the individual as they are within him. When, for example, Jung in 1916 had the vision of his anima flying away, the "soul crisis" that immediately followed this was something that engulfed the whole Jung household. Jung, we saw, did not just have disturbing dreams, but rather his whole household was subjected to a full-scale haunting. The threatening situation with which Jung, his family, and his servants were confronted—the situation that Jung would himself have to exorcise—was present as much in the environment as it was in his psyche, much as were the equally threatening situations that confronted Philip Metman and, in another case, Bolen's female analysand in the form of car accidents.

A second point to be considered in relationship to this theme is the way in which synchronistic phenomena transform our understanding of the bonding that develops between analyst and analysand. In the analytical relationship, it is the case that a very powerful bonding develops between the analyst and analysand, and one of the distinguishing features of Jung's method, from the time of its inception, was his positive evaluation of this bonding. Analysis, Jung argued, should be a type of dialectical process in which both the conscious and unconscious experiences and insights of the analyst and analysand come into play. Accordingly, in contrast to the Freudian couch technique, Jung's idea was that all such physical and psychic barriers should be removed. Analyst and analysand, Jung held, should directly face each other so that in their direct interaction each might bring the fullness of his own personality, both in the conscious and unconscious sense, more completely to bear on the work.

Anathema to Jung was any attempt on the analyst's part to "shield" himself from his patient "with a smoke-screen of fatherly and professional authority." Much as the shaman heals by taking the illness of his patient into himself, for Jung the analyst must too allow himself to be susceptible to the affliction of his patient. Only in this way, Jung argued, can the analyst have any effect as a healer. "In any effective psychological treatment," Jung writes, "the doctor is bound to influence the patient; but this influence can only take place if the patient has a reciprocal influence on the doctor. You can exert no influence if you are not susceptible to influence." For Jung, therefore, if the analyst is to accompany his analysand in true shamanic fashion, he must be prepared for the fact that he, like his analysand, will at times be threatened and frightened by what appears before them. He must be prepared for the "psychic disturbances or even injuries peculiar to the profession" to which he may very well fall victim as he journeys with his patient. He must be prepared to be transformed, as his analysand will also be, by what they encounter in the course of their journey and by what unfolds between them as they walk the path together. With direct reference to the latter point, Jung writes, "For two personalities to meet is like mixing two different chemical substances: if there is any combination at all, both are transformed."[2]

With the analytical process, then, a powerful and intimate bonding of analyst and analysand takes place. What we shall now consider is how this analytical bonding is carried to quite a different level with the introduction of synchronistic experiences in which both analyst and analysand are contained.

In his autobiography Jung describes such a case. The example involves a man, a former patient of Jung's, whom Jung "had pulled out of a psychogenic depression." Shortly after the completion of his therapy, the man returned home and married. The marriage, however, was not one Jung felt good about. Indeed, after having met his patient's wife just once Jung was left with "an uneasy feeling." Describing this further, Jung writes, "Her husband was grateful to me, and I observed that I was a thorn in her side because of my influence over him." As things turned out, the couple had been married just a year when the man again fell into a serious depression. Having anticipated the possibility that such a relapse might occur, Jung had directed his patient to contact him the moment "he observed his spirits sinking." This, however, was something he did not do, "partly," Jung explains, "because of his wife, who scoffed at his moods." Describing what then took place, Jung writes:

> At that time I had to deliver a lecture in B. I returned to my hotel around midnight. I sat with some friends for a while after the lecture, then went to bed, but I lay awake for a long time. At about two o'clock—I must have just fallen asleep—I awoke with a start, and had the feeling that someone had come into my room; I even had the impression that the door had been hastily opened. I instantly turned on the light, but there was nothing. Someone might have mistaken the door, I

thought, and I looked into the corridor. But it was still as death. "Odd," I thought, "someone did come into the room!" Then I tried to recall exactly what had happened, and it occurred to me that I had been awakened by a feeling of dull pain, as though something had struck my forehead and then the back of my skull. The following day I received a telegram saying that my patient had committed suicide. He had shot himself. Later, I learned that the bullet had come to rest in the back wall of his skull.[3]

Bolen describes a similar synchronistic exchange between an American analyst and her analysand. With her example, however, the situation is somewhat reversed, as here it is the analysand who has insight into a situation greatly troubling the analyst. During a time in which the analyst was on vacation, she received the shattering news that her parents, who were themselves travelling outside the United States, had taken their own lives. Because her parents lived on the east coast of the United States and their double suicide occurred outside of the country, it was, of course, not reported in San Francisco, where she had her practice. When she returned to work at the time she had been scheduled to return following her vacation, she decided only to tell her patients "that her planned vacation had been cut short by a tragedy in her family. A patient," Bolen continues, "then reported a dream in which she was traveling in a bus with her therapist (her therapist was with relatives) when the bus began to fill with poison gas. Since the double death of her parents was through carbon monoxide, it seemed to my colleague that her patient had picked up on details of her emotional situation and incorporated them into a dream."[4]

As with Freud's case history involving "Mr. Foresight," with Bolen's above example we seem to again have a situation where the analysand is functioning as the "oracle" for the analyst. Along this same line, it should not be forgotten that during the time of Jung's serious illness in 1944, Jung himself, as patient, similarly obtained knowledge about a tragic situation that his doctor, Dr. H., would soon face. While in a state of unconsciousness, Jung learned that his doctor's life—the man who was then working to save Jung's own life—was endangered. Jung, it should be recalled, was concerned about Dr. H. because he had appeared to him in his "primal form," and, as time was to reveal, his concern was not unjustified. At the turning point of his recovery, on the very day Jung sat up in his bed for the first time, Dr. H. was confined to his with a fatal illness. Forming something of a parallel to Jung's experience is the following shamanic account related by Eliade. Of particular interest is its depiction of the close bonding that exists between patient and healer—a bonding that here enabled a patient who had "suddenly died" to be informed of the death of a shaman who was actually working to restore her to life. The text reads:

> A shaman was trying to bring back the soul of a woman who had died suddenly, when he fell dead himself from a terrible wound in his stomach. A second shaman entered the scene and revived the woman, whereupon she related that she had seen the first shaman's spirit crossing a lake in the form of a walrus [his primal form?], and that someone had hit him with a weapon, the effect of the blow being visible on the corpse.[5]

With respect to synchronistic experiences within which both analyst and analysand, healer and patient, are contained, they do seem to increase, Jung suggests, in proportion to the degree of unconscious identification between the analyst and analysand.[6] The closer, in other words, the analyst and analysand are related to each other on the unconscious level, that is to say, the more intricately their respective destinies entwine, the more frequent such synchronistic phenomena will be. The bonding that unites analyst and analysand goes beyond conventional notions of countertransference and transference. It is not a case of the analytical relationship beginning and ending on the hour, for the analytical relationship that is being pursued within a clearly defined time- and space-bound framework is also unfolding in a dimension outside of space and time. It is with the latter in mind, it seems, that Jung told Charles Baudouin the following. "We were speaking one evening," Baudouin relates,

> of "telepathic" dreams where, between persons who are emotionally close, a mutual unconscious communication and penetration appears to take place. Jung finally, to sum up his thoughts on the matter, acted them out as follows: with brief, firm gestures he touched first my forehead, then his own, and thirdly drew a great circle with his hand in the space between us; the three motions underscored the three clauses of this statement; "In short, one doesn't dream here, one doesn't dream here, one dreams there." And *there* the hand kept turning.[7]

In closing this section on the ritual dimension of Jung's psychology of religion, I would like to return to a point made in chapter 1. In that chapter it was emphasized that within the Jungian model the idea of vicarious atonement gives way to the belief that the individual must consciously take upon himself the suffering that will invariably be part of his individuation journey. Individuation in its fullest sense is a tremendous burden, as Jung always emphasized. Related to this, it is certainly not the case that the synchronicity principle, as some might wrongly imagine, in some way lightens this burden. The integration of the compensatory messages of synchronistic phenomena is, to be sure, as demanding as the integration of the compensatory messages of dreams. Accordingly, with "immediate religious experience," either in the intrapsychic or synchronistic sense of that concept, the heavy burden of integration falls directly on the individual. The individual, it should be emphasized, in both instances is the one who must himself walk the path.

Doctrinal Dimension

One subject that Jung does not treat with a great deal of sympathy is the subject of metaphysics. Commenting on Jung's much-emphasized aversion to things metaphysical, Dourley writes: "Jung repeatedly disavows any metaphysical import in his psychology. Jung usually means by the term 'metaphysical' a position or doctrine without any basis in human experience, so he often relates it to an inadequate model of belief."[8] For Jung, as Dourley indicates, metaphysics is not simply a discipline that seeks to produce carefully developed theoretical constructs of the nature of reality; rather it is regarded by Jung as producing something akin to statements of faith, that is to say, statements that lack any experiential basis. "Psychology," Jung thus writes, "as the science of the soul has to confine itself to its subject and guard against overstepping its proper boundaries by metaphysical assertions or other professions of faith."[9]

In all fairness to Jung, something he most certainly sought to achieve—even though his critics often fail to appreciate this, especially those not familiar with the practical workings of the unconscious—was to have theory flow from clinical experience. This is not to say, however, as Jung himself would like to, that the theories which were so generated were themselves always devoid of metaphysical import—I am specifically thinking here of Jung's theorizing about synchronistic phenomena.

Concerning the question of the metaphysical import of the synchronicity theory, there are those, we should perhaps note, who believe that even this concept of Jung's is completely without such content. Heisig, for instance, writes, "The claim that the principle of synchronicity represents an excursion into theological metaphysics quite misses the point of Jung's intentions."[10] Although the wording of Heisig's statement is somewhat ambiguous, Heisig's essential point is that not only did Jung not intend the synchronicity theory to be an excursion into metaphysics, but that Jung's theorizing about synchronistic phenomena does not in fact constitute such an excursion. Heisig's point is, of course, one that the material presented in this work does not support. My own impression is that those, like Heisig, who fail to see the metaphysical import of this concept either have simply followed Jung's own statements to this effect or have failed to grasp what Jung had in mind in his description of the archetype as a psychoid factor. Bender has, I believe, in contrast to this, hit the mark in writing, "Jung attempts, as a metaphysical background to synchronicity, a hypothesis of a [unus mundus], a unitary aspect of being."[11] Similarly, Rao writes, "For Jung, synchronicity is a metaphysical principle and is intended to explain more than what we now regard as parapsychological phenomena."[12]

In chapter 2, we saw how the archetype was lifted out of the strictly intrapsychic realm and, in its most advanced theoretical form, came to be regarded by Jung as a psychophysical continuum of meaning present in nature as a whole. Clearly this progression from an intrapsychic to a "transcendental meaning" is a theoretical development that is not without metaphysical import, as Jung himself tacitly concedes in the following. "We are so accustomed," Jung writes in his principal essay on synchronicity, with reference to his concept of the psychoid archetype, "to regard meaning as a psychic process or content that it never enters our heads to suppose that it could exist outside the psyche. . . . If, therefore, we entertain the hypothesis that one and the same (transcendental) meaning might manifest itself simultaneously in the human psyche and in the arrangement of an external and independent event, we at once come into conflict with the conventional scientific and epistemological views."[13] With this progression from the intrapsychic to the transcendental—a theoretical development undertaken by Jung on the basis of his study of synchronistic phenomena—what we indeed have, in part, is a progression from "metapsychology" to "metaphysics," for what Jung is now theorizing about with his concept of the psychoid archetype is not simply the structure of the psyche, but the nature of reality itself.

In our study of synchronistic experiences, we have seen that the transcendental meaning of the psychoid archetype is sometimes experienced both inwardly and outwardly, while at other times just outwardly. In the case of the former, where one attains knowledge of a specific objective event via the unconscious, Jung speaks of an experience of the "absolute knowledge" of the archetype. As we have also seen, however, what is "absolute knowledge" in the unconscious may be far from "absolute"—in the sense of a strict mirroring of the inner and outer events—by the time it reaches consciousness. Indeed, en route it often undergoes specific compensatory transformations. Concerning this point, it was suggested in chapter 3 that a strict mirroring of inner and outer events only takes place when it serves, so to speak, the compensatory objectives of the constellated archetype; otherwise the two events will diverge, and as a consequence of this need to be interpreted in terms of their compensatory interplay. Freud, as was demonstrated, in actual practice took much the same approach in analyzing telepathic communications between individuals.

With respect to such experiences of the "absolute knowledge" of the constellated archetype, Jung makes the very interesting suggestion that an intrapsychic experience of the archetype's "absolute knowledge" may very well give rise to the more common experience of déjà vu.[14] In the case of déjà vu, the idea would be that the "absolute knowledge" one achieves of a future event is forgotten by the individual, perhaps upon waking. When, therefore, the individual is confronted at a later point with the parallel objective event and in turn is deeply impressed with its seeming familiarity, the individual nevertheless is unable to connect the event to the initial intrapsychic experience. In contrast to this, however, sometimes it is the case that when a synchronistic dream has been initially forgotten it is recalled when the individual encounters the objective parallel event, much as one can be "reminded" of a previous night's dream by something that happens to one the following day. Esther Harding describes such a case where a woman first had an experience of déjà vu when confronted with a parallel objective situation, but then almost immediately things came more sharply into focus for her, and she was able to recall her dream and indeed make use of its information in a manner that perhaps saved the woman and her friend from a serious car accident.[15]

Whether or not the compensatory activities of the constellated archetype are, in connection with synchronistic events, experienced both inwardly and outwardly or outwardly only, it should be emphasized that for Jung the meaning that one encounters, and often feels overwhelmed by, is an objective meaning, a transcendental meaning present in nature itself. As von Franz explains, "Synchronistic events constitute moments in which a 'cosmic' or 'greater' meaning becomes gradually conscious in an individual; generally this is a shaking experience."[16] Similarly, Marion Woodman characterizes a synchronistic encounter as an encounter with "that greater Reality."[17] Here we are also reminded of Bolen's previously cited statement, "Every time I have become aware of a synchronistic experience, I have had an accompanying feeling that some grace came along with it."

It is rather ironic that Jung, in keeping with the developments that took place in connection with his study of synchronistic phenomena, would find himself talking about the collective unconscious in a manner that in earlier years would have been a source of considerable annoyance to him coming from the lips of others. Indeed when Jung first spoke of the idea of the collective unconscious he often found himself having to correct the then incorrect way in which his term was interpreted. Rather than simply understanding the term to refer to a collective level in each individual's psyche, it was at times wrongly understood by others to refer to the idea of a single unconscious shared by all. As it has now turned out, however, with the theoretical extension of his concept of the archetype, what was previously an incorrect interpretation of the concept of the collective unconscious is now not at all off the mark. Jung's above-described comments to Charles Baudouin, for example, about where we dream, certainly give us a sense of this. So also does the following taken from a letter of Jung's dated July 10, 1946. "Your view that the collective unconscious," Jung writes to his correspondent,

> surrounds us on all sides is in complete agreement with the way I explain it to my pupils. It is more like an atmosphere in which we live than something that is found *in* us. . . . Also, it does not by any means behave merely psychologically; in the cases of so-called synchronicity it proves to be a universal substrate present in the environment rather than a psychological premise. Wherever we come into contact with an archetype we enter into relationship with transconscious, metapsychic fac-

tors which underlie the spiritualist hypothesis as well as that of magical actions.[18]

Even though the "universal substrate present in the environment" to which Jung refers can be described as the collective unconscious, it is nevertheless the case that the term more commonly used by Jung to describe this "universal substrate" is, as previously indicated, the *unus mundus*, the unitary world of the psychoid archetype. Furthermore, just as the psyche as a whole is understood by Jung to function in a unitary manner in relationship to the central archetype, the self, so too for Jung does the *unus mundus* function as a unitary substrate coextensive with nature in its entirety. "If mandala symbolism," Jung writes, emphasizing the oneness of the psyche and the *unus mundus* and, moreover, the presence in both of a unitary orderedness, "is the psychological equivalent of the *unus mundus*, then synchronicity is its parapsychological equivalent."[19] Arguing much along the same line, von Franz writes: "The most essential and certainly the most impressive thing about synchronistic occurrences . . . is the fact that in them the duality of soul and matter seems to be eliminated. They are therefore an *empirical* indication of an ultimate unity of all existence, which Jung, using the terminology of medieval natural philosophy, called the *unus mundus*."[20]

One of the most notable challenges to Jung's concept of the *unus mundus* comes from James Hillman. The problem, as Hillman sees it, with the use of concepts such as the *unus mundus* and the self, is an ideational one. For Hillman, to be sure, it is the problem of giving free rein to our cultural bias toward monotheism at the expense of what he considers to be the essentially polytheistic character of the psyche. "The question 'polytheism or monotheism,' " Hillman thus argues, "represents a basic ideational conflict in Jungian psychology today."[21]

In contrast to what he describes as the monotheistic tendency to gather psychic events into a unity, the polytheistic perspective, Hillman writes, aims at "integrating each fragment according to its own principle, giving each God its due over that portion of consciousness, that symptom, complex, fantasy which calls for an archetypal background."[22] Multiplicity, for Hillman, is the genuine form of psychic reality. "Babel," he writes, "may be a religious decline from one point of view but it may also be a psychological improvement since through the many tongues complete psychic reality is being reflected."[23] The monotheistic perspective, by contrast, as

Hillman sees it, devours the many, thus silencing those other voices: "The one God swallows all the others."[24]

Contrary to the general integrative approach of the classical Jungian method, which is often described in terms 'of an upward spiralling movement around the center—a movement in which psychic contents are consciously brought into relationship with the larger pattern of one's individuation—the general thrust of Hillman's approach is to compartmentalize. Clearly, Hillman diverges from the classical integrative approach. The question, however, of exactly how radically Hillman diverges in this manner and to what degree he would include, as Fordham puts it, "deintegrative states in the process of individuation,"[25] is something open to interpretation. In the following, we are, nevertheless, given a good indication of where Hillman's sentiments lie in this regard. Writing in a "Postscript" to his "Psychology: Monotheistic or Polytheistic," written, by the way, ten years after the appearance of that paper, Hillman comments:

> For a long time I was not able to understand why clinicians had such an investment in the strong ego, the suppressive integration of personality, and the unified independence of will at the expense of ambivalence, partial drives, complexes, imagos, vicissitudes—to say nothing of hallucinations and split personality—until I heard sounding through this clinical language the ancient and powerful basso profundo of the One.[26]

Hillman's charge that that which he characterizes as the monotheistic perspective of the classical Jungian method invariably leads one to ride roughshod over the multiplicity of psychic contents—"The one God swallows all the others"—strikes one as a considerable distortion of what actually takes place in the analytical process. In the individuation process, Adler writes in direct response to Hillman's charge, "an internal splitting and reuniting [is] going on all the time, so that the self is never the Wholeness but the container of the work, the focus, the point of reference, the IDENTITY of the individual."[27] Interestingly enough, something one senses in connection with Hillman's thesis is that his objective is not so much to keep the monotheistic perspective from devouring the polytheistic one, as he claims it does, but rather to use the latter himself to devour the former. It was perhaps Marvin Spiegelman's perception of this point that led him to conclude that Hillman's concern about the monotheistic perspective is misplaced. What Hillman should indeed be concerned with, Spiegelman suggests, is not monotheism as such, but those authoritarian tendencies characteristic of the senex consciousness which can just as easily take possession of a polytheistic orientation as a monotheistic one.[28]

In contrast to Hillman's assessment of the role that the monotheistic/monistic perspective plays in Jung's psychology, I would argue that for Jung "complete psychic reality" is to be found in the conscious study of the particular, in its uniqueness, as viewed against the background of the larger pattern, the latter being defined as one's successively unfolding experiences of the self as totality, running from the intrapsychic through to the *unus mundus.* I thus think it is the case, in contrast to Hillman, that elements associated with both the monotheistic and polytheistic perspective come into play in Jung's analytical method. In this regard, I am very much in agreement with James Olney when he writes in his major study of the work of Yeats and Jung: "Yeats, like Jung, was a monist who would not—who *could* not—deny mundane pluralism."[29]

In closing this section on the doctrinal dimension of Jung's psychology of religion, I would like to comment further on two points that were raised in chapter 1: first, the charge against Jung of psychologism, and second, Jung's concept of the self as archetype.

In chapter 1, it was explained that one of the central criticisms levelled against Jung's psychology of religion is that while it opens up, on the one hand, a completely new dimension of religious meaning through its interpretation of religious phenomena in terms of specific psychological processes, it seems also to discredit, on the other hand, the objective reality of the phenomena described. Homans, it was pointed out, has identified this "reductive" aspect of Jung's psychology of religion, as have Spinks, Hostie, Goldbrunner, and Wulff, to name but a few. The latter, we should recall, writes in his extensive survey of research in the psychology of religion that "Jung has . . . been sharply criticized for foreclosing the question of religion's objective validity." This same issue, we should note, was very much at the center of the bitter exchange that took place between Buber and Jung. With reference to what he regarded as Jung's religious reductionism, Buber wrote: "If religion is a relation to psychic events, which cannot mean anything other than to events of one's own soul, then it is implied by this that it is not a relation to a Being or Reality which, no matter how fully it may from time to time descend to the human soul, always remains transcendent to it. More precisely, it is not the relation of an I to a Thou."[30] Concerning this charge, Jung, for his part, never could comprehend why for Buber, and for that matter those others with similar concerns about his psychology of religion, the archetypal unconscious was not itself a transcendent enough reality for their tastes. "The so-called 'forces of the unconscious,' " Jung thus wrote in response to Buber, "are not intellectual concepts that can be arbitrarily manipulated, but dangerous antagonists which can, among other things, work frightful devastation in the economy of the personality. They are everything one could wish for or fear in a psychic 'Thou.' "[31]

In contrast to the above assessments of Jung's position and, furthermore, in spite of the line of defense that Jung himself took against such accusations of psychologism, something that we have come to understand through our study of the synchronicity concept is that in his psychology of religion Jung ultimately came to view religious contents as arising not from a strictly intrapsychic ground—the divine ground of the psyche as Goldbrunner describes it—but rather from "a universal substrate present in the environment," that is to say, from the transcendental world of the psychoid archetype. Here, then, with this very significant theoretical step, we are indeed carried beyond the projectionism of Jung's strictly intrapsychic model and find ourselves face to face with that transcendent "Thou," the transcendent "Reality" to which Buber referred above.

Not unrelated to this is the theoretical movement of Jung's concept of the archetype of the self from the intrapsychic to the metaphysical level. With specific reference to the former, it was explained in chapter 1 how the self, as the archetype of order and unity for the psyche as a total phenomenon, "might equally be called the 'God within us.' " For Jung, the self is indeed the source and goal of our psychic lives. Furthermore, as an archetype, the self is not a fixed image, but rather that which gives rise to those myriad expressions of transcendent wholeness that appear in the course of the individuation process, and have characterized religious phenomenology from time immemorial. It is the case, therefore, as noted in chapter 1, that just as "the ancients saw the *imago Dei* in man not as a mere imprint, as a sort of lifeless, stereotyped impression, but as an active force," so too, Jung emphasized, should we view the archetype of the self.

Not surprisingly, Jung's concept of the self, when characterized as a strictly intrapsychic phenomenon, has been very much at the center of the psychologism debate. Singling this particular concept out for special treatment, Buber writes: "He [Jung] conceives of Him in general as an 'autonomous psychic content.' This means he conceives of God not as a Being or Reality to which a psychical content corresponds, but rather as this content itself."[32] In contrast to Buber, not everyone has come to see in Jung's concept of the self such a radical formulation. At least one reason for this, it seems to me, is that a number of individuals have simply failed to grasp, or tendentiously chosen not to emphasize, what Jung really means by the self as archetype. More specifically, they have failed to distinguish, or have chosen not to emphasize, the great difference between Jung's description of the functional emergence of the self into consciousness—as discussed in the experiential section in chapter 1—and his description of the archetype of the self as such.

For example, John de Gruchy writes about the self in his "theological assessment" of Jung's work: "The Self represents a purely human wholeness,"[33] by which he means something situated entirely within the scope of consciousness. Nothing, as we have seen, is further from the truth when we regard the self in terms of its status as archetype. Of some interest is the point, revealed by de Gruchy's footnotes, that this particular notion of the self has come to de Gruchy from Gebhard Frei via White. In his *God and the Unconscious*, we are told by White that a paper by Frei—a paper included as an appendix to White's book—"should straighten out once and for all what has proved one of the most considerable tangles which confronts the theologically-minded student of Jung, namely his conception of the 'Self' in its religious aspects."[34] Regarding Frei's paper, it is very clear that the author has, in seeking to make Jung more palatable to the Catholic theologian, played down Jung's description of the self as archetype. Thus, after having briefly touched on certain parallels that exist between the way in which the self is experienced and described and the way in which Christ is experienced and described, Frei summarizes, "We should not forget that, despite these parallels, the 'self' represents a purely *human* wholeness; it is not, as Christ is, also God."[35] Much along the same line as the above, Heisig himself, curiously enough, either chose to play down, or simply failed to grasp, the very critical role that the self as archetype plays in Jung's psychology. Thus, in his *Imago Dei* Heisig writes with reference to an argument put forward by Edinger: "My only complaint against his analysis is the identification of God the Father with the Self. This is justifiable only in terms of Jung's occasional use of the term 'Self' to refer to an unconscious archetype."[36] It is, of course, the use of the word "occasional" that causes one to have doubts about Heisig's assessment of Jung's concept.

In contrast to the above assessments, and more in keeping with the interpretation that has been presented in this work, Adler writes about the archetype of the self:

> The most powerful archetypal experience of man is that of the 'Deity.' As a matter of fact, from the standpoint of psychology this statement has to be reversed, and we have to say that man has called his most powerful [archetypal] experience: 'God.' It is the experience of a supra-individual centre of existence, of a power that gives and takes life, of a point from which life springs and towards which it aims, and in which the meaning and purpose of creation and man's place in it seem to become apparent.[37]

For Jung, the archetype of the self is not the mere image, in the fixed sense of that word, of that which is called God. Rather, it is the living reality itself; it is the living reality from which all things we call "God" flow. For Jung, therefore, the archetype of the self is indeed " 'God within.' " Accordingly, and consistent with this characteristically Jungian notion of the psychic immediacy of "God," von Franz states about the analytical process: "To us the experience of God is greater and more unknown [than fixed law] and therefore we consult Him each time. We have not the idea that He has uttered His last word. That is the great contrast between psychology and theology. We think of God as a reality who can speak in our psyche. One never knows what God may ask of an individual. That is why every analysis is an adventure, because one never knows what God is going to ask of this particular person."[38] We might also recall in this regard a statement made by Jung during his 1959 BBC interview for television. When asked by John Freeman if he believed there was a God, Jung's reply to this question was: " 'I don't believe, I know.' "[39]

If, therefore, for Jung, the archetype of the self is the inner equivalent of that which is called God, that is to say, " 'God within,' " the question that naturally follows from this is whether or not the self, as metaphysical principle, might in the same way also be the outer equivalent to that which is called God. My own answer to this question would be yes, it is equivalent. If indeed the self is, as an intrapsychic factor, the central archetype of meaning and order for the psyche as a whole, if the self is the *spiritus rector* of our psychic lives, if the self is described as the beginning and end of our psychic existence, it seems to me that when, through the synchronicity concept, this same role is transported to the metaphysical level, it is certainly hard to imagine that the self as archetype is not equivalent to what is described as God without.

The self, Jung writes, with specific reference to the functional emergence of the central archetype, "is in need of help and must be perceived, protected, and as it were built up by the conscious mind, just as if it did not exist at all and were called into being only through man's care and devotion. As against this," Jung continues, now describing the archetype of the self as such in its form as both an intrapsychic and metaphysical factor,

> we know from experience that it has long been there and is older than the ego, and that it is actually the secret *spiritus rector* of our fate. The self does not become conscious by itself, but has always been taught, if at all, through a tradition of knowing (the *purusha/atman* teaching, for instance). . . . The self, moreover, is an archetype that invariably expresses a situation within which the ego is contained. Therefore, like every archetype, the self cannot be localized in an individual ego-consciousness, but acts like a circumambient atmosphere to which no definite limits can be set, either in space or in time. (Hence the synchronistic phenomena so often associated with activated archetypes).[40]

If as an intrapsychic factor, the self is for Jung the atman, that is to say, "the ultimate as discovered introspectively," the self as metaphysical principle is, to be sure, equivalent to Brahman, that is to say, "the ultimate as discovered objectively."[41] Very much in the same manner, von Franz, it should be recalled, was quoted in the previous section in this chapter as stating that to concentrate and attempt to get a sign from the self, either inwardly or outwardly, "is tantamount to paying constant attention to Tao, whether what I am now doing is right, in Tao." That von Franz is here using, in her description of the characteristic religious attitude, the traditional Chinese term Tao as an equivalent to the word God, there can be no question, for as Jung himself does, von Franz uses these words interchangeably. Reflecting this very understanding, Jung thus commented to Georges Duplain in an interview given in the late fifties: "The collective unconscious, it's not for you, or me, it's the invisible world, it's the great spirit. It makes little difference what I call it: God, Tao, the Great Voice, the Great Spirit. But for people of our time God is the most comprehensible name with which to designate the Power beyond us."[42] For Jung, I would thus say in conclusion, the self is most certainly that to which others refer as God.

Experiential Dimension

In chapter 1, it was explained how Jung places a very high value on experientially based knowledge, particularly that which has as its ground a direct encounter with the unconscious. To experience life through the unique perspective that a direct encounter with the unconscious yields is, for Jung, to experience life in its fullness. It is to open oneself to an experience of reality as it exists in its "suchness," that is to say, for Jung, to experience consciously the underlying patterns that conjoin the myriad and seemingly unrelated events of phenomenal reality. That such an encounter with reality was at the heart of Jung's own experience of life, there can be little doubt. Furthermore, that this same encounter with life constitutes the most salient feature of the experiential dimension of the Jungian worldview, we can be equally sure. "Life," Jung tells us in the prologue of his autobiography,

> has always seemed to me like a plant that lives on its rhizome. Its true life is invisible, hidden in the rhizome. The part that appears above ground lasts only a single summer. Then it withers away—an ephemeral apparition. When we think of the unending growth and decay of life and civilizations, we cannot escape the impression of absolute nullity. Yet I have never lost a sense of something that lives and endures underneath the eternal flux. What we see is the blossom, which passes. The rhizome remains.
>
> In the end the only events in my life worth telling are those when the imperishable world irrupted into this transitory one. That is why I speak chiefly of inner experiences, amongst which I include my dreams and visions. These form the *prima materia* of my scientific work. They were the fiery magma out of which the stone that had to be worked was crystallized.[43]

Sharing Jung's fascination with the rhizome metaphor, Olney, in his book that is appropriately titled *The Rhizome and the Flower: The Perennial Philosophy—Yeats and Jung*, takes it upon himself to trace, as best as he can, that archetypal root system of which, we are told, the works of Pythagoras, Heraclitus, Parmenides, Empedocles, Plato, Blake, Jung, and Yeats are but flowers. "Its flowers are of a day," Olney writes about the luminous works of these figures, "blossoming and fading in a man's lifetime, but the rhizome itself is as ancient as thought, as deep as psyche, whose limits, as Heraclitus says, 'you would not find even by travelling along every path: so deep a *logos* does it have.' "[44] As much as I am myself fascinated by the rhizome metaphor and both Olney's and Jung's descriptions of its centrality to the latter's life and psychology, there is something of no small importance of which we are not informed by either Olney, in his book, or Jung, in his above statement. Jung's life and psychology clearly were shaped by Jung's experience of the archetypal rhizome, yet something of which we must be fully cognizant with regard to this point is 'hat this rhizome, this "imperishable world," was experienced by Jung as much outwardly in the synchronistic patterning of events as it was inwardly in the form of dreams and visions. In his encounter with life, Jung's gaze was indeed fixed on the rhizome, but it was, to be sure, directed toward this rootlike, subterranean archetypal world not just by his experiences of its intrapsychic flowers, but by his experience of its synchronistic flowers as well.

If, therefore, one's gaze is fixed on the archetypal rhizome, as Jung's was, and one thus becomes conscious of the rootlike patterns underlying phenomenal reality, experientially, nature as a whole acquires a decidely unitary character. Writing with reference to the attainment of such a unitary experience of reality in the individuation process, Edinger reflects: "A twofold split is healed to the extent individuation is achieved; first the split between conscious and unconscious which began at the birth of consciousness, and second the split between subject and object. The dichotomy between outer and inner reality is replaced by a sense of unitary reality."[45] If indeed such a unitary experience of reality is characteristic of the individuation process, the question that then arises in connection with this is, How does this particular experience of nature differ, if it does at all, from the phenomenon that Jung, having borrowed the term from Lucien Lévy-Bruhl, characterizes as *participation mystique?*

According to Jung's developmental model, as Edinger alluded to above, individual consciousness is understood to develop "out of an original state of unconsciousness and therefore of nondifferentiation." "Differentiation," Jung accordingly writes, "is the essence, the *sine qua non* of consciousness. Everything unconscious is undifferentiated, and everything that happens unconsciously proceeds on the basis of non-differentiation—that is to say, there is no determining whether it belongs or does not belong to oneself."[46] The latter point in particular is what Jung has in mind when he uses the term *participation mystique.*

One thing about participation mystique is that it is not regarded by Jung as pathological in every instance. The projection of one's unconscious contents onto others, and/or into one's environment is, Jung maintains, quite normal, and everyone experiences a certain degree of such subject/object identification. As a simple example of just how fundamental to human nature this tendency to project is, Jung cites the common assumption that people untrained in analytical methods have about their dream figures. The fact that these individuals take it as "self-evident from the start that when [they dream] of Mr. X this dream-image is identical with the real Mr. X" demonstrates, Jung suggests, the fundamental human propensity to project. It is thus the case, Jung explains, that "every normal person of our time, who is not reflective beyond the average, is bound to his environment by a whole system of projections." And even those, on the other hand, who are "reflective beyond the average," can never hope to put an end to all of their projections—projections that will be invariably unleashed in moments of anger, and so forth.[47] The experience of participation mystique is not, therefore, pathological in every instance. Rather, the pathological element seems to be more a question of the degree of one's participation mystique with the people and events of one's life. In small doses, it could be said, subject/object identification is relatively harmless. When, however, one's life is largely dominated by such a state of identification, when there is an ongoing experience of participation mystique with the world as a whole, it is at this point that this phenomenon becomes, for Jung, pathological.

Having said this, we can now return to our original question, which is, How does the unitary experience of nature, characteristic of the synchronistic perspective, differ, if it does at all, from participation mystique? Neumann has given serious thought to this matter, and I would, therefore, like to quote him here at some length. "We are accustomed to explain participation mystique," Neumann writes,

> by the presence of projections, and, in reverse, to say that a projection is a piece of unconscious identification that leads to *participation mystique.* When a primitive says he gets his knowledge from a bird that told him a secret, we call this a projection. This theory can be stated as follows: We say that this

knowledge was present "in him" but unconscious, that he, however, experiences it as coming from outside, and that the connection with the bird is accidental. Hence, we say that he has "projected" something inner to the outside. These assertions of our ego-consciousness, however, are not really correct, although satisfactory to our ego-centered cognition. The inexactness begins with the statement that the knowledge had been present "in him." We further assume in opposition to this inner, a separate outer, which we associate with the bird, while the bird, the main thing for the primitive (which for this reason he calls "doctor bird"), is left out of our interpretation as an "accidental" phenomenon.

In our attempt to improve the interpretation by the term "exteriorization," we lay stress on the primary "outwardness" of the experience, while the concept of projection presupposes its primary "inwardness." But this outwardness, too, is understood not as a real but only as a phenomenal outwardness. The correct description of the actual situation would be that the knowledge imparted to the primitive by means of the bird was a field knowledge, an extrane knowing, present or emergent in a living field wherein both bird and primitive are enclosed.[48]

Neumann's above point that the existence of a type of "field knowledge"—a knowledge that he goes on to explain is characteristic of synchronistic phenomena—challenges established notions of participation mystique is a point well taken. With synchronistic phenomena, as has been repeatedly demonstrated, subject and object, individual and bird, to use Neumann's example, are both enclosed within the same archetypal field. Accordingly, a common meaning, a type of "extrane knowledge," an "absolute knowledge," does conjoin subject and object. This being so, are we not then led to believe that the synchronistic perspective, the synchronistic way of relating to the world is essentially the same as participation mystique? To this I would reply that there most certainly is a fundamental difference between participation mystique and the synchronistic way of seeing. A difference, I would add, that is of no small importance.

With synchronistic phenomena, even though the intrapsychic and external events are enclosed within the same archetypal field, that is to say, they are understood to give expression to the meaning of the constellated archetypal pattern in question, the two or more

events are not identical in every aspect. Both are meaningfully related to each other, but the nature of their relationship is along the
line of a type of mutual complementarity rather than that of mutual
identity. Both are players in the larger drama of the archetypal pattern, yet the roles they play within that pattern differ. In this manner, even though the scarab was an expression of the same
archetypal pattern in which the analysand's then psychic situation
was contained—the archetypal pattern out of which her dream of
the golden scarab had arisen the night before—the scarab is not understood to have appeared at the window of Jung's office, as emphasized earlier, simply for the sake of the analysand. From the
synchronistic perspective, in spite of the fact that they are contained
within the same archetypal pattern, both the scarab and the
analysand are understood to have, beyond their shared archetypal
ground, an existence and meaning quite independent of each other.
For this reason, with synchronistic phenomena, the complementary
or compensatory interplay of events in the constellated archetypal
pattern are to be interpreted symbolically and not concretely.

If, therefore, we are to take participation mystique as defined
by Jung above to refer to the nondifferentiation of subject and object, it is certainly not the case that the synchronistic perspective is
the same as participation mystique, for with the synchronistic perspective subject and object ultimately are differentiated. With synchronistic events, the subject should indeed know what "belongs"
to him and what does not, that is to say, one should be able to
separate the specific compensatory value of the object from what
the object is in itself. With reference, then, to our original assertion
that the synchronistic perspective provides one with an experience
of the unitary character of nature, we can now say, in keeping with
the conclusions made about the participation-mystique question,
that this should not be taken to refer to an experience in which subject and object are not differentiated. Rather, the experience one has
of nature's unitary character takes the form more of a conscious recognition that subject and object are interrelated as complementary
players in the larger archetypal pattern.

If, then, as we have seen above, the "normal" reaction to synchronistic phenomena requires one ultimately to differentiate subject and object, that is to say, the specific compensatory value of the
object from what the object is in itself, the "abnormal" reaction, by
contrast, would be not to differentiate the two. In the case of the
abnormal reaction, the subject thus would not distinguish what
"belongs" to him, in the compensatory sense, from what belongs to

the object. Somewhat similar to this, Edward Whitmont, writing with reference to the magical fantasies typical of the schizophrenic state, explains how for the schizophrenic the associations he has in connection with a particular object actually become for the patient indistinguishable from the object itself. In demonstrating his point, Whitmont writes: "For example, to the question: 'Who was the first president of the United States?' a schizophrenic patient answered 'White House.' Through association, 'White House' and 'President' became identical." For the schizophrenic patient, as this example indicates, the "associated quality or part" comes to represent the whole. Accordingly, it is the case, as Whitmont concludes, "That in the schizophrenic state . . . 'as though' is the equivalent of 'is.' "[49]

In terms of the synchronistic perspective, the " 'as though' " would be the specific compensatory meaning of the object for the subject, which is ultimately to be differentiated from what the object " 'is' " in itself. Something, however, for which we have to allow, as Whitmont himself mentions, is the use of metaphor. When, for example, the scarab came flying into Jung's office and Jung, catching it in his hand, placed it on the lap of his analysand with the words, " 'Here is your scarab,' " Jung was speaking metaphorically, and justifiably so, as he wished to draw his analysand's full attention to the compensatory meaning of nature's synchronistic pattern. From one angle, the scarab flying into the room was indeed the patient's scarab, and metaphor gives expression to the specific compensatory meaning with which nature itself objectively presents one. On the other hand, the object does have an existence and meaning quite independent of its compensatory import for the subject and this difference must equally be consciously recognized. Accordingly, if one is to use the language of metaphor in this manner to describe synchronistic phenomena, one must ultimately be able to distinguish between that which "belongs" to one, in the sense of that with which nature has presented one through its compensatory patterning, from that which belongs to the object, that is to say, what the object is in its own right.

If, therefore, as it is understood to be the case with synchronistic phenomena, nature does present one with a specific compensatory meaning through the interplay of subject and object in the archetypal pattern, it follows from this that the "abnormal" reaction to these events would not only involve the concrete identification of this compensatory meaning with what the object is in itself, as explained above, but that an equally "abnormal" reaction to the synchronistic experience would be to misinterpret the specific compensatory meaning with which one is presented. In the following, von Franz presents a very good example of how such a misinterpretation of a synchronistic experience resulted in the pathological distortion of what otherwise would have been a normal and valuable compensatory message. The case involved a man who, on the verge of a psychotic break, attacked his wife. She in turn called a doctor and the police. When they arrived and entered the house with the intention of forcibly removing the man to a clinic, "the lamp in the corridor shattered with a bang, so that suddenly they were all standing in darkness in the midst of the broken glass. The patient," von Franz continues,

> saw clearly that what had happened was a supernatural sign: just as the sun grew dark when Christ was crucified, this event was to him a confirmation that he was a savior who was being unjustly arrested. We, on the other hand, would say that he had projected his delusion into the event. Thus the synchronistic phenomenon, in itself meaningful, was instead covered by a projection. To a person with normal consciousness the 'meaning' of the occurrence would be quite different. A lamp, in contrast to the sun, is not a cosmic principle but an appliance invented by man; it usually symbolizes ego-consciousness in dreams and fantasies. The meaning of the unusual event would then more probably be expressed thus: In the moment of intense agitation caused by his imminent arrest the patient's ego-consciousness was shattered and a 'mental blackout' resulted. The patient, however, could not grasp this meaning.[50]

Had the patient properly interpreted the synchronistic event that took place in his environment, its compensatory content would have provided him with an objective look at the degree to which his Messianic complex was threatening ego-consciousness. The patient, however, failed to do this and simply used the synchronistic experience, as one can equally do with dreams, to feed his own delusion.

Consistent with the two points made above, Jung tells us that with synchronistic experiences, much as is also the case with the appearance of archetypal contents themselves, if we are to identify a pathological element in connection with these experiences, it would be found not in the fact of their occurrence, but rather in the improper reaction of the subject to them. "Since archetypal situations," Jung explains,

> are not uncommon in schizophrenia, we must also suppose that corresponding synchronistic phenomena will occur which follow exactly the same course as with so-called normal persons. The difference lies simply and solely in the interpretation. The schizophrenic's interpretation is morbidly narrow because it is mostly restricted to the intentions of other people and to his own ego-importance. The normal interpretation . . . is based on the philosophic premise of the sympathy of all things, or something of that kind. . . . If synchronicities occur in these cases it is because an archetypal situation is present, for whenever archetypes are constellated we find manifestations of the primordial unity. Thus the synchronistic effect should be understood not as psychotic but as a normal phenomenon.[51]

Rather than view synchronistic phenomena as a compensatory activity of nature that complements but functions independently of ego-consciousness, the psychotic tends to overvalue his own role or the role of others in the process. In this way, he tends to see the synchronistic event as a manifestation of his or another individual's personal power. Such an interpretation is "morbidly narrow," and the effect would be, furthermore, to remove the individual even further from a genuine experience of life.

For Jung, therefore, we can say in summary, the pathological element of the synchronistic experience, if it exists at all, is found not in the occurrence of these experiences but rather in one's reaction to them. In keeping with this, three types of abnormal reactions to synchronistic events have been identified: first, the tendency of the subject to enter into a type of participation mystique with the object, that is to say, for the subject not to differentiate the specific compensatory import that the object has for him from what the object is in itself; second, the failure to interpret correctly the compensatory meaning of the synchronistic event, such as was the case with von Franz's example where the patient incorrectly interpreted the shattering of the lamp as a sign that he, like Christ, was a savior being unjustly arrested; and third, wrongly seeing the synchronistic event as a manifestation of one's or another individual's, personal power.

A final point that I would like to make in this section concerns what has been described as the functional emergence of the self. As was indicated in chapter 1, Jung likens the experience of the functional emergence of the self to an experience of religious conversion, and in connection with this it was pointed out that central to Jung's own "conversion" experience was his 1927 "Liverpool dream." The importance of the Liverpool dream to Jung's experiential understanding of the self cannot be overstated. However, something we have also seen is that for those who consciously follow the path of individuation, "conversion" is never a static state but rather takes the form of an ongoing process. Accordingly, following his 1927 experience, new vistas of understanding were still to be opened to Jung. Indeed, it could perhaps be argued that whereas the 1927 experience was Jung's most dramatic experience of the self as " 'God within,' " the experiences Jung had in connection with his 1944 illness were his most dramatic experiences of the self as "God without," as *unus mundus*. "What he describes in these visions," von Franz writes with reference to this latter point, "is a feeling experience of the *unus mundus*, in which everything happening in time is experienced as if gathered up into a timeless objective oneness."[52] What I would now like to consider is the specific impact the 1944 experiences had on Jung.

It is a curious fact that Jung's experiences in 1944 served to awaken in him two distinct orientations—orientations which to some would appear to be contradictory, but are indeed complementary when considered, as they should be, in terms of the functional unfoldment of the self, that is to say, in terms of what is experienced by one who cultivates a living relationship to the self. First, and this is what one would imagine Jung's experience to have been, Jung had a tremendous sense of expansiveness. It was, as von Franz relates, an experience of opening to the transcendental, an "awakening to the Tao," an experience which the medieval alchemist Gerhard Dorn describes "as the opening of a 'window on eternity' or of an 'air-hole' into the eternal world." Second, as von Franz notes, and this is the aspect of Jung's experience that most would not anticipate and would perhaps regard as contradictory of the first one, Jung experienced a concentration of his being. When one penetrates the *unus mundus*, as Jung himself did in 1944, one experiences, von Franz explains, "a glimpse through the 'window on eternity' but [it] is at the same time [an experience of the] concentration of one's own being in the 'stone,' at one and the same time a boundless enlargement and the narrowest of limitations."[53]

That Jung had such an experience of both expansion and concentration of his being in connection with his illness in 1944 tells us, I believe, a very great deal about the synchronistic perspective itself. It tells us that when one genuinely realizes a living relationship to the self in its most expansive sense as *unus mundus*, as the synchronistically ordered totality, one's experience is not that of being swept away from this world, as some would imagine. There is, to be sure, a tremendous sense of expansiveness, but there is also at the same time, as a necessary counterposition to this, a tremendous concentration of the personality—a concentration of one's being that cannot be realized in the absence of considerable ego strength. If, therefore, one is to attain such a living relationship to the self in its form as totality, if one is to open oneself fully to the synchronistic perspective, considerable ego strength is demanded of one. Accordingly, after Jung had been through the expansive experiences that arose in connection with his illness in 1944, after he had perhaps journeyed as far away from this space- and time-bound life as one possibly can without turning away from it completely, Jung would write in his autobiography with reference to these events: "It was only after the illness that I understood how important it is to affirm one's own destiny. In this way we forge an ego that does not break down when incomprehensible things happen; an ego that endures, that endures the truth, and that is capable of coping with the world and with fate."[54]

Ethical Dimension

For Jung, as was indicated in chapter 1, individuation is a task imposed on one by nature. Accordingly, the general moral challenge associated with the individuation process is for one consciously to receive nature's command to realize one's full potential "as a binding personal commitment." It is the moral challenge, we could say with the synchronicity theory in mind, of consciously bringing oneself into accord with the unique pattern of meaning that not only underlies one's inner life, but one's outer life as well.

Certainly one synchronistic experience that left Jung with an indelible sense of this specific moral responsibility was the 1916 haunting of the Jung household. Hannah, it should be recalled, remarked about this synchronistic experience that because the ghostly chaos in Jung's home subsided as soon as he attempted to raise the meaning of these events to consciousness, Jung became convinced of the great moral responsibility one has to come fully to terms with one's individuation, for when one fails to do so it is not just one's psychic equilibrium that is threatened, but the equilibrium of one's environment as well. Consistent with Hannah's assessment, Jung was himself to write in his autobiography with reference to his "confrontation with the unconscious"—a period within which the 1916 haunting conspicuously figures—that it was only with the unfoldment of the events of this period that he came to understand the moral commitment that individuation entails. Both inwardly and outwardly, Jung came to acknowledge during those years, nature was directing him to fulfill consciously a unique destiny. To this "calling," Jung realized, he now owed the highest degree of commitment he could offer. Indeed, for Jung, it seemed as if his life was no longer simply his own to do with as he pleased. "It was then," Jung writes in his memoirs with reference to the time of his "confrontation with the unconscious,"

> that I ceased to belong to myself alone, ceased to have a right to do so. From then on, my life belonged to the generality. The knowledge I was concerned with, or was seeking, still could not be found in the science of those days. I myself had to undergo the original experience, and, moreover, try to plant the results of my experience in the soil of reality. . . . It was then that I dedicated myself to service of the psyche. I loved it and hated it, but it was my greatest wealth. My delivering myself over to it, as it were, was the only way by which I could endure my existence and live it as fully as possible.[55]

Beyond the emergence of this general, yet vital sense of moral responsibility to one's individuation, the individuation process also gives rise to a rather comprehensive moral framework that is quite different from that which is associated with the Judeo-Christian tradition. Accordingly, Neumann has suggested that we can speak in terms of an "old ethic," by which he means the traditional Judeo-Christian values, and a "new ethic," by which he means the values that the process of individuation produces. Writing in the foreword to Neumann's *Depth Psychology and a New Ethic*, Jung very accurately describes what the author has in mind in speaking of the "new ethic" of depth psychology. "We might . . . define the 'new ethic' as a development and differentiation within the old ethic, confined at present to those uncommon individuals who, driven by unavoidable conflicts of duty, endeavour to bring the conscious and the unconscious into responsible relationship."[56]

One thing that we do know from chapter 1 is that pivotal to the individuation process, that is to say in following Jung, pivotal to the task of bringing "the conscious and the unconscious into responsible relationship," is the considerable problem of coming to terms with what Jung characterizes as the "shadow"—that which constitutes, in the main, the inferior and even evil aspects of one's personality. The problem of the shadow is, as we have seen, no small matter. It is, however, largely through such "shadow work" that the more comprehensive moral position characteristic of the individuation process emerges. Accordingly, Neumann, in acknowledgement of the centrality of such "shadow work" to his own concept of the new ethic, writes, "The only person who is morally acceptable in the eyes of the new ethic is the person who has accepted his shadow problem—the person, that is to say, who has become conscious of his own negative side."[57] What I would now like to look at in some detail is how the synchronistic perspective greatly alters the more conventional understanding of what exactly "shadow work" entails.

Certainly one of the values of the "old ethic," specifically the Christian ethic, is for one to experience compassion and love for one's enemies. As a general principle, this value, which can be used to illustrate the nature of the problem under consideration, is not at odds with the values of the "new ethic." There is a difference, however, Neumann argues, between the "old ethic" and the "new ethic" with respect to how such a compassionate understanding is to be reached. Very much along the line that Jung himself argues, Neumann maintains that for one truly to feel compassion for one's "enemy," one first must be able to experience the reality of that "enemy" within oneself, that is to say, one must know exactly how one is like the individual who is one's "enemy." More specifically, acceptance of the other can only genuinely take place when one accepts those aspects of one's own shadow that the "enemy" personifies. And to this we should add that such acceptance is, for Jung and Neumann, hardly possible to achieve in the absence of an analysis of the unconscious, simply because the shadow contents in question are buried too deeply to touch from the side of consciousness alone. This is the reason why the Jungian notion of compassion, although it has a certain ring of the Christian ethic of love, takes, in practice and in terms of degree, quite a different form.

In contrast to the "old ethic," shadow work is a comprehensive process that is carried out under the direction of the unconscious and carries one on far-reaching expeditions into the dark,

inferior areas of one's personality. Systematically, the inferior areas
are uncovered; responsibly, they are embraced as one's own. With
the "new ethic," therefore, compassion for one's "enemy" flows, as
Neumann suggests, from what might be characterized as "a paradoxical form of 'self-love.' "[58] With the "new ethic," healing first
takes place within through directly coming to terms with one's own
shadow. Only in this manner, it is believed, can genuine compassion be felt for the other.

As the above indicates, then, with the "new ethic" there is
clearly a movement away from what might be described as a scapegoat morality,[59] that is to say, a morality in which one's own inferior
traits are projected onto others. This is the case, moreover, not only
in situations where such projections are totally unjustified by the
conduct of an individual or individuals, such as tends to happen
with minority groups, but it is also the case where the conduct of
the other individual provides, so to speak, cause for such projections, such as when another does one harm. In both instances, the
point of the "new ethic" is that one must aim not to lose touch with
one's own shortcomings. One must aim not to make the other the
moral scapegoat for one's own inadequacies. The pursuit of such a
moral position does, however, demand a very great deal of the individual, for not only is considerable consciousness required, such
as one obtains through an analysis of the unconscious, but an abun-
dance of moral courage is required as well. This is particularly true
when one is confronted outwardly with synchronistic intrusions of
the shadow.

One case that we have examined that serves as a very good
example of an individual coming to terms with such a synchronistic
intrusion of the shadow is the case of the American Buddhist
monks Heng Sure and Heng Ch'au, presented in chapter 3. It
should be recalled that Heng Ch'au was able to identify, through
studying his dreams, the synchronistic interplay between the activities of his own shadow, which inwardly was working to sabotage
his and Heng Sure's pilgrimage, and the appearance on two occasions of actual thieves whose activities outwardly threatened to
bring their journey to a halt. The first time around, as we saw,
Heng Ch'au's inner thief had his way, and likewise so too did the
outer thief. On the second occasion, however, when Heng Ch'au
had successfully brought the inner thief under control, the outer
thief left empty-handed. By confronting the thief within himself,
Heng Ch'au therefore was able to avoid the danger that threatened
the pilgrimage from without. By confronting the thief within him-

self, moreover, Heng Ch'au did not make the outer thief a moral scapegoat for his own shortcomings. In this manner, Heng Ch'au grasped the spirit of his Master's teaching: "Other's faults are just your own—Being one with everyone is called great compassion."

In her book *Addiction to Perfection: The Still Unravished Bride,* Woodman examines, among other things, the various types of regressive relationships that arise when men and women mutually succumb to shadow contamination. Of particular interest to our study is the case history of Ingrid, which, like the above case, is a very striking example of a synchronistic shadow intrusion—specifically, the synchronistic intrusion of what Woodman describes as the "demon lover complex." Although Woodman does not directly refer to the events of this case as synchronistic, the approach that she takes with respect to the interpretation of its meaning is, as we shall see, very synchronistic indeed. The case of Ingrid, Woodman explains, demonstrates "both the kind of danger the demon lover complex can constellate and the feminine harnessing of strength that is required to break free of it."[60] The circumstances of the case are as follows.

Ingrid, who had been travelling alone by train, found herself late one evening in a strange city having to make her way from one railway station to another. As she walked along a deserted street, Woodman tells us, "a powerfully-built man . . . forced her into an alleyway, saying he was going to rape and kill her. Her initial reaction was panic, and she tried to fight back. But he was stronger. Then in a flash she saw the situation she was in; she saw the man; she saw herself. She accepted her death, her body relaxed and she looked straight into the man's eyes. Immediately, his fingers loosened on her throat." Ingrid's assailant was now confused. Sensing this, she took hold of his hands and slowly removed them from her throat. As she did this he began to cry.[61]

This, however, was not the end of her ordeal, for her assailant forced Ingrid to accompany him to a nearby bar where they sat and talked about what had taken place. There it was disclosed by the man that he had actually been on the train with Ingrid prior to the assault. Travelling in the same coach, he had been in a position to observe her for some time. His impression was that Ingrid "was casting a spell on him. What *he* saw", Woodman explains, "was a woman pretending to read while secretly concentrating on luring him into her feminine web. . . . The rape and murder in the alleyway would be at once the gratification of the desire that her witchery had aroused in him and his release from it."[62] Not until the man, whom Woodman believes was most probably psychopathic, went to the washroom was Ingrid able to escape.

Turning now to the inner experiences of her analysand at the time of the attack and presenting her interpretation of these experiences, Woodman continues:

> The woman herself was not entirely blameless. She was in fact a dreamer who had blocked out the real world on the train and was lost in fantasies of her demon lover. She had undertaken the trip in an effort to overcome the pain of a broken relationship, and fasting had been part of the purifying plan. This city was her last stop on her homeward journey. Six weeks of near starvation had brought her to an almost bodiless state. . . . [S]he was more ready to free herself into death than to move back into the reality of her responsibilities at home. What she was so "innocently" dreaming as she watched the world pass by, the man was picking up. She was willing to be sacrificed; he was willing to be sacrificer. Together, they were one. Unconsciously, at opposite ends of the coach, they constellated the wound and the sword.[63]

Ingrid, Woodman tells us, lived in a world in which she sought control of its every aspect as a means of achieving an egocentric perfectionism. Her desire was to find "the perfect lover" who would make everything in their life together right and perfect. "She had believed," Woodman writes, "that if she could be as perfect as possible, and love as perfectly as possible, and yearn as perfectly as possible—somehow that perfect yearning would magically be returned in perfectly possessing."[64] It was the case, however, that rather than finding the experience of perfect possessing that she had so greatly wanted, Ingrid had herself become perfectly possessed. Her controlling orientation, her perfectionism had simply served to feed the sadomasochistic energies of the demon lover complex, thus giving it greater opportunity to take possession of consciousness as it had done in the course of her trip. The death, therefore, to which Ingrid had resigned herself before she came face to face with her assailant in the alleyway, the death to which six weeks of near starvation had brought her that much closer, was a masochistic death at the hands of her demon lover.

When, however, her "demon lover" literally had his hands on her throat and objectively confronted her with such a death, Ingrid immediately perceived the meaninglessness and unreality of that state. Ingrid, to be sure, as Woodman indicated, did surrender herself to a type of death when she was being actually strangled by her assailant, but the death to which she surrendered herself was not a masochistic death, that is to say, the death that destroys and annihilates; rather, it was the death that gives life. The death she experienced was the collapse of the ego's false sense of control in unconditional surrender to the self. "Something entirely new," Woodman explains,

> had penetrated her, something so vast that she had no choice but to surrender. In accepting that impersonal power, she saw how egocentric and manipulative her yearning had been. She set out on her journey a still unravished bride; she returned home unraped but ravished. She returned with a depth-experience of the feminine mysteries—the recognition that when what is inside naturally comes together with what is outside, that is a miracle—not magic. She inadvertently had opened herself to that greater Reality.[65]

With the case of Ingrid and the above case involving the American Buddhist monks, we are certainly led into very deep water in raising the issue of the moral responsibility of the "victim," much deeper water indeed than most would ever choose to venture into today. To keep things in perspective, I would like, therefore, to make every effort to indicate exactly what I believe these examples of synchronistic shadow intrusions contribute to the problem of the "new ethic." I will present my summary in terms of three points.

First, it should be emphasized that the fact that these events are described as synchronistic shadow intrusions does not in any way lessen the responsibility that the assailant, in the second instance, and the thieves, in the first instance, must assume for their actions. Woodman makes exactly the same point when she writes that she has no intention whatsoever of "minimizing the guilt of the rapist."[66] In this regard, I think it is important to bear in mind the point made in the experiential section about the need to differentiate what the object represents to the subject, that is to say, what the object represents in terms of its synchronistic compensatory import, from what the object is in itself. Second, I would like to emphasize that it should not be concluded from the above that all synchronistic experiences that outwardly resemble the cases we have examined here are necessarily compensating a shadow problem. As was indicated in chapter 4, there are synchronistic experiences in which considerable suffering falls on one as a means, for instance, of tempering the personality or leading one to an understanding that one would not otherwise attain. I would suggest, then, that with certain synchronistic experiences that outwardly resemble these cases there may very well be situations where the subject is equally blameless. Third, having said this, it has been argued that when an individual is in fact presented with synchronistic shadow intrusions such as we have seen with the above two cases, the subject, from the point of view of the "new ethic," must not make the offender the moral scapegoat for his own shortcomings. In that the events in question are manifestations of the compensatory activities of nature, there is something to be learned by the subject. Accordingly, to see the evil as existing only outside oneself in the person of the offender is to turn away from the healing, compensatory activities of nature itself. And to do this, is, from the Jungian point of view, to commit a very great moral sin indeed. We are, Woodman writes with reference to the case of Ingrid, "as answerable to our own unconscious as we are to moral and legal codes."[67] With synchronistic intrusions of the shadow, therefore, each individual has a responsibility to come fully to terms with his own darkness. In meeting the moral demands of the "new ethic," each individual must recognize that with such synchronistic shadow intrusions, the "offender," in terms of the journey of the soul, is not simply the one who is guilty in the eyes of the law.

Social Dimension

In chapter 1, we saw how within the Jungian worldview considerable tension is understood to exist between the individual and society. Accordingly, the problem of how exactly the individual is to come to terms with the collective or societal consciousness without sacrificing his own individual values is one of the fundamental concerns of the individuation process. Commenting on this problem, Homans relates:

> Jung's thought followed the pattern laid down by his life experiences: it authorized a deep suspicion of the social order as a source for authentic living. At the heart of Jung's system lies a firm distinction between the persona, collective ideals, and the collective consciousness on the one hand, and the individuation process and all it involves on the other. . . . In all fairness to Jung, we should recognize that he always specified that in-

dividuation presupposed a firm commitment to social ideals, and Jungian therapists nowadays speak of the need to strengthen the persona. But in spite of these caveats, the force of the Jungian system on the whole moves against the social order. . . . Jungian therapy is for people who choose not to adapt entirely to the world of social convention.[68]

As mentioned in chapter 1, it is very difficult to assess the nature and degree of Jung's sense of conflict with the collective. On the one hand, it seems at times that Jung "moves against the social order" in the sense of simply rejecting the established social order that in its present form he regards as psychologically and spiritually impoverished. On the other hand, one is led at times to believe that Jung is fundamentally hostile to collective or group activities, much as he initially opposed the establishment of a Jungian training institute in Zurich.[69] Homans, it seems, inclines toward the latter view in his assessment of Jung. "In the world of Jung's thought," Homans thus writes, going somewhat further than the above, "the mind became society and church—a world within a world."[70]

Although there can be little doubt that the authority of the church and society are superseded by the psyche in Jung's thought, and that the psyche itself is turned to as the primary source of one's sense of meaning and purpose in life, there still is to be found within the Jungian worldview, it has been argued in this work, a very definite sense of social responsibility. The Jungian worldview does not rule out social action, but rather simply maintains that social action should flow from psychological wholeness. Similarly, relationship to the psyche is not understood to supplant one's need for relationship to society. Clearly, there is a tension in the Jungian worldview between the values of the individual and those of society, but this tension is not to be dealt with by simply turning one's back on the collective. The challenge is rather to engage the collective in a manner that is commensurate with one's personal experience of wholeness. For Jung, therefore, the inner world of the psyche is not so much a vehicle of escape from the collective, rather it is the means of obtaining special access to the latter. What we shall now examine is how the synchronicity theory extends this characteristically Jungian notion.

If we are to say in following Freud that dreams are the "royal road" to the unconscious,[71] we might equally say about synchronicity that it is, for the highly introverted Jungian worldview, something of the "royal road" to the collective. As indicated in chapter 1, for the introvert, whose primary concern is with life's "inner pattern," encounters with the collective are highly problematic, largely because the meaning that is experienced in relationship to the inner world is not understood to extend to the outer world. For the introvert, accordingly, the outer world is something of an enigma which in its strangeness gives rise to confusion and even terror. In contrast to this, the synchronicity theory bridges the chasm between the inner and the outer worlds in that it informs the introvert of the existence of a genuine link between his experience of the "inner pattern" and outer life. It infuses outer life, to put it differently, with a meaning that is coextensive with the "inner pattern." In this way, therefore, the synchronicity theory becomes for the introvert, something of the "royal road" to the collective.

As was emphasized in chapter 4 in connection with the discussion of the *I Ching*, the synchronicity principle is understood by Jung to be the instrument, so to speak, through which individuals find their way into relationships that are mutually complementary. Along this line, and very much consistent with the Chinese worldview, Jung, we saw, in seeking to emphasize this synchronistic aspect of social relationship, cited the following words of an old alchemist: " 'No matter how isolated you are and how lonely you feel, if you do your work truly and conscientiously, unknown friends will come and seek you.' " Similarly, Bolen, writing with reference to both her personal and professional experience of the synchronicity principle in its role as social "matchmaker," states: "Synchronicity can pave the way for people coming together. By unraveling the circumstances through which two people meet to enter a *significant* relationship, the delicate unseen hand of fate, destiny, synchronicity, or underlying Tao—by whatever name the matchmaker is called—can be discerned."[72] One example of this synchronistic "matchmaking" that Bolen cites from her professional experience as a psychiatrist concerns an Episcopalian priest. The priest, Bolen tells us, was having considerable emotional problems and turned to a friend—an individual who was an analysand of Bolen's—for help. Because Bolen was the only psychiatrist the priest's friend knew, it was, understandably, suggested that she be consulted. The priest, however, who "had considerable difficulty trusting women," was not inclined to take his friend's advice. Indeed, it was only under the pressure of his sense of "increasing desperation" that he was driven to do so. Describing the curious twist events were to take from here, Bolen writes:

Knowing me only as Dr. Jean Bolen, [Bolen being her husband's surname] and assuming that I would be a Caucasian from my name, he sat in the waiting room fearing this appointment was a terrible mistake. Then I came down the stairs, and he unexpectedly met a five-foot-tall Japanese-American woman, which altered the situation remarkably.

The only positive feminine image of women that he had—thanks to an idolized uncle's stories from being in the American occupation in Japan—was that of a Japanese woman. . . . His initial relief later gave way to wonder, as the synchronicity of it all became further evident. . . . It seemed to him that a female, Japanese, Jungian psychiatrist was precisely what he needed. If so, synchronicity had to have been finely tuned to have arranged our meeting, since I was the only Japanese woman Jungian analyst to be found anywhere.[73]

Consistent with both Bolen's characterization of the synchronicity principle as social matchmaker, and Jung's own position on this matter, von Franz speaks of *"the social function of the Self.* Each person," von Franz relates, "gathers around him his own 'soul family,' a group of people not created by accident or by mere egoistic motivation but rather through a deeper, more essential spiritual interest or concern." This gathering together of one's 'soul family,' von Franz reflects, is experienced as one of the great mysteries of individuation, for "this kind of relationship, by way of the Self, has something strictly objective, strangely transpersonal about it." In this "gathering together," one becomes conscious, von Franz explains, of the genuine experience of "relatedness to one's fellowmen" that attends the individuation process, provided, and this is a critical point, one is able to transcend emotional bonds and view things in terms of the objective meaning that underlies these relationships.[74] Here, of course, is the point where the "inner pattern" and the outer social world unite.

The idea that psychological wholeness should precede social action is, as we have seen, central to the Jungian worldview. Although the synchronicity principle does not take anything away from this fundamental position, it does extend this notion by indicating that, in certain cases, the unfoldment of the individuation experience of a single person is actually synchronistically linked to the unfoldment of the collective destiny of a social group. "Not infrequently," Neumann writes with reference to the interplay be-

tween the psychic struggle of a single individual and the problems
that threaten the collective consciousness,

> a sensitive person falls ill because of his incapacity to deal
> with a problem which is not recognized as such by the world
> in which he lives, but which is, in fact, a future problem of
> humanity which has confronted him and forced him to wrestle
> with it.
>
> This explains the lack of contemporaneity, the remoteness
> and the eccentric isolation of these people—but also their pro-
> phetic role as forerunners. Their fate and their often tragic
> struggle with their problems is of crucial significance for the
> collective, since both the problem and the solution, the criti-
> cism which destroys the old and the synthesis which lays
> the foundation for the new, are performed by these same in-
> dividuals for the collective, which in fact takes over their
> work.[75]

Similar to the manner in which shamans, as Eliade informs us,
"have played an essential role in the defense of the psychic integrity
of the community,"[76] it seems to be the case that certain individuals
are synchronistically thrust into the position of having to grapple
with the psychic conflicts—those invisible powers—which, as much
as any pestilence, threaten the existence of the collective. Jung himself, it is believed by many, underwent such an experience during
his "confrontation with the unconscious," or, to use Ellenberger's
term, during the period of his "creative illness." Describing the
events that took place at the very beginning of this period in 1913,
events that presaged the magnitude of the problem that fatefully
awaited him, Jung, writing in his autobiography, relates:

> In October, while I was alone on a journey, I was suddenly
> seized by an overpowering vision: I saw a monstrous flood
> covering all the northern and low-lying lands between the
> North Sea and the Alps. When it came up to Switzerland I saw
> that the mountains grew higher and higher to protect our
> country. I realized that a frightful catastrophe was in progress.
> I saw the mighty yellow waves, the floating rubble of civiliza-
> tion, and the drowned bodies of uncounted thousands. Then
> the whole sea turned to blood. This vision lasted about one
> hour. I was perplexed and nauseated, and ashamed of my
> weakness.[77]

After a period of two weeks the same vision, Jung tells us, recurred. It was, however, different from the first one in three respects. First, the blood in the second vision "was more emphasized" than in the first one. Second, the vision generally had a more realistic, lifelike quality. Third, as Jung watched the events of this second vision unfold he heard an "inner voice" say: " 'Look at it well; it is wholly real and it will be so. You cannot doubt it.' " Reflecting on the meaning of these words, Jung initially wondered if perhaps the visions were referring to something external to him, like a revolution that would soon be taking place. This possibility seemed, however, too remote. The visions, he reasoned, could only be referring to his own situation. "I drew the conclusion," Jung writes, "that they had to do with me myself, and decided that I was menaced by a psychosis."[78]

Again during the spring and earlier part of the summer of 1914, Jung found himself once more haunted by images of vast destruction. This time he had a dream that repeated itself three times. The dream first took place in April and then recurred in May and June of 1914. Jung dreamt that "in the middle of summer an Arctic cold wave descended and froze the land to ice. I saw, for example, the whole of Lorraine and its canals frozen and the entire region totally deserted by human beings. All living green things were killed by frost." The three dreams in this series all took essentially the same form with the exception of the third one. In contrast to the images of total devastation that were presented in the other dreams, and in Jung's previous visions, for that matter, in the third dream there was an element of hope. At the end of the third dream, an image of healing emerged. Describing this "unexpected" ending, Jung writes: "There stood a leaf-bearing tree, but without fruit (my tree of life, I thought), whose leaves had been transformed by the effects of the frost into sweet grapes full of healing juices. I plucked the grapes and gave them to a large, waiting crowd."[79] Against a background of suffering and destruction that dominated Jung's visions and dreams, the appearance of this image of healing clearly was encouraging. Its real meaning, though, was not to be revealed to Jung until the end of the following month.

Near the end of July 1914, Jung, at the invitation of the British Medical Association, travelled to Aberdeen, where he delivered a lecture titled "On the Importance of the Unconscious in Psychopathology." At the time, Jung thought it to be a very curious development that he would be asked to speak on this subject when he was so deeply troubled with concerns about his own sanity. "In my state of mind just then," Jung reflects in his memoirs, "with the fears that were pursuing me, it seemed fateful to me that I should have to talk on the importance of the unconscious at such a time!"[80] Something, Jung felt, was about to break, and while Jung was in Scotland something did.[81] On July 28, 1914, Austria-Hungary declared war on Serbia, thus beginning the First World War.[82] With the outbreak of war, the meaning of Jung's visions and dreams of vast devastation and destruction suddenly became clear. These horrific images, Jung now realized, were not strictly his own. They were not, as he had once believed, pointing to a psychotic break. "Now my task," Jung explains, "was clear: I had to try to understand what had happened and to what extent my own experience coincided with that of mankind in general. Therefore my first obligation was to probe the depths of my own psyche."[83]

"As a shaman often suffers from the plight of his people," von Franz relates, "so Jung was afflicted with dreams of blood-baths and catastrophes in Europe."[84] In the form of these terrifying visions and dreams, the challenge that was soon to concern mankind as a whole was revealed to Jung—a challenge, moreover, whose real importance has become even that much clearer in our present age. It is the challenge to realize a level of consciousness, self-understanding, that leads away from the destructive path that the world found itself on in 1914 and has yet to take itself off. Jung's journey into the unconscious would be an attempt, his synchronistic visions and dreams told him, to provide mankind with the means to bridge what Ross Woodman describes as "the discrepancy . . . between the demands of our global village—the earth as one country and mankind its citizens—and the level of consciousness at which we continue to function. Jung's attempt," Woodman continues, "to raise his own awareness and that of his analysands was, I believe, an attempt to create a consciousness commensurate to the demands that our century with increasing urgency imposes upon it."[85] Like the archetypal shaman-hero, Jung's task was now to undertake the journey into the darkness of the yet uncharted areas of the unconscious, not simply for his own sake, but for that of mankind as a whole. "I plucked the grapes," Jung dreamt, "and gave them to a large, waiting crowd."

In closing this section on synchronicity and the social dimension of the Jungian worldview, I would like to examine one further way in which Jung believed the wholeness one attains with the unfoldment of the individuation process might be of benefit to others. In the course of the individuation process, as has been emphasized, one acquires a considerable level of self-knowledge. Accordingly, one is given the means both to read accurately, and be responsive to, the compensatory activities of nature as they manifest themselves both inwardly and outwardly. Beyond the more obvious benefits that such insight into things would accrue for the subject, this ability to raise the progressive, compensatory flow of nature to consciousness is, in terms of the synchronicity principle, something from which others stand to benefit considerably as well, particularly when the situation in question involves adverse synchronistic conditions. With respect to the synchronistic patterning of events, in certain cases it seems that when one individual raises the compensatory meaning of a constellated archetypal pattern to consciousness the pattern as whole is transformed. If, then, it is the case that the psychophysical pattern in question constitutes a potentially harmful situation, such a progressive transformation of the pattern by a single individual would, of course, greatly benefit others.

As at least two of the synchronistic cases presented in this work suggest, the way in which just one individual reacts to the compensatory message of the constellated archetypal pattern means a great deal as to how that archetype will continue to manifest itself in the environment. With the case of the haunting of the Jung household, for instance, we saw the negative turn events in the environment took when Jung failed to recognize the compensatory message that was seeking recognition. When Jung failed to respond to the compensatory message of the archetypal pattern—which was strongly constellated at the time of his vision of his anima having flown away—the whole house filled up with spirits threatening everyone within it. When, however, Jung allowed the archetype to dictate its compensatory message to him, peace was again restored to the Jung household.

Similarly, with the case of Ingrid, we saw how Ingrid and her assailant were at first possessed by the constellated psychological pattern of the "demon lover complex". Although Ingrid and her assailant had no direct hand in the part being acted out by the other, both were in fact fulfilling in the psychophysical pattern, interdependent, mutually destructive roles: "She was willing to be sacrificed; he was willing to be sacrificer." Once, though, Ingrid was confronted with the possibility of her own murder, she snapped out of her state of unconscious identification with the complex, and in so doing, as Woodman tells us, "she freed them both from the possession." By conjoining herself consciously with the compensatory movement of the self that was seeking to release her from the grips of the demon lover complex, not only was the hold that the complex had on Ingrid broken, but so too was the hold that the complex had on her assailant.

It should perhaps be pointed out here that further support for the interpretation that Woodman gives to the case of Ingrid is to be found in the new model of the complex theory that has been promoted by von Franz. In keeping with the insights that the synchronicity theory has provided, it has been suggested by von Franz that a complex is not a strictly intrapsychic factor. Indeed, the hypothesis being advanced by von Franz characterizes a complex as something that is "unattached" and "free-floating" in the environment as a whole. The implications of this hypothesis are clearly of very great importance to the future study of parapsychological phenomena, particularly to the study of the spiritualistic-type manifestations. Commenting on this, von Franz writes:

> The much discussed question of whether the "manifestations" in seances represent unconscious complexes belonging to the participants or are "real spirits" becomes, from this point of view, irrelevant; they simply represent autonomous complexes that can belong either to the living or to the dead. But in this connection even the word "belong" is really imprecise, since "autonomous" means that such complexes are largely unattached and free-floating.[86]

Given the close relationship known to exist between the complex and the archetype, the argument being put forward by von Franz could be regarded as a type of necessary move to keep the complex theory in line with Jung's concept of the archetype as a psychoid factor. As true as this may be, von Franz's hypothesis nevertheless does have its own clinical basis. One case that she cites concerns "the analysis of a woman whose brother had 'disintegrated' into incurable schizophrenia"; specifically, he had fallen under the possession of autonomous complexes. "I was actually able to observe," von Franz states,

> how partial souls [complexes] belonging to her brother had activated parapsychological semi-material haunting incidents in the patient's neighborhood. When I related this story to Jung, he told me that he had often witnessed such phenomena and considered it possible that partial complexes were capable of 'haunting' a living person.[87]

The new understanding of the complex being advanced by von Franz indicates, then, that an encounter with a complex is not unlike encountering what is traditionally described as a spirit, for the complex with which one is confronted exists as much outwardly as inwardly and, moreover, can potentially manipulate ego-consciousness through its activity in either one or both of these areas.

The image of a free-floating complex active in the environment as a whole creates a very sinister picture indeed. A Chinese story that is presented by von Franz serves to give one a sense of just how serious a threat such a complex poses. The story is based on "the ancient Chinese folk belief that the souls of people who commit suicide are condemned to wander about carrying a rope, trying to coerce others to commit suicide as well."[88] This story, von Franz points out, is especially meaningful because it demonstrates how the successful action on the part of a single individual to integrate the free-floating complex benefits not only that particular individual, but the "universal psyche" as well.[89] Describing the story, von Franz writes:

> One day a soldier who is quartered in a strange town looks through a window and sees a distraught young woman sitting inside her house. Above her head an evil spirit dangles a rope to induce her to kill herself. The soldier wages a ferocious battle against the wicked ghost and finally defeats it, but as a sign of his nocturnal fight with the suicide devil he subsequently bears a ring of red flesh around his arm. It consists of the rope, which became a part of his flesh and can perform no more mischief. Here the evil concatenation exerted by the autonomous suicide complex is literally "integrated" by the soldier. It becomes a living part of him, which "distinguishes" but does not injure him.[90]

In a confrontation with a free-floating complex, such as the suicide complex, the greatest danger would be for the individual to believe wrongly that integration could be achieved through the sole efforts of his ego. Such an attitude would be the direct road to possession by the complex. Clearly, the strength of personality that is actually required to make such a free-floating complex conscious is not to be found in the independent efforts of the ego, but rather in the ego's ability to work in conjunction with the more comprehensive plan of the archetype of wholeness, the self, just as Ingrid did.

"It [integration of a complex]," von Franz emphasizes "must be achieved *deo concedente*, so that the greater powers of the Self assist the ego and act in harmony with it."[91] In the above Chinese story, this type of coordinated action on the part of the ego and the self is symbolized by the fact that the one who is able after a "ferocious battle" to integrate the suicide complex is a soldier, that is, an individual who is acting in service of a greater authority.[92]

With the above examples, we have seen how, in certain cases, when one individual acting in harmony with the self raises the compensatory meaning of a constellated archetypal pattern to consciousness, all who are contained within that same archetypal pattern benefit. Through the efforts of one individual the pattern as a whole is transformed. It could be said, then, as Jung himself does, that from a synchronistic point of view the social contribution of a single individual pursuing his own wholeness may be far greater than one would otherwise imagine it to be. Commenting on this specific point in a letter to Miguel Serrano dated September 14, 1960, Jung writes:

> Whoever is capable of such insight [like that achieved in the individuation process], no matter how isolated he is, should be aware of the law of synchronicity. As an old Chinese saying goes: "The right man sitting in his house and thinking the right thought will be heard a 100 miles away." . . . If the archetype, which is universal, i.e., identical with itself always and anywhere, is properly dealt with in one place only, it is influenced as a whole, i.e., simultaneously and everywhere.[93]

In seeking to illustrate the above in a somewhat more dramatic manner, Jung often referred to a story that was given to him by Wilhelm—a story based on events to which Wilhelm was himself witness during his stay in China. Wilhelm's account of "the rainmaker" was a story that Jung highly valued and told regularly. Jung, Hannah explains, felt so strongly about the importance of this story that he actually advised her "never to give a course of lectures without relating to it." While in China, Wilhelm visited a small village that had been struck by a severe drought. "Everything," Hannah relates, "had been done to put an end to it, and every kind of prayer and charm had been used, but all to no avail." Finally, it was decided that there was no alternative but to send for the rainmaker, a man who lived a considerable distance away. Wilhelm was present when the old man arrived in his covered cart, "sniffed the air in distaste," and then simply asked that he be left alone in a hut on the outskirts of the village. On the third day of his seclusion, the village was awakened by a downpour of rain. Wilhelm, who was, of course, fascinated with what he had witnessed, took it upon himself to question the rainmaker about his methods. "Wilhelm," Hannah writes,

> asked him [the rainmaker] in wonder: 'So you can make rain?' The old man scoffed at the very idea and said *of course* he could not. "But there was the most persistent drought until you came," Wilhelm retorted, "and then—within three days— it rains?" "Oh," replied the old man, "that was something quite different. You see, I come from a region where everything is in order, it rains when it should and is fine when that is needed, and the people also are in order and in themselves. But that was not the case with the people here, they were all out of Tao and out of themselves. I was at once infected when I arrived, so I had to be quite alone until I was once more in Tao and then naturally it rained!"[94]

With the story of the rainmaker we once again see how others benefit when the "right man sitting in his house . . . [thinks] the right thought." The "right man" in this case is the rainmaker. He is the right man because he is the one who has the consciousness to understand the compensatory flow of events in nature, much as von Franz says about the shaman that he would have been "the most individuated, that is, the most conscious, person of the group to which he belonged."[95] The rainmaker knows the village is out of harmony with the Tao and he also knows what must be done to restore the balance. The rainmaker is the one who has sufficient self-knowledge to think the "right thought," that is to say, to raise the progressive compensatory flow of the Tao, the self, to consciousness. Just as Ingrid released herself and her assailant from the grip of the demon lover complex by acting in harmony with the self, just as Jung freed his household from the haunting by making the compensatory pattern conscious, so too did the rainmaker, through his consciousness, release the progressive flow of nature that the villagers in their onesidedness had so persistently blocked. The story of the rainmaker is a story, Max Zeller writes, "Jung loved to tell . . . as often as anyone wanted to hear it."[96] Looking at the story of the rainmaker from a synchronistic perspective, it is not hard to understand why it was so highly valued by Jung, for in it we see how the wholeness just one individual achieves synchronistically benefits others.

Mythological Dimension

As indicated in chapter 1, myth is viewed by Jung as fulfilling an indispensible role for the various religious and secular world-views. Analogous to the symbol, which pointing beyond itself draws the individual to a higher level of consciousness—a synthesis in which the personal is enriched by the transpersonal—so too does myth function in the case of a worldview as a type of collective symbol. Far from being a mere fiction, as some would imagine it to be, for Jung myth gives expression to, in symbolical terms, the transpersonal truth that forms, so to speak, the background to one's particular experience of life. "Let no man say," Olney writes with reference to Jung, " . . . that his myth was a fiction . . . or that his system, because symbolic, was therefore less exactly conformed to the highest reality."[97] Myth, Olney emphasizes, drawing on Yeats, is for Jung "not a fiction but a statement with its own mode of truth."[98]

For Jung myth has the power to transform and heal by making the individual aware of the transpersonal dimension of his particular life experience. Conversely, the individual without a myth, Jung writes, "is like one uprooted, having no true link either with the past, or with the ancestral life which continues within him."[99] Not surprisingly, then, as Edinger explains, one of the fundamental concerns of the individuation process is for the analysand to "seek the myth or archetypal image which expresses his individual situation."[100] More precisely stated, as Jung himself puts it, the analysand must raise to consciousness the myth that is, as it were, "forming" him.[101] "We grow up, we blossom and we wilt," Jung writes to Serrano, here returning again to his metaphor of the rhizome,

> and death is ultimate quietude—or so it seems. But much depends upon the spirit, i.e., the meaning or significance, in which we do and make or—in another word—live. This spirit expresses itself or manifests itself in a Truth [myth], which is indubitably and absolutely convincing to the whole of my being in spite of the fact that the intellect in its endless ramblings will continue forever with its "But, ifs," which however should not be suppressed but rather welcomed as occasions to improve the Truth.[102]

The "Truth" or myth that was Jung's life took, we know, principally the form of an inner journey. This being so, it was not the case, however, that Jung's experience of life's meaning was confined to his experience of his inner world. Rather, it was the case that the inner journey became the means of opening a new route to the outer. Through exploring his inner nature, Jung discovered a new path linking him to outer nature. And here, I would suggest, was exactly the point where the "Truth" that was seeking expression in Jung's life fully flowered. The "Truth" that Jung had been led toward from the beginning, and ultimately would find by way of the unconscious with the formulation of the synchronicity theory, was, it seems to me, not simply an intrapsychic meaning, but rather a cosmological meaning.

Indeed this was the religious meaning that Jung was so deeply moved to have witnessed in the person of Ochwiay Biano (Mountain Lake) when he visited the Taos Pueblos of New Mexico in January of 1925.[103] It is the experience of religious meaning upon which, Jung would write, "the 'dignity,' the tranquil composure of the individual Indian, [is] founded."[104] Recalling in his autobiography his experiences in New Mexico, Jung describes how one day, as he sat with Mountain Lake in the blazing sun on the fifth story of an adobe building, he was told by the Pueblo chief that the religious practices of the Taos Pueblos are not carried out for the benefit of their people alone, but for the benefit of " 'the whole world.' " Sensing from the emotion shown by Mountain Lake as he spoke that their conversation was "approaching extremely delicate ground . . . verging on the mysteries of the tribe," Jung listened very attentively as Mountain Lake continued speaking: " 'We are a people who live on the roof of the world; we are the sons of Father Sun, and with our religion we daily help our father to go across the sky. We do this not only for ourselves, but for the whole world. If we were to cease practicing our religion, in ten years the sun would no longer rise. Then it would be night forever.' "[105]

Mountain Lake's description of the Taos Pueblos' religion made an impression on Jung that would remain the rest of his life. Knowing what we now know about Jung's synchronistic worldview, it is not hard to understand why. Mountain Lake had given Jung a glimpse of the "Truth" that Jung would himself seek through his journey into the unconscious, and would ultimately realize in his theory of synchronicity. He had shown Jung in his person what it is to experience one's life as "cosmologically meaningful."[106] Each individual, Jung had learned through his encounter with Mountain Lake's "Truth,"is supported by and in turn must be supportive of the whole of nature. With the Taos Pueblos, the idea that the whole supports the individual is expressed in the belief that each person is a son of Father Sun. The whole, on the other hand, requires the support of each individual. Each person must act as a type of facilitator of the unfoldment of the events in nature itself. For the Taos Pueblos this takes the form of helping Father Sun daily to go across the sky. "The idea, absurd to us," Jung reflects in his memoirs,

> that a ritual can magically affect the sun is, upon closer examination . . . far more familiar to us than might at first be assumed. Our Christian religion—like every other, incidentally—is permeated by the idea that special acts or a special kind of action can influence God—for example, through certain rites or by prayer, or by a morality pleasing to the Divinity.
>
> The ritual acts of man are an answer and reaction to the action of God upon man; and perhaps they are not only that, but are also intended to be "activating." . . . That man feels capable of formulating valid replies to the overpowering influence of God, and that he can render back something which is essential even to God, induces pride, for it raises the human individual to the dignity of a metaphysical factor.[107]

Mountain Lake had provided Jung with a description of the unique relationship of mutual interdependence between man and his Creator—between the individual and the sacred circle of nature as a whole. This, of course, is the same "Truth" that Jung would himself come to acknowledge in his own theory of synchronicity. The idea that the individual is both supported by and in turn must act in support of the progressive compensatory flow of nature is central to the synchronistic worldview. On the one hand, nature works both inwardly and outwardly to further the realization of one's unique personality. In this work, we have seen numerous examples of this compensatory synchronistic activity of nature. On the other hand, the individual, through actions consistent with his heightened consciousness, actions that are in harmony with the self, returns to nature something that is of genuine importance to the progressive unfoldment of the whole. With the example of the haunting of the Jung household, with the case history of Ingrid, and with Jung's much-treasured story of the rainmaker, we have seen the pivotal role that a single conscious individual can play in facilitating the progressive unfoldment of events in nature. At first glance, as Jung notes above, the idea of a single individual playing such a role seems inconceivable. Yet when looked at more thoughtfully, it becomes clear that it does have its parallel in the more accepted notion of the efficacy of prayer—a notion that Jung, significantly, elsewhere describes as a belief "based on the experience of concomitant synchronistic phenomena."[108] Much along this line, Hannah, who similarly views both the rainmaker story and Mountain Lake's account as depictions of the activities of the synchronicity principle,[109] suggests that for prayers to be efficacious one must be in Tao when one prays, that is to say, one must be acting in harmony with the compensatory flow of nature. As Hannah relates, speaking here with direct reference to the rainmaker story, "the first necessity of praying the right prayer is to be in oneself, in Tao as the Chinese call it."[110]

Some thirty-five years after his visit with the Taos Pueblos of New Mexico, Jung could say that he had himself found the "Truth" that he had so greatly admired in the person of Mountain Lake. Jung, it is clear, had come to experience his life as cosmologically meaningful. Now, like Mountain Lake, Jung felt his task was to do what he could to "guard" this "Truth." In the same letter to Miguel Serrano that has been cited twice above—once in connection with Jung's description of how the "law of synchronicity" makes the insight of each individual of significance to the whole and again in connection with his description of the concept of mythological "Truth" that we have given considerable attention to in this section—Jung, writing at the age of eighty-five, less than a year before his death, reflects about man's search for wholeness:

> We are sorely in need of a Truth . . . which I have found still living with the Taos Pueblos. Their chief of ceremonies, old Ochwiah Biano (Mountain Lake) said to me: "We are the people who live on the roof of the world, we are the sons of the Sun. . . . We help him daily to rise and to cross over the sky. We do this not only for ourselves, but for the Americans also. Therefore they should not interfere with our religion. But if they continue to do so . . . and hinder us, then they will see that in ten years the Sun will rise no more." . . . I [Jung here speaking about himself] tried to find the best truth and the clearest light I could attain to, and since I have reached my highest point I can't transcend any more, I am guarding my light and my treasure, convinced that nobody would gain and I myself would be badly, even hopelessly injured, if I should

lose it. It is most precious not only to me, but above all to the darkness of the creator, who needs man to illuminate His creation.[111]

The highest point reached by Jung, the clearest light he was able to attain, that which he was most careful to guard during the time of his own life, yet that which has now become Jung's legacy to the world, is his concept of individuation understood as a search for meaning in relationship to the sacred circle of nature as a whole. In contrast to Jung's intrapsychic model of his psychology of religion, wherein the search for spiritual wholeness is largely to be pursued in relationship to the inner world, with the synchronistic model, nature as a whole has become the sacred retort of the work. The "Truth," therefore, to which the synchronistic Jungian worldview has given birth is clearly of a different sort than its intrapsychic counterpart, for in contrast to the latter, the "Truth" that the synchronistic worldview discloses is most certainly a cosmological meaning.

In closing this section, I would like to point out as a footnote to the above that Jung, as Dourley tells us, "understands the role or function of the prophet to be that of bringing to birth, through the depths of his own person, the symbolic expression or myth that responds to the spiritual needs and aspirations of the age."[112] It is certainly the case that the "Truth" or "myth" to which Jung's synchronistic worldview has given birth is of considerable import "to the spiritual needs and aspirations" of this age, for we live in an age in which man's alienation from nature, both inwardly and outwardly, threatens to end life on this planet, either with nuclear war or through the sheer abuse of the global environment.

Conclusion 🍂

The purpose of this study has been to examine the synchronicity theory in relationship to the individuation process in order to reveal the import of this concept for Jung's psychology of religion.

In this work, a model has been introduced that identifies the key aspects of the synchronistic event. Furthermore, utilizing this same framework, we have been able to explore in considerable detail the theorizing about the synchronicity principle that has been carried out by Jung and others. In this way, both the strengths and the weaknesses of the theoretical models associated with the synchronicity concept have been revealed. Jung, as we have seen, never developed a satisfactory, comprehensive theory to account for the key features of the synchronistic event, on the one hand, and the activities of the synchronicity principle, on the other. As a consequence of this, it seems to me that his discussion of this phenomenon was greatly inhibited. Perhaps this is one of the reasons why Jung delayed the writing of the principal essay on synchronicity for some twenty years. Perhaps it is also partly the reason why he focused away from the human element when he finally found his way to writing that paper. Clearly, the presentation of synchronistic case material, if it is to be done in any detail, requires a comprehensive theoretical understanding of synchronicity—a comprehensive theoretical overview that Jung's writings on this subject suggest he did not have. In the same manner, the literature that has followed the principal essay has been equally held back by the absence of such a theoretical overview. Hopefully, this work makes a contribution toward resolving that particular problem.

Having made the above point, it should be added that this is not to take anything away from Jung's practical knowledge of the workings of the synchronicity principle, nor is it intended to take anything away from the practical knowledge of these events that other analysts may have. Clearly, one can have a highly developed practical understanding of a phenomenon without having come to terms with it theoretically. Accordingly, when, for instance, I criticize Jung and von Franz's theorizing about the time factor, as I did in chapters 2 and 4, this is certainly not to say that I believe that their practical knowledge of these events is in anyway deficient. I have no doubts that Jung's handling of synchronistic phenomena in analysis was masterful, and I am sure the same is true of von Franz, Bolen, and many other analysts.

Beyond, then, the theoretical weaknesses of Jung's understanding of this concept, I would suggest that another factor equally served to obstruct a complete disclosure of Jung's position on the synchronicity theory in the principal essay. Jung, I would suggest, had difficulties coming to terms with the broader implications of the synchronicity theory for his psychology as a whole. More specifically, Jung had difficulties coming to terms with the problem of how this new synchronistic perspective and its attendant implications for his psychology should be introduced into the public domain. In chapter 4, we saw that Jung referred to this very problem in a letter to W. P. Witcutt. In his letter, Jung indicated that ideas that he then had about synchronistic phenomena—ideas that Jung told Witcutt the "public today is incapable of understanding"—would not be disclosed to the general public by him, but would have to be presented by others at a later point. Similarly, in a letter to J. B. Rhine, Jung writes with reference to his study of parapsychological-type phenomena: "I have arrived at the conviction that the main difficulty doesn't consist in the question of how to tell, but rather in how not to tell it. . . . I prefer not to communicate too many of my experiences. They would confront the scientific world with too upsetting problems."[1]

Having been able to observe in this study the extent to which the Jungian worldview, as it is generally understood, is transformed by the synchronicity theory, we are certainly in a position to appreciate why Jung may have been somewhat hesitant to lay his complete findings and their implications for his psychology before the public. As has been evidenced in this work, Jung's psychology is radically transformed with the introduction of the synchronicity concept. When you add to this the fact Jung had spent most of his professional life attempting to gain the acceptance of his unique understanding of the workings of the inner world of the psyche, the problem of the synchronicity theory, which emphasizes the interplay of both the inner and outer worlds, would have been that much more difficult for Jung to come to terms with himself and, moreover, put into a perspective that would be acceptable to his professional audience. Such a dramatic change of course would be very difficult for anyone to come to terms with. What Jung had learned about the synchronicity concept in his life and work certainly constituted a paradigmatic leap for analytical psychology—a paradigmatic leap, Jung realized, whose full import would have to be disclosed not by him, but by others following afterward.

It is a curious fact that Freud himself, with his work on telepathy, struggled with a problem similar to the one described above. Freud, it was shown, was deeply concerned for some time that if he were to publish his observations of telepathic phenomena, this would have a damaging effect on his psychology as a whole. In connection with this, the influence of Jones, who strongly opposed such publication, was quite significant. Finally, however, Freud decided that it was a matter of conscience that he be more forthright about his findings, regardless of the public reaction. One further point that comes to mind after having examined, as we did in chapter 3, the points of agreement and disagreement between the positions of Freud and Jung on the subject of telepathy is that one cannot help but wonder what both men might have achieved together had not their professional collaboration come to an end. In the absence of the schism in the psychoanalytical world that was to result from their parting of the ways, it is certainly possible that the fear of the charge of mysticism that is to be found in both schools would not be so great. A more unified front would have served to strengthen the professional standing of depth psychology, thus giving its adherents a greater confidence. Perhaps as a consequence of this, the study of parapsychological phenomena itself would not be the taboo subject it tends to be. It is certainly conceivable to me that had Freud and Jung worked together in this area they would have accomplished a great deal. I think Jung would have pushed Freud further in his thinking about telepathy; I think Freud would have pushed Jung to give more definite shape to some of his own ideas, particularly with respect to their clinical application.

In light of the fact that in his principal essay on synchronicity Jung focused away from the human element, those individuals who have used that paper as their primary source of information on the synchronicity concept have been left with no real sense of just how prevalent these experiences were in Jung's life and work. Reading the principal essay, one could easily imagine that the synchronistic events Jung described were very rare. Indeed, Jung himself furthered this misconception when he wrote about the case history of the "golden scarab": "I must admit that nothing like it ever happened to me before or since, and that the dream of the patient has remained unique in my experience."[2] However, characteristic of the tangle Jung often left his reader to unwind, he wrote about this same case in another paper, "This story is meant only as a paradigm of the innumerable cases of meaningful coincidence that have been observed not only by me but by many others."[3] In this work, it has, of course, been demonstrated that Jung's second statement is the more accurate one of the two. In both Jung's life and work, synchronistic phenomena came to play a very significant role. In demonstrating just how significant a role they came to play, we have had to draw on a great variety of sources beyond Jung's principal essay. These sources have included *The Collected Works of C. G. Jung*, Jung's correspondence, interviews, lectures, his autobiography, and secondary source material as well. From these sources bits and pieces of information were assembled to create a comprehensive picture of the very great role that the concept of synchronicity played in Jung's life and work. It was, moreover, through the utilization of these same sources that we were able to pursue the third and final objective of this work, which was to disclose the import of the synchronicity concept for Jung's psychology of religion.

One of the fundamental assumptions of this study has been that the full picture of Jung's psychology of religion is largely to be found outside of Jung's formal writings on that subject. Much as Homans has suggested that the individuation process was the lens through which Jung viewed Christianity, it has been held in this work that the individuation process was the lens through which Jung viewed all religious experience. Going further than this, it has also been held in this work that Jung actually regarded the individuation process as a spiritual journey in its own right, as von Franz suggests herself in the following. Writing in her biographical account of Jung's life and work, von Franz reflects:

> "When I once remarked to Jung that his psychological insights and his attitude to the unconscious seemed to me to be in many respects the same as those of the most archaic religions—for example shamanism, or the religion of the Naskapi Indians who have neither priest nor ritual but who merely follow their dreams which they believe are sent by the "immortal great man in the heart"—Jung answered with a laugh: "Well, that's nothing to be ashamed of. It's an honor!" The pastor's son, for whom the church now meant only death, came early to the painful recognition that ecclesiastical religion could give him no answers.[4]

It is true, as von Franz suggests above, that Jung personally rejected Christian ecclesiasticism. And it is also true, moreover, that Jung's sense of the spiritual life became inextricably tied to what von Franz describes here as Jung's characteristic "attitude to the unconscious." As we saw in chapter 1, essentially both of these points were made by Jung in his 1937 Terry lectures at Yale University. Speaking on the subject of psychology and religion, Jung, it should be remembered, called upon his Yale audience to accept the challenge of what he described as "immediate religious experience," by which he meant a religious experience based on a direct encounter with the unconscious. What Jung wished to convey to his Yale audience, especially to those for whom the rituals of established religion had lost their meaning and efficacy, was that the individuation process itself might very well meet their spiritual needs in a way that the more traditional Western religious practices no longer could. In 1937, Jung therefore introduced his Yale audience to what in effect was, and here is where we assess things somewhat differently than von Franz does above, a new form of religious ritual—a ritual involving the religious-like observation of the contents of the unconscious.

This notion of "immediate religious experience" is, to be sure, the pivotal factor of Jung's psychology of religion. Accordingly, one of the central problems of this study has been to identify the specific transformation that this concept undergoes with the introduction of the synchronicity theory. In endeavoring to come to terms with this problem, that which has been described in this work as the intrapsychic and synchronistic models of Jung's psychology of religion have been comparatively examined using Smart's six-dimensional model for the analysis of worldviews.

Perhaps the most important general conclusion that has been reached through following this particular methodology is that when we move from the intrapsychic model to the synchronistic one it is the case that the fundamental concepts of the former are not so much overthrown and done away with as extended. For instance, as we have seen with Jung's notion of psychic compensation, this principle, which in the intrapsychic model is applied strictly to the interaction of the conscious and the unconscious is, with the synchronistic model, extended to include the compensatory interplay between the individual and nature as a whole. Here, then, a very radical step is taken, but it is done, interestingly enough, without violating the structure central to the intrapsychic model. The implications of this type of extension of the intrapsychic model for

Jung's psychology of religion are, of course, very far-reaching, and a good number of them have been dealt with as we have moved through the six-dimensional framework. The major finding, however, concerns Jung's concept of "immediate religious experience," which is now to be taken to refer not merely to an encounter with the compensatory contents of the unconscious, but to a direct encounter with the compensatory patterning of events in nature as a whole, both inwardly and outwardly. With the introduction of the synchronicity concept, therefore, Jung's notion of "immediate religious experience" is dramatically transformed. Through it, one is drawn into an encounter with nature that has, as was demonstrated in chapter 4, a very strong parallel in the type of encounter with nature that characterizes the unitary worldview of traditional Chinese philosophy. It should be emphasized, however, that this particular notion of "immediate religious experience" is, in the final analysis, uniquely Jungian.

The synchronistic worldview, I would like to say in closing, opens the door to a completely new understanding of the meaning of life. Although it has, as part of Jung's legacy, been given considerable attention, its full import most certainly has yet to be raised to consciousness, even amongst Jung's followers. It is hoped, therefore, that this work constitutes a contribution to that venture.

Notes

Introduction

1. C. G. Jung, *Dream Analysis: Notes of the Seminar Given in 1928–1930 by C. G. Jung*, ed. William McGuire (London: Routledge & Kegan Paul, 1984), pp. 43–45.

2. *The Secret of the Golden Flower*, trans. Richard Wilhelm, trans. from the German by Cary F. Baynes, commentary by C. G. Jung (New York: Harcourt, Brace & World, 1962), pp. 138ff.

3. The principal paper, "Synchronizität als ein Prinzip akausaler Zusammenhänge," was published together with a monograph by W. Pauli entitled "Der Einfluss archetypischer Vorstellungen auf die Bildung naturwissenschaftlicher Theorien bei Kepler" in the volume *Naturerklarung und Psyche* (Studien aus dem C. G. Jung-Institut, IV; Zurich, 1952). This volume was translated as *The Interpretation of Nature and Psyche* (New York [Bollingen Series LI] and London, 1955). See editor's note in C. G. Jung, "Synchronicity: An Acausal Connecting Principle," *Collected Works* (hereafter cited as *C.W.*), vol. 8, trans. R. F. C. Hull (Princeton: Princeton University Press, 1978), p. 417.

4. Jung, "Synchronicity: An Acausal Connecting Principle," *C.W.*, vol. 8, par. 816, p. 419.

5. Michael Fordham, *New Developments in Analytical Psychology* (London: Routledge & Kegan Paul, 1957), p. 42.

6. Ira Progoff, *Jung, Synchronicity, and Human Destiny* (New York: Dell, 1973), p. 143.

7. The "Astrological Experiment" appears in "Synchronicity: An Acausal Connecting Principle," *C.W.*, vol. 8, pars. 867–915, pp. 453–84. A shortened version can be found in *C.W.*, vol. 18, pars. 1174–1192, pp. 494–501.

Jung, who had been deeply impressed with the results achieved by Rhine's ESP experiments (see "Synchronicity: An Acausal Connecting Principle," *C.W.*, vol. 8, pars. 833ff, pp. 432ff) sought to develop similar statistical proof for the synchronicity theory, hence the "Astrological

Experiment." As things turned out, however, the experiment did not yield the results Jung had hoped it might. In other words, no statistical proof for the synchronicity theory was obtained.

I am personally not qualified to evaluate either Jung's use of statistics or his use of astrological material. Fordham, it can be noted, however, does examine Jung's use of both in his article "Reflections on the Archetypes and Synchronicity" in *New Developments in Analytical Psychology*.

The "Astrological Experiment" has been widely criticized. Some individuals have expressed serious doubts about Jung's use of statistics, which Fordham himself euphemistically describes as "highly original and peculiarly his own" (Ibid., p. 36.). Others have criticized the experiment on the grounds that the case material used by Jung was not a truly random sampling, since it was drawn from a group whose members had demonstrated an interest in astrology prior to Jung's experiment. Finally, and this is a critical point, Jung himself came to believe that the statistical method itself was not appropriate for the study of synchronistic phenomena in terms of its clinical applications. Writing to Abrams in a letter dated June 20, 1957, Jung comments, "As far as I can see, there are only two ways of approach to parapsychology: the one is the experimental way without psychology, and the other the psychological approach without hope of a statistical method." (Gerhard Adler and Aniela Jaffé, eds., *C. G. Jung Letters*, vol. 2, trans. R. F. C. Hull (Princeton: Princeton University Press, 1975), pp. 374–75).

8. Robert S. McCully, "The Rorschach, Synchronicity, and Relativity," in Robert William Davis, ed., *Toward a Discovery of the Person* (Burbank, Calif.: The Society for Personality Assessment, 1974), p. 33.

9. C. A. Meier, "Psychosomatic Medicine from the Jungian Point of View," *Journal of Analytical Psychology* 8, no. 2 (1963), p. 103.

10. Mary R. Gammon, " 'Window into Eternity': Archetype and Relativity," *Journal of Analytical Psychology* 18, no. 1 (1973), pp. 11–24.

11. Marie-Louise von Franz, *Number and Time: Reflections Leading towards a Unification of Psychology and Physics,* trans. Adrea Dykes (London: Rider & Company, 1974).

12. Carolin S. Keutzer, "Archetypes, Synchronicity and the Theory of Formative Causation," *Journal of Analytical Psychology* 24 (1982), pp. 255–62; Keutzer, "The Power of Meaning: From Quantum Mechanics to Synchronicity," *Journal of Humanistic Psychology* 24, no. 1 (1984), pp. 80–94.

13. L. Zinkin, "The Hologram as a Model for Analytical Psychology," *Journal of Analytical Psychology* 32 (1987), pp. 1–21.

14. Hans Bender, "Meaningful Coincidences in the Light of the Jung-Pauli Theory of Synchronicity and Parapsychology," in Betty Shapin and Lisette Coly, eds., *The Philosophy of Parapsychology* (New York: Parapsychology Foundation, 1976), pp. 66–81.

15. Lila L. Gatlin, "Meaningful Information Creation: An Alternative Interpretation of Psi Phenomenon," *The Journal of the American Society for Psychical Research* 71, no. 1 (1977), pp. 1–17.

16. K. Ramakrishna Rao, "On the Nature of PSI: An Examination of Some Attempts to Explain ESP and PK," *Journal of Parapsychology* 41 (1977), pp. 294–351.

17. Gustav Jahoda, "Jung's 'Meaningful Coincidences,' " *The Philosophical Journal* 4, no. 1 (1967), pp. 35–42.

18. Aniela Jaffé, *From the Life and Work of C. G. Jung*, trans. R. F. C. Hull (New York: Harper & Row, 1971); Jaffé, *Apparitions: An Archetypal Approach to Death, Dreams and Ghosts* (Irving, Tex.: Spring, 1978).

19. Marie-Louise von Franz, *Number and Time*; Franz, *On Divination and Synchronicity: The Psychology of Meaningful Chance* (Toronto: Inner City Books, 1980).

20. Franz, *Number and Time*, p. 13.

21. J. F. Zavala, "Synchronicity and the Mexican Divinatory Calendar 'Tonalamatl,' " *Quadrant* 15, no. 1 (1982), pp. 55–70.

22. Progoff, op. cit.

23. Jean Shinoda Bolen, *The Tao of Psychology: Synchronicity and the Self* (San Francisco: Harper & Row, 1979).

24. Mary Williams, "An Example of Synchronicity," *Journal of Analytical Psychology* 1 (1955–56), pp. 93–96.

25. Michael Fordham, "An Interpretation of Jung's Thesis about Synchronicity," *British Journal of Medical Psychology* 35 (1962), pp. 205–10; Fordham, *New Developments in Analytical Psychology*. See chap. 4.

26. Carolin S. Keutzer, "Synchronicity in Psychotherapy," *Journal of Analytical Psychology* 29 (1984), pp. 373–81.

27. James W. Heisig, *Imago Dei: A Study of C. G. Jung's Psychology of Religion* (Lewisburg, Pa.: Bucknell University Press, 1979).

28. Harold Coward, *Jung and Eastern Thought* (Albany: State University of New York Press, 1985).

29. Ninian Smart, "The Scientific Study of Religion in Its Plurality," in Frank Whaling, ed., *Contemporary Approaches to the Study of Religion*, vol. 1 (Berlin: Mouton, 1983), p. 377.

30. Ninian Smart, *Concept and Empathy: Essays in the Study of Religion*, ed. Donald Wiebe (London: Macmillan Press, 1986), p.74.

31. Smart's six-dimensional model is outlined in the following works: Ninian Smart, *The Religious Experience of Mankind* (New York: Scribner,

1969), and Smart, *Worldviews: Crosscultural Explorations of Human Beliefs* (New York: Charles Scribner's Sons, 1983).

32. Donald Capps, Lewis Rambo, and Paul Ransohoff, eds., *Psychology of Religion: A Guide to Information Sources* (Detroit: Gale Research Company, 1976). Also see Donald Capps, "Contemporary Psychology of Religion: The Task of Theoretical Reconstruction," *Social Research* 41 (1974), pp. 362–83. Capps does not use Smart's doctrinal and ethical dimensions. Rather he uses in their place what he describes as the dispositional and directional dimensions. The dispositional dimension, Capps writes, captures "the element of arranging and structuring systems of meaning, and the directional centering on the process of individual and group realization in terms of these systems" ("Contemporary Psychology of Religion" p. 381). To my mind, Smart's doctrinal dimension handles quite well what Capps refers to as the dispositional dimension. And, likewise, Smart's experiential dimension covers what Capps refers to as the directional dimension. Beyond this, I have found Smart's ethical dimension, an area that I do not think Capps's model adequately addresses, to be of fundamental importance to this particular study of the Jungian worldview.

Chapter I

1. Smart, *The Religious Experience of Mankind*, p. 7.

2. C. G. Jung, *Psychology and Religion* (New Haven: Yale University Press, 1978), p. 52.

3. Ibid., p. 21.

4. Ibid., p. 63.

5. Victor White, *God and the Unconscious* (London: The Harvill Press, 1953), p. 49.

6. C. G. Jung, "Answer to Job," *C.W.*, vol. 11, trans. R. F. C. Hull (Princeton: Princeton University Press, 1977), par. 757, p. 469.

7. Mircea Eliade, *Shamanism: Archaic Techniques of Ecstasy*, trans. Willard R. Trask (Princeton: Princeton University Press, 1964), pp. 3–8.

8. Ibid., p. 8.

9. Josef Goldbrunner, *Individuation: A Study of the Depth Psychology of Carl Gustav Jung* (Notre Dame: University of Notre Dame Press, 1966), p. 92.

10. Jung, *Psychology and Religion*, pp. 54–59.

11. Eliade, op. cit., p. 109.

12. Henri F. Ellenberger, *The Discovery of the Unconscious* (New York: Basic Books, 1970), p. 889.

13. Ibid., p. 890.

14. Eliade, op. cit., p. 13. Eliade writes about shamanism in Central and North Asia: "A shaman is not recognized as such until after he has received two kinds of teaching: (1) ecstatic (dreams, trances, etc.) and (2) traditional (shamanic techniques, names and functions of the spirits, mythology and genealogy of the clan, secret language, etc.). This twofold course of instruction, given by the spirits and the old master shamans, is equivalent to an initiation."

15. Marie-Louise von Franz, *Alchemy: An Introduction to the Symbolism and the Psychology* (Toronto: Inner City Books, 1980), p. 254.

16. Eliade, op. cit., See chapter 2, pp. 33–66.

17. Jung, "Transformation Symbolism in the Mass," *C.W.*, vol. 11, par. 448, p. 294.

18. Ibid., par. 410, p. 271.

19. Eliade, op. cit., p. 36. Eliade, writing about a Yakut account, states: "The evil spirits carry the future shaman's soul to the underworld and there shut it up in a house for three years (only one year for those who will become lesser shamans). Here the shaman undergoes his initiation."

20. Peter Homans, *Jung in Context* (Chicago: The University of Chicago Press, 1979), p. 184.

21. C. G. Jung, *Symbols of Transformation*, *C.W.*, vol. 5, trans. R. F. C. Hull (Princeton: Princeton University Press, 1976), p. xxiii.

22. Jung, "On Psychic Energy," *C.W.*, vol. 8, par. 35, p. 19.

23. Sigmund Freud, *Totem and Taboo, Standard Edition*, vol. 13, trans. James Strachey (London: Hogarth Press, 1964); pp. 156 and 161.

24. Jung, "On Psychic Energy," *C.W.*, vol. 8, par. 35, p. 19.

25. Jung, "General Aspects of Dream Psychology," *C.W.*, vol. 8, par. 456. p. 241.

26. C. G. Jung, Prefaces to *Collected Papers on Analytical Psychology*, *C.W.*, vol. 4, trans. R. F. C. Hull (Princeton: Princeton University Press, 1979), par. 687, p. 295.

27. Sigmund Freud, *The Future of an Illusion, The International Psycho-Analytical Library*, no. 15, trans. W. D. Robson-Scott (London: Hogarth Press, 1978), p. 39.

28. Jung, "On Psychic Energy," *C.W.*, vol. 8, par. 43, p. 23.

29. Jung, "General Aspects of Dream Psychology," *C.W.*, vol. 8, par. 471, p. 246.

30. Jung, "On Psychic Energy," *C.W.*, vol. 8, par. 88, p. 46.

31. C. G. Jung, *Mysterium Coniunctionis, C.W.*, vol. 14, trans. R. F. C. Hull (Princeton: Princeton University Press, 1976), par. 667, p. 468.

32. Jung, Prefaces to *Collected Papers on Analytical Psychology, C.W.*, vol. 4, par. 675, p. 291.

33. Jung, "On Psychic Energy," *C.W.*, vol. 8, pars. 46–47, pp. 24–25.

34. Jung, Prefaces to *Collected Papers on Analytical Psychology, C.W.*, vol. 4, pars. 674–75, p. 291.

35. C. G. Jung, "The Relations between the Ego and the Unconscious," *C.W.*, vol. 7, trans. R. F. C. Hull (Princeton: Princeton University Press, 1977), par. 275, pp. 177–78.

36. Jung, "On the Nature of Dreams," *C.W.*, vol. 8, par. 546, p. 288.

37. Jung, "General Aspects of Dream Psychology," *C.W.*, vol. 8, par. 489, pp. 253–54.

38. Jung, "On the Nature of Dreams," *C.W.*, vol. 8, par. 550, pp. 289–90.

39. C. G. Jung, *Memories, Dreams, Reflections,* recorded and edited by Aniela Jaffé, trans. Richard and Clara Winston (New York: Vintage Books, 1965), p. 196.

40. Jung, "On the Nature of Dreams," *C.W.*, vol. 8, par. 557, p. 292.

41. C. G. Jung, *Aion, C.W.*, vol. 9, pt. 2, trans. R. F. C. Hull (Princeton: Princeton University Press, 1978), pars. 1–2, p. 3.

42. Jung, "The Structure of the Psyche," *C.W.*, vol. 8, par. 321, pp. 151–52.

43. C. G. Jung, "Symbols and the Interpretation of Dreams," *C.W.*, vol. 18, trans. R. F. C. Hull (Princeton: Princeton University Press, 1976), par. 523, p. 228.

44. C. G. Jung, "Psychological Aspects of the Mother Archetype," *C.W.*, vol. 9, pt. 1, trans. R. F. C. Hull (Princeton: Princeton University Press, 1977), pars. 156–57, pp. 81–82.

45. Jung, *Symbols of Transformation, C.W.*, vol. 5, par. 30, p. 25.

46. John P. Dourley, *C. G. Jung and Paul Tillich: The Psyche as Sacrament* (Toronto: Inner City Books, 1981), pp. 23–24.

47. Jung, "A Psychological Approach to the Dogma of the Trinity," *C.W.*, vol. 11, par. 238, p. 160.

48. Jung, "Transformation Symbolism in the Mass," *C.W.*, vol. 11, par. 400, p. 263.

49. Jung, "A Psychological Approach to the Dogma of the Trinity," *C.W.*, vol. 11, par. 289, p. 194.

50. Jung, *Aion*, *C.W.*, vol. 9, pt. 2, par. 59, p. 31.

51. Ibid., par. 356, p. 226.

52. Jung, "The Relations between the Ego and the Unconscious," *C.W.*, vol. 7, par. 399, p. 238.

53. Jung, "Transformation Symbolism in the Mass," *C.W.*, vol. 11, par. 391, p. 259.

54. Jung, *Aion*, *C.W.*, vol. 9, pt. 2, par. 411, p. 260.

55. Jung, Psychological commentary on *The Tibetan Book of the Great Liberation*, *C.W.*, vol. 11, par. 773, pp. 483–84.

56. *The Secret of the Golden Flower*, pp. 133–34.

57. Jung, Foreword to Suzuki's *Introduction to Zen Buddhism*, *C.W.*, vol. 11, par. 902, p. 553.

58. Jung, *Memories, Dreams, Reflections*, p. 215.

59. Murray Stein, "The Significance of Jung's Father in His Destiny as a Therapist of Christianity," *Quadrant* 18, no. 1 (1985), p. 24.

60. Jung, Psychological commentary on *The Tibetan Book of the Great Liberation*, *C.W.*, vol. 11, par. 780, p. 489.

61. Jung, "The Transcendent Function," *C.W.*, vol. 8, par. 157, p. 82.

62. Jung, "The Tavistock Lectures," *C.W.*, vol. 18, par. 396, p. 171.

63. Jung, "On The Nature of the Psyche," *C.W.*, vol. 8, par. 400, p. 202.

64. Jung, *Memories, Dreams, Reflections*, p. 181.

65. Jung, *Mysterium Coniunctionis*, *C.W.*, vol. 14, par. 752, p. 528.

66. Jung, "The Tavistock Lectures," *C.W.*, vol. 18, par. 397, p. 171.

67. Jung, "The Transcendent Function," *C.W.*, vol. 8, par. 167, p. 82.

68. Ibid., par. 181, p. 87.

69. Jung, *Mysterium Coniunctionis*, *C.W.*, vol. 14, pars. 753–74, pp. 528–29.

70. Ibid., par. 753, p. 529.

71. Ibid., par. 778, p. 545.

72. Ibid., par. 759, p. 533.

73. Jung, "The Transcendent Function," *C.W.*, vol. 8, par. 183, pp. 87–88.

74. Ibid., par. 134, p. 69.

75. Jung, "A Study in the Process of Individuation," *C.W.*, vol. 9, pt. 1, par. 621, p. 351.

76. Franz, *Alchemy*, p. 217.

77. Jung, *Mysterium Coniunctionis*, *C.W.*, vol. 14, par. 756, p. 531.

78. Jung, *Aion*, *C.W.*, vol. 9, pt. 2, par. 257, p. 167.

79. Jung, "Transformation Symbolism in the Mass," *C.W.*, vol. 11, par. 400, p. 263.

80. Jung, *Memories, Dreams, Reflections*, pp. 197–99.

81. *The Secret of the Golden Flower*, p. 132.

82. Ibid., pars. 77–78, p. 52.

83. Jung, *Aion*, *C.W.*, vol. 9, pt. 2, par. 125, p. 70.

84. Jung, Foreword to White's *God and the Unconscious*, *C.W.*, vol. 11, par. 460, p. 307.

85. Jung, *Mysterium Coniunctionis*, *C.W.*, vol. 14, par. 778, p. 545.

86. Jung, *Memories, Dreams, Reflections*, p. 189.

87. Adler and Jaffé, eds., *C. G. Jung Letters*, vol.. 2, p. 486.

88. Jung, *Aion*, *C.W.*, vol. 9, pt. 2, pars. 422–23, p. 266.

89. Jung, *Mysterium Coniunctionis*, *C.W.*, vol. 14, par. 710, p. 499.

90. Ibid., pars. 739–40, p. 520.

91. Jung, *Aion*, *C.W.*, vol. 9, pt. 2, par. 14, p. 8.

92. Ibid., par. 42, p. 22.

93. *The Secret of the Golden Flower*, p. 118.

94. C. G. Jung, ed., *Man and His Symbols* (Garden City, N.Y.: Doubleday, 1979), p. 85.

95. Jung, "A Psychological Approach to the Dogma of the Trinity," *C.W.*, vol. 11, par. 292, p. 198.

96. Jung, *Aion*, *C.W.*, vol. 9, pt. 2, par. 74, p. 41.

97. Ibid., par. 104, p. 58.

98. Jung, "A Psychological Approach to the Dogma of the Trinity," *C.W.*, vol. 11, par. 261, p. 176.

99. C. G. Jung, "Fundamental Questions of Psychotherapy," *C.W.*, vol. 16, trans. R. F. C. Hull (Princeton: Princeton University Press, 1977), par. 241, pp. 117–18.

100. Jung, *Memories, Dreams, Reflections*, p. 3.

101. Aniela Jaffé, ed., *C. G. Jung: Word and Image*, trans. Krishna Winston (Princeton: Princeton University Press, 1979), p. 3.

102. Jung, *Psychology and Religion*, pp. 16, 32–33.

103. Volodymyr Walter Odajnyk, *Jung and Politics: The Political and Social Ideas of C. G. Jung*, foreword by Marie-Louise von Franz (New York: Harper & Row, 1976), pp. 44–45.

104. C. G. Jung, "The Undiscovered Self (Present and Future)," *C.W.*, vol. 10, trans. R. F. C. Hull (Princeton: Princeton University Press, 1978), par. 536, p. 276.

105. Jung, "The Relations between the Ego and the Unconscious," *C.W.*, vol. 7, par. 240, p. 153.

106. Jung, Introduction to Wolff's *Studies in Jungian Psychology*, *C.W.*, vol. 10, par. 891, p. 471.

107. Jung, "A Psychological Approach to the Dogma of the Trinity," *C.W.*, vol. 11, par. 276, p. 184.

108. Jung, "The Relations between the Ego and the Unconscious," *C.W.*, vol. 7, par. 239, p. 151.

109. Goldbrunner, op. cit., p. 169.

110. Barbara Hannah, *Jung: His Life and Work* (London: Michael Joseph, 1977), p. 290.

111. Jung, "On the Nature of the Psyche," *C.W.*, vol. 8, par. 432, p. 226.

112. Ellenberger, op. cit., p. 733.

113. This quote, which appears in Ellenberger, op. cit., p. 733, is taken from "Bill's Story," in *Alcoholics Anonymous* (New York: Works Publishing, 1939), pp. 10–26.

114. Adler and Jaffé, eds., *C. G. Jung Letters*, vol. 2, pp. 623–25.

115. Odajnyk, op. cit., p. x.

116. Jung, "The Undiscovered Self (Present and Future)," *C.W.*, vol. 10, par. 540, p. 278.

117. Adler and Jaffé, eds. *C. G. Jung Letters*, vol. 2, p. 488.

118. Jung, "A Psychological Approach to the Dogma of the Trinity," *C.W.*, vol. 11, par. 233, p. 157.

119. Jung, *Mysterium Coniunctionis*, *C.W.*, vol. 14, par. 778, p. 546.

120. William Blake, "To God," in Richard Wilbur, ed., *Blake* (New York: Dell, 1973), p. 90.

121. Gerhard Adler and Aniela Jaffé, eds., *C. G. Jung Letters*, vol. 1, trans. R. F. C. Hull (Princeton: Princeton University Press, 1973), n. 1, p. 236.

122. Jung, "The Psychology of the Transference," *C.W.*, vol. 16, par. 400, p. 200.

123. Jung, "Psychotherapists or the Clergy," *C.W.*, vol. 11, par. 497, p. 330–31.

124. Jung, *Aion*, *C.W.*, vol. 9, pt. 2, par. 125, p. 70.

125. Viktor E. Frankl, *Man's Search for Meaning*, trans. Ilse Lasch (New York: Pocket Books, 1974), pp. 121–24.

126. Homans, op. cit., p. 183–84.

127. David Wulff, "Psychological Approaches," in Frank Whaling, ed., *Contemporary Approaches to the Study of Religion*, vol. 2 (Berlin: Mouton, 1985), p. 44.

128. G. S. Spinks, *Psychology and Religion: An Introduction to Contemporary Views* (London: Methuen, 1963), p. 100.

129. Raymond Hostie, *Religion and the Psychology of Jung*, trans. G. R. Lamb (London: Sheed and Ward, 1957), p. 160.

130. Jung, Psychological commentary on *The Tibetan Book of the Great Liberation*, *C.W.*, vol. 11, par. 771, p. 482.

131. Ibid., par. 759, p. 476.

132. Jung, "Psychology and Religion," *C.W.*, vol. 11, par. 2, p. 6.

133. Jung, Psychological commentary on *The Tibetan Book of the Great Liberation*, *C.W.*, vol. 11, par. 760, p. 476.

134. Goldbrunner, op. cit., pp. 171–72.

135. Smart, "The Scientific Study of Religion in Its Plurality," pp. 373–74.

Chapter II

1. Jung, "Instinct and the Unconscious," *C.W.*, vol. 8, pars. 273 and 280, pp. 135 and 137–38.

2. Ibid., par. 282, p. 138.

3. Ibid., pars. 268 and 276, pp. 132 and 137.

4. Anthony Stevens, *Archetype: A Natural History of the Self* (London: Routledge & Kegan Paul, 1982), pp. 48–49.

5. Jung, "Instinct and the Unconscious," *C.W.*, vol. 8, par. 270, p. 133.

6. Jung, "On the Nature of the Psyche," *C.W.*, vol. 8, par. 406, p. 206.

7. Ibid., par. 414, p. 212.

8. Ibid., par. 414, p. 211.

9. Ibid., pars. 414–15, pp. 211–12.

10. Jung, *Mysterium Coniunctionis*, *C.W.*, vol. 14, par. 742, p. 522.

11. Jung, "On the Nature of the Psyche," *C.W.*, vol. 8, par. 418, p. 215.

12. Jung, *Mysterium Coniunctionis*, *C.W.*, Vol. 14, par. 768, p. 538.

13, Fritjof Capra, *The Tao of Physics* (London: Fontana, 1977), p. 64.

14. Ibid., p. 67.

15. Ibid., p. 71.

16. Jung, "On the Nature of the Psyche," *C.W.*, vol. 8, par. 438, p. 229.

17. Capra, op. cit., p. 86.

18. Jung, "Synchronicity: An Acausal Connecting Principle," *C.W.*, vol. 8, par. 948, p. 506.

19. Ibid., par. 912, p. 481.

20. Adler and Jaffé, eds., *C. G. Jung Letters*, vol. 2, p. 398.

21. Jung, "Synchronicity: An Acausal Connecting Principle," *C.W.*, vol. 8, par. 964, p. 515.

22. Jung, "A Psychological View of Conscience," *C.W.*, vol. 10, par. 851, pp. 451–52.

23. Jung, "On the Nature of the Psyche," *C.W.*, vol. 8, par. 440, p. 231.

24. Jung, "A Psychological View of Conscience," *C.W.*, vol. 10, par. 852, p. 452.

25. Progoff, op. cit., p. 158.

26. Hannah, op. cit., p. 293.

27. Jung, *Memories, Dreams, Reflections*, p. 314.

28. Jung, "On Synchronicity," *C.W.*, vol. 8, pars. 984–85, p. 526.

29. Ibid., par. 986, p. 527.

30. Fordham, "An Interpretation of Jung's Thesis about Synchronicity," p. 210.

31. Jung, "Synchronicity: An Acausal Connecting Principle," *C.W.*, vol. 8, par. 850, p. 441.

32. Bolen, op. cit., p. 7.

33. Jung, *Memories, Dreams, Reflections*, pp. 315–16.

34. Adler and Jaffé, eds., *C. G. Jung Letters*, vol. 2, p. 289.

35. Jung, "On Synchronicity," *C.W.*, vol. 8, par. 982, pp. 525–26.

36. Jung, "Synchronicity: An Acausal Connecting Principle," *C.W.*, vol. 8, par. 845, p. 439.

37. Ibid., par. 843, p. 438.

38. Jung, *Memories, Dreams, Reflections*, p. 377.

39. Jung, "Synchronicity: An Acausal Connecting Principle," *C.W.*, vol. 8, par. 855, p. 444.

40. Jung, "On Synchronicity," *C.W.*, vol. 8, par. 995, p. 531.

41. Zavala, op. cit., p. 55.

42. Arthur Koestler, *The Roots of Coincidence* (London: Hutchinson & Co., 1972), p. 95.

43. Jung, "Synchronicity: An Acausal Connecting Principle," *C.W.*, vol. 8, par. 912, p. 481.

44. Jung, "On Synchronicity," *C.W.*, vol. 8, par. 969, p. 520.

45. Jung, "Synchronicity: An Acausal Connecting Principle," *C.W.*, vol. 8, par. 912, p. 481.

46. Jung, "On the Nature of the Psyche," *C.W.*, vol. 8, par. 440, p. 231.

47. Jung, *Mysterium Coniunctionis, C.W.*, vol. 14, par. 662, p. 464.

48. Jung, "On Synchronicity," *C.W.*, vol. 8, par. 995, p. 531.

49. Ibid.

50. Jung, "Synchronicity: An Acausal Connecting Principle," *C.W.*, vol. 8, par. 840, p. 435.

51. Ibid., par. 916, p. 485.

52. Jung, *Memories, Dreams, Reflections,* p. 305.

53. Jung, "Synchronicity: An Acausal Connecting Principle," *C.W.,* vol. 8, par. 967, p. 519.

54. Ibid., par. 855, pp. 445–46.

55. Antony Flew, "Coincidence and Synchronicity," *Journal of the Society for Psychical Research* 37, no. 677 (1953), pp. 198–99.

56. Rao, op. cit., p. 339.

57. Marie-Louise von Franz, *Projection and Re-Collection in Jungian Psychology: Reflections of the Soul,* trans. William H. Kennedy (LaSalle, Ill.: Open Court, 1980), p. 197.

58. Jung, "Synchronicity: An Acausal Connecting Principle," *C.W.,* vol. 8, par. 849, p. 441.

59. Adler and Jaffé, eds., *C. G. Jung Letters,* vol. 2, p. 495.

60. *The Secret of the Golden Flower,* p. 147.

61. Jung, *Memories, Dreams, Reflections,* p. 376.

62. Ibid., p. 376.

63. *The Secret of the Golden Flower,* p. 149.

64. Jung, *Memories, Dreams, Reflections,* p. 376.

65. Ibid., p. 377.

66. Jung, "On the Nature of the Psyche," *C.W.,* vol. 8, par. 405, pp. 205–6.

67. Jung, *Mysterium Coniunctionis, C.W.,* vol. 14, par. 745, p. 524.

68. Jung, "Synchronicity: An Acausal Connecting Principle," *C.W.,* vol. 8, par. 859, p. 448. The square brackets in this passage are Jung's. This quote is taken from Albertus Magnus, *De mirabilibus.* Incunabulum, undated, in the Zentralbibliothek, Zurich.

69. Ibid., par. 860, p. 449.

70. Ibid., par. 845, p. 439.

71. Jung, "On the Psychology of the Unconscious," *C.W.,* vol. 7, par. 130, p. 84.

72. Bender, op. cit., p. 67.

73. Fordham, "An Interpretation of Jung's Thesis about Synchronicity," p. 207.

74. Bolen, op. cit., pp. 37ff.

75. Jung, "Synchronicity: An Acausal Connecting Principle," *C.W.*, vol. 8, par. 942, pp. 501–2.

76. Ibid., par. 856, p. 447.

77. Ibid., par. 847, p. 440.

78. Ibid., par. 845, p. 439.

79. Ibid., par. 844, p. 438.

80. Ibid., par. 850, p. 442.

81. Hannah, op. cit., p. 202. See note K.

82. Ferne Jensen, ed., *C. G. Jung, Emma Jung and Toni Wolff: A Collection of Remembrances* (San Francisco: The Analytical Psychology Club of San Francisco, 1982), p. 21.

83. Progoff, op. cit., pp. 34–35.

84. Jaffé, *Apparitions: An Archetypal Approach to Death, Dreams and Ghosts,* p. 204.

85. Adler and Jaffé, eds., *C. G. Jung Letters,* vol. 2, p. 415.

86. Jensen, ed., op. cit., p. 21.

Chapter III

1. Ernest Jones, *Sigmund Freud: Life and Work,* vol. 2 (London: Hogarth Press, 1967), pp. 56–57. Jung and his wife, Emma, stayed in Vienna from March 25 to March 30, 1909.

2. Jung, *Memories, Dreams, Reflections,* pp. 155–56.

3. Ibid., p. 156.

4. Ibid., p. 149.

5. William McGuire, ed., *The Freud/Jung Letters,* trans. Ralph Manheim and R. F. C. Hull (London: Hogarth Press and Routledge & Kegan Paul, 1974), pp. 196–97.

6. Ellenberger, op. cit., p. 728. The text reads: "Jung never accepted Freud's ideas about the role of sexuality in neurosis, sexual symbolism, and the Oedipus complex."

7. McGuire, ed., op. cit., p. 217.

8. Jung, *Memories, Dreams, Reflections,* pp. 149–50.

9. Although Jung states in *Memories, Dreams, Reflections* that this conversation "took place some three years later (in 1910), again in Vienna" (p. 150), there is other evidence that suggests that this conversation actually took place in 1909. First, in *Memories, Dreams, Reflections* Jung, in reference to this conversation, states: "After that second conversation in Vienna" (p. 153). As indicated previously Jung's second visit to Vienna (see *The Freud/Jung Letters*, pp. 557–59) was from March 25 to March 30, 1909. (Jones, *Sigmund Freud: Life and Work*, vol. 2, pp. 56–57). Second, if this conversation did take place in Vienna, it must have occurred in 1909, simply because "there is no other evidence that Jung visited Freud in Vienna after 1909." (*The Freud/Jung Letters*, p. 216, n. 4).

10. Jung, *Memories, Dreams, Reflections*, pp. 150–51.

11. C. G. Jung, "On the Psychology and Pathology of So-called Occult Phenomena," *C.W.*, vol. 1, trans. R. F. C. Hull (Princeton: Princeton University Press, 1978), par. 136, p. 79.

12. McGuire, ed., op. cit., p. 217.

13. Ibid., p. 218. See n. 2.

14. *The Oxford English Dictionary* (Oxford University Press, 1961) defines "poltergeist" in the following manner: "[Ger. f. *polter* noise, uproar + *geist* ghost] A spirit which makes its presence known by noises; a noisy spirit".

15. McGuire, ed., op. cit., pp. 218–19.

16. Ibid., p. 220.

17. Joseph L. Henderson, "Ancient Myths and Modern Man," in C. G. Jung, ed., *Man and His Symbols* (Garden City, N.Y.: Doubleday, 1979), p. 149 and p. 151.

18. Jung, "On the Psychology of the Trickster-Figure," *C.W.*, vol. 9, pt. 1, par. 457, p. 256.

19. Jung, *Memories, Dreams, Reflections*, pp. 216–19.

20. This is the period Jung refers to as his "confrontation with the unconscious". See chapter 6, pp. 170–99, of *Memories, Dreams, Reflections*. Ellenberger refers to this period as Jung's "creative illness." See chapter 1 of this work, pp. 13–14.

21. McGuire, ed., op. cit., p. 246.

22. Ernest Jones, *Sigmund Freud: Life and Work*, vol. 3 (London: Hogarth Press, 1967), pp. 411–12.

23. McGuire, ed., op. cit., p. 255.

24. Jones, *Sigmund Freud: Life and Work*, vol. 3, pp. 412–14.

25. McGuire, ed., op. cit., p. 421.

26. Jones, *Sigmund Freud: Life and Work*, vol. 3, p. 415.

27. McGuire, ed., op. cit., p. 429.

28. Jones, *Sigmund Freud: Life and Work*, vol. 3, p. 425 and p. 429.

29. Ibid., p. 419.

30. Ernst L. Freud, ed., *Letters of Sigmund Freud 1873–1939*, trans. Tania and James Stern (London: Hogarth Press, 1961), pp. 339–40.

31. Sigmund Freud, "Psycho-analysis and Telepathy," *Standard Edition* (hereafter cited as *S.E.*), vol. 18, trans. James Strachey (London: Hogarth Press, 1964). See editor's note, pp. 175–76.

32. Jones, *Sigmund Freud: Life and Work*, vol. 3, p. 429 and p. 420.

33. Sigmund Freud, "Psycho-analysis and Telepathy," *S.E.*, vol. 18, p. 179.

34. Ibid., p. 180.

35. Ibid., p. 181.

36. This same case appears in two other papers: Sigmund Freud, "The Occult Significance of Dreams" (1925), *S.E.*, vol. 19, trans. James Strachey (London: Hogarth Press, 1964), pp. 135–38, and also in Sigmund Freud, "Dreams and Occultism" (1933), *S.E.*, vol. 22, trans. James Strachey (London: Hogarth Press, 1964), pp. 31–56.

37. Jones, *Sigmund Freud: Life and Work*, vol. 3, p. 414. Another case presented by Freud in this essay was also in his possession as early as November 22, 1910 (p. 413).

38. Sigmund Freud, "Psycho-analysis and Telepathy," *S.E.*, vol. 18, pp. 185–87.

39. Ibid., pp. 187–88.

40. Ibid., pp. 188–89.

41. Ibid., p. 189.

42. Sigmund Freud, "Dreams and Occultism," *S.E.*, vol. 22, p. 42.

43. Jones, *Sigmund Freud: Life and Work*, vol., 3, p. 420.

44. Sigmund Freud, "Dreams and Telepathy," *S.E.*, vol. 18, p. 197.

45. Ibid., p. 219.

46. Ibid.

47. Ibid., pp. 219–20.

48. Ibid., p. 199.

49. Ibid., pp. 200–201.

50. Ibid., pp. 205–6.

51. Ibid., p. 206.

52. Ibid., p. 207.

53. Jones, *Sigmund Freud: Life and Work*, vol. 3, p. 422. Also see Editor's Note to Sigmund Freud, "Psycho-analysis and Telepathy," *S.E.*, vol. 18, p. 176. With reference to the paper "The Occult Significance of Dreams," the editor writes: "This was apparently designed for inclusion in *The Interpretation of Dreams* and it was actually first printed as part of an appendix in Volume III of the *Gesammelte Schriften* edition of that work, but was not included in any of its later editions."

54. Sigmund Freud, "The Occult Significance of Dreams," *S.E.*, vol. 19, p. 136.

55. Ibid., p. 137.

56. Jones, *Sigmund Freud: Life and Work*, vol. 3, pp. 420–21.

57. Sigmund Freud, "The Occult Significance of Dreams," *S.E.*, vol. 19, p. 138.

58. Jones, *Sigmund Freud: Life and Work*, vol. 3, p. 422.

59. Ibid., p. 423.

60. Sigmund Freud, "Dreams and Occultism," *S.E.*, vol. 22, p. 33.

61. Ibid., pp. 54–55.

62. Ibid., p. 47.

63. Ibid., pp. 55–56.

64. Jung, "Synchronicity: An Acausal Connecting Principle," *C.W.*, vol. 8, par. 931, p. 493.

65. Ibid., par. 948, p. 506.

66. Lao Tzu, *Tao Te Ching*, pt. 47. The *Tao Te Ching* (the *Classic of the Way and its Virtue*) is generally attributed to the sixth-century B.C. Chinese philosopher Lao Tzu. See Wing-Tsit Chan, trans. and comp., *A Source Book in Chinese Philosophy* (Princeton: Princeton University Press, 1973), p. 137.

67. Jung, "Synchronicity: An Acausal Connecting Principle," *C.W.*, vol. 8, par. 923, p. 489.

68. Ibid., pars. 950–52, pp. 507–9.

69. Ibid., par. 995, pp. 509–10.

70. Jung, "On the Nature of Dreams," *C.W.*, vol. 8, par. 557, p. 292.

71. Jung, *Memories, Dreams, Reflections*, p. 289.

72. Ibid., pp. 290–91.

73. Ibid., p. 291.

74. Ibid.

75. Hannah, op. cit., p. 277. Hannah identifies Dr. H. as Dr. Theodor Haemmerli-Schindler, "perhaps the most famous heart specialist of his time . . . in Switzerland."

76. Jung, *Memories, Dreams, Reflections*, p. 292. Kos is the site of the medical school of the great fifth century B.C. physician Hippocrates. "Hippocrates," Hannah relates, "was the first Basileus of Kos (which came to mean prince of medicine). This title was then given to the greatest doctors, who were thought to be divinely appointed." Hannah, op. cit., n. e, p. 57.

77. Hannah, op. cit., p. 57.

78. Jung, *Memories, Dreams, Reflections*, p. 292.

79. Ibid.

80. Ibid.

81. Ibid., p. 293.

82. Ibid.

83. Hannah, op. cit., p. 277.

84. Jung, *Memories, Dreams, Reflections*, p. 297.

85. *With One Heart Bowing to the City of 10,000 Buddhas*, vols. 1–9 (San Francisco: Sino-American Buddhist Association, 1977–83) and Heng Sure and Heng Ch'au, *News from True Cultivators: Letters to the Venerable Abbot Hua*, vol. 1 (San Francisco: Sino-American Buddhist Association, 1983).

86. Heng Sure and Heng Ch'au, op. cit., p. 2.

87. Ibid., p. 111.

88. *With One Heart Bowing to the City of 10,000 Buddhas*, vol. 2, p. 242.

89. Ibid.

90. Ibid., p. 244.

91. Ibid., p. 245.

92. Ibid., pp. 244–45.

93. Sigmund Freud, "Dreams and Occultism," *S.E.*, vol. 22, p. 47.

94. Ibid., p. 48.

95. Jones, *Sigmund Freud: Life and Work*, vol. 3, p. 4.

96. Sigmund Freud, "Dreams and Occultism," *S.E.*, vol. 22, p. 53.

97. Ibid., p. 48.

98. Ibid., p. 51.

99. Ibid., p. 48.

100. Ibid., p. 49.

101. Ibid., pp. 49–50.

102. Ibid., p. 50.

103. Ibid., p. 51.

104. Ibid., pp. 51 and p. 54.

105. Ibid., p. 52.

106. Ibid., pp. 53–54.

107. Ibid., p. 52.

108. Jones, *Sigmund Freud: Life and Work*, vol. 3, p. 8.

109. Ernst L. Freud, op. cit., p. 330.

110. Sigmund Freud, "Dreams and Occultism," *S.E.*, vol. 22, p. 50.

111. Jones, *Sigmund Freud: Life and Work*, vol. 3, p. 435.

112. Ibid., p. 5

113. Ibid., p. 34.

114. Ibid., p. 19.

115. Ibid.

116. Ibid., p. 21.

117. Ibid., pp. 19–20.

118. Ibid., p. 94.

119. Ibid., pp. 233ff.

120. Ibid., p. 96.

121. Ibid., p. 242.

122. Ibid., p. 258.

123. Ibid., p. 242.

124. Ibid., p. 245.

125. Ibid., p. 239.

126. Ibid., p. 249.

127. Ibid., p. 260.

128. Ernst L. Freud, op. cit., p. 453.

129. Jones, *Sigmund Freud: Life and Work*, vol. 3, p. 435.

Chapter IV

1. Jung, *Mysterium Coniunctionis*, *C.W.*, vol. 14, par. 767, pp. 537–38.

2. Fung Yu-Lan, *A Short History of Chinese Philosophy*, ed. Derk Bodde (New York: Free Press, 1966), p. 8.

3. Ibid., p. 8.

4. *The Secret of the Golden Flower*, p. 11.

5. Wing-Tsit Chan, trans. and comp., *A Source Book in Chinese Philosophy* (Princeton: Princeton University Press, 1973), n. 1, p. 136.

6. *The Secret of the Golden Flower*, p. 11.

7. Ibid., p. 12.

8. Ibid., p. 11.

9. Nathan Sivin, *Chinese Alchemy: Preliminary Studies* (Cambridge: Harvard University Press, 1968), pp. 5–6.

10. Joseph Needham, *Science and Civilisation in China*, vol. 2 (Cambridge: Cambridge University Press, 1956), p. 281.

11. Ibid., p. 289.

12. Ibid., pp. 290–91. This idea is taken from the writings of Marcel Granet, *La Pensée Chinoise* (Paris: Albin Michel, 1934).

13. Adler and Jaffé, eds., *C. G. Jung Letters*, vol. 1, p. 395.

14. Jung, "On the Nature of Dreams," *C.W.*, vol. 8, par. 554, p. 290.

15. Erich Neumann, "The Psyche and the Transformation of the Reality Planes," trans. Hildegard Nagel, *Spring* (1956), pp. 81–111.

16. Ibid., p. 101.

17. Jung, "Synchronicity: An Acausal Connecting Principle," *C.W.*, vol. 8, par. 924, p. 489. This idea is taken from Granet, *La Pensée Chinoise.*

18. Needham, op. cit., pp. 280–81.

19. Franz, *On Divination and Synchronicity*, p. 8.

20. William McGuire and R. F. C. Hull, eds., *C. G. Jung Speaking: Interviews and Encounters* (London: Pan Books, 1980), p. 241.

21. Jung, *Memories, Dreams, Reflections*, pp. 122–23.

22. Ibid., p. 123.

23. Edward F. Edinger, *Ego and Archetype* (Baltimore, Md.: Penguin Books, 1974), p. 93.

24. Holmes Welch, *The Practice of Chinese Buddhism 1900–1950* (Cambridge: Harvard University Press, 1973), Glossary Index, p. 545. The quotations from Hsu Yun's autobiography, *Hsu-yun ho-shang nien-p'u*, that appear in this work are taken from *The Practice of Chinese Buddhism 1900–1950*. An English translation of Hsu Yun's autobiography is published in *World Buddhism*, vol. 11, no. 12 (July 1963) through vol. 14, no. 4 (November 1965), under the title "The Story of Ch'an Master Hsu Yun—From Master Hsu Yun's Autobiography," trans. Upasaka Lu K'uan Yu (Charles Luk).

25. John Blofeld, *The Wheel of Life: The Autobiography of a Western Buddhist* (London: Rider and Company, 1972), pp. 74–75.

26. The publisher's note on the cover page of Lu K'uan Yu [Charles Luk], ed., trans. *Ch'an and Zen Teaching* (Berkeley: Shambhala, 1970) reads: "The book C. G. Jung was reading on his deathbed was Charles Luk's *Ch'an and Zen Teaching: First Series*, and he expressly asked his secretary to write to tell the author that 'He was enthusiastic. . . . When he read what Hsu Yun said, he sometimes felt as if he himself could have said exactly this! It was just *it!*' Unpublished letter from Dr. Marie-Louise von Franz to Charles Luk dated September 12, 1961."

27. Welch, op. cit., pp. 82–83.

28. Ibid., p. 83. Suzuki presents the following analogous image of enlightenment: "When a Master was asked what Buddhahood consisted in, he answered, 'The bottom of a pail is broken through.' " (D. T. Suzuki, *Essays in Zen Buddhism*, First Series [London: Rider & Company, 1949], p. 229).

29. Needham, op. cit., p. 286.

30. *The Secret of the Golden Flower*, p. 141.

31. *The I Ching or Book of Changes*, trans., Richard Wilhelm, trans. from the German by Cary F. Baynes, foreword by C. G. Jung (Princeton: Princeton University Press, 1977).

32. *The Secret of the Golden Flower*, p. 143.

33. *The I Ching or Book of Changes*, p. lix. Wilhelm states: "According to general tradition . . . the present collection of sixty-four hexagrams orig-

inated with King Wen, progenitor of the Chou dynasty [1150–249 B.C.]. . . .
The text pertaining to the individual lines originated with his son, the Duke
of Chou. This form of the book, entitled the Changes of Chou (*Chou I*), was
in use as an oracle throughout the Chou period, as can be proven from a
number of the ancient historical records."

34. Ibid., p. xlvii.

35. Ibid., p. lvi.

36. Ibid., p. liv.

37. Ibid., pp. 721–24. Alternative methods to the two mentioned here
for consulting the *I Ching* are found in Kwok Man Ho, Martin Palmer, and
Joanne O'Brien, *The Fortune Teller's I Ching* (London: Guild, 1986).

38. Ibid., p. liv.

39. Adler and Jaffé, eds., *C. G. Jung Letters*, vol. 1, p. 155.

40. Jung, *Memories, Dreams, Reflections*, pp. 373–75.

41. Ibid., p. 374.

42. *The Ching or Book of Changes*, p. xxix.

43. Fordham, *New Developments in Analytical Psychology*, p. 49.

44. Adler and Jaffé, eds., *C. G. Jung Letters*, vol. 2, p. 344.

45. Jung, *Memories, Dreams, Reflections*, p. 374.

46. Hannah, op. cit., pp. 165ff.

47. Progoff, op. cit., pp. 21–45.

48. *The I Ching or Book of Changes*, p. xxi.

49. Fordham, *New Developments in Analytical Psychology*, p. 49.

50. *The I Ching or Book of Changes*, pp. xxiv–xxv.

51. Ibid., p. xxv.

52. Franz, *On Divination and Synchronicity*, pp. 8–9.

53. Adler and Jaffé, eds., *C. G. Jung Letters*, vol. 2, p. 584.

54. Welch, op. cit., p. 169.

55. Ibid., p. 155.

56. Ibid., p. 169.

57. Ibid.

58. Ibid., pp. 169–70.

59. Ibid., pp. 155–56.

60. Ibid., p. 170.

61. *The I Ching or Book of Changes,* p. liv.

62. Ibid., p. xxxv.

63. Franz, *Number and Time,* p. 6.

64. *The I Ching or Book of Changes,* pp. lvii–lviii.

65. Ibid., p. 28.

66. Ibid., pp. 28–29.

67. Ibid., n. 9, p. 8.

68. Ibid., p. 37.

69. Ibid., p. 39.

70. Adler and Jaffé, eds., *C. G. Jung Letters,* vol. 2, p. 595. In prefacing this statement, Jung writes the following: "But whoever is capable of such insight, no matter how isolated he is, should be aware of the law of synchronicity. As the old Chinese saying goes: 'The right man sitting in his house and thinking the right thought will be heard a 100 miles away.' " The accompanying editorial note 4 reads: "Cf. *I Ching* (3rd edn., 1967), p. 305: 'The Master said: The superior man abides in his room. If his words are well spoken, he meets with assent at a distance of more than a thousand miles.' "

71. *The I Ching or Book of Changes,* pp. 198–99.

72. Ibid., p. 199.

73. Adler and Jaffé, eds., *C. G. Jung Letters,* vol. 1, pp. 139–40.

74. Ibid., p. 201.

75. Jaffé, ed., *C. G. Jung: Word and Image,* pp. 34–35.

76. Hannah, op. cit., p. 236.

77. *The I Ching or Book of Changes,* p. liii.

78. Adler and Jaffé, eds., *C. G. Jung Letters,* vol. 2, pp. 161–62.

79. Bolen, op. cit., pp. 45–46.

80. Ibid., p. 46.

81. Jung, *Memories, Dreams, Reflections,* p. 191.

82. Ibid., p. 190.

83. Ibid., pp. 190–91.

84. Ibid., p. 191.

85. Ibid., pp. 378ff.

86. Ibid., p. 192.

87. Hannah, op. cit., p. 121.

88. McGuire and Hull, eds., op. cit., p. 242.

89. Jung, "Answer to Job," C. W., vol. 11, par. 648, p. 409.

Chapter V

1. Franz, *Alchemy*, p. 95.

2. Jung, "Problems of Modern Psychotherapy," C.W., vol. 16, par. 163, pp. 71–72.

3. Jung, *Memories, Dreams, Reflections*, pp. 137–38. Certain details of this case correspond with a case presented by Jung in "Synchronicity: An Acausal Connecting Principle," C.W., vol. 8, par. 852, pp. 442–43 and par. 857, p. 447.

4. Bolen, op. cit., p. 34.

5. Eliade, op. cit., p. 383.

6. Jung, *Memories, Dreams, Reflections*, p. 137.

7. McGuire and Hull, eds., op. cit., p. 91.

8. Dourley, op. cit., pp. 24–25.

9. Jung, "Introduction to the Religious and Psychological Problems of Alchemy," C.W., vol. 12, trans. R. F. C. Hull (Princeton: Princeton University Press, 1977), par. 15, p. 14.

10. Heisig, op. cit., p. 75, and n. 33, p. 180.

11. Bender, op. cit., p. 80.

12. Rao, op. cit., p. 340.

13. Jung, "Synchronicity: An Acausal Connecting Principle," C.W., vol. 8, par. 915, p. 482.

14. Jung, "On Synchronicity," C.W., vol. 8, par. 974, p. 522.

15. M. Esther Harding, *The "I" and the "Not-I": A Study in the Development of Consciousness* (London: Conventure, 1977), p. 45.

16. Marie-Louise von Franz, "Meaning and Order: Concerning Meeting Points and Differences between Depth Psychology and Physics," in Renos K. Papadopoulos and Graham S. Saayman, eds., *Jung in Modern Perspective* (Hounslow, Middlesex: Wildwood House, 1984), p. 272.

17. Marion Woodman, *Addiction to Perfection: The Still Unravished Bride* (Toronto: Inner City Books, 1982), p. 154.

18. Adler and Jaffé, eds., *C. G. Jung Letters*, vol. 1, p. 433.

19. Jung, *Mysterium Coniunctionis*, C.W., vol. 14, par. 662, p. 464.

20. Marie-Louise von Franz, *C. G. Jung: His Myth in Our Time*, trans. William H. Kennedy (London: Hodder and Stoughton, 1975), p. 247.

21. James Hillman, "Psychology: Monotheistic or Polytheistic," *Spring* (1971), p. 193.

22. Ibid., p. 197.

23. Ibid., p. 200.

24. Ibid., p. 202.

25. Michael Fordham, "Responses and Discussion" to James Hillman, "Psychology: Monotheistic or Polytheistic," *Spring* (1971), p. 212.

26. James Hillman, "Appendix: 'Psychology: Monotheistic or Polytheistic,' " in David L. Miller, *The New Polytheism: Rebirth of the Gods and Goddesses* (Dallas, Tex.: Spring, 1981), p. 135.

27. Gerhard Adler, "Responses and Discussion" to James Hillman, "Psychology: Monotheistic or Polytheistic," *Spring* (1971), p. 209.

28. J. Marvin Spiegelman, "Responses and Discussion" to James Hillman, "Psychology: Monotheistic or Polytheistic," *Spring* (1971), p. 221.

29. James Olney, *The Rhizome and the Flower: The Perennial Philosophy—Yeats and Jung* (Berkeley: University of California Press, 1980), p. 122.

30. Martin Buber, *Eclipse of God: Studies in the Relation between Religion and Philosophy* (New York: Harper & Row, 1957), p. 79.

31. Jung, "Religion and Psychology: A Reply to Martin Buber," C.W., vol. 18, par. 1504, p. 665.

32. Buber, op. cit., p. 80.

33. John W. de Gruchy, "Jung and Religion: A Theological Assessment," in Papadopoulos and Saayman, eds., op. cit., p. 202.

34. White, op. cit., p. 71.

35. Gebhard Frei, "Appendix: On Analytical Psychology—'The Method and Teaching of C. G. Jung,' " in White, op. cit., p. 248.

36. Heisig, op. cit., n. 151, p. 176.

37. Gerhard Adler, *Studies in Analytical Psychology* (London: Hodder and Stoughton, 1966), p. 191.

38. Franz, *Alchemy*, p. 139.

39. Hannah, op. cit., p. 124.

40. Jung, *Aion*, C.W., vol. 9, pt. 2, par. 257, pp. 167–68.

41. Sarvepalli Radhakrishnan and Charles A. Moore, eds., *A Source Book in Indian Philosophy* (Princeton: Princeton University Press, 1973), p. 38.

42. McGuire and Hull, eds., op. cit., p. 375.

43. Jung, *Memories, Dreams, and Reflections*, p. 4.

44. Olney, op. cit., pp. 52–53.

45. Edinger, op. cit., p. 96.

46. Jung, "The Relations between the Ego and the Unconscious," C.W., vol. 7, par. 329, p. 206.

47. Jung, "General Aspects of Dream Psychology," C.W., vol. 8, pars. 507–8, pp. 265–66.

48. Neumann, "The Psyche and the Transformation of the Reality Planes," pp. 86–87.

49. Edward Whitmont, "The Magic Level of the Unconscious," *Spring* (1956), p. 58.

50. Franz, *Projection and Re-Collection in Jungian Psychology*, pp. 196–97.

51. Adler and Jaffé, eds., *C. G. Jung Letters*, vol. 2, p. 409.

52. Franz, *C. G. Jung: His Myth in Our Time*, p. 252.

53. Ibid., pp. 250–51.

54. Jung, *Memories, Dreams, Reflections*, p. 297.

55. Ibid., p. 192.

56. Erich Neumann, *Depth Psychology and a New Ethic*, trans. Eugene Rolfe, foreword by C. G. Jung (New York: G. P. Putnam's Sons, 1969), p. 15.

57. Ibid., p. 91.

58. Ibid., p. 95.

59. Ibid. Neumann speaks of the "psychology of the scapegoat."

60. Woodman, op. cit., p. 152.

61. Ibid., pp. 152–53.

62. Ibid., p. 153.

63. Ibid.

64. Ibid., p. 154.

65. Ibid.

66. Ibid., p. 155.

67. Ibid.

68. Homans, op. cit., p. 200.

69. Hannah, op. cit., p. 295.

70. Homans, op. cit., p. 201.

71. Sigmund Freud, *The Interpretation of Dreams (Second Part)*, S.E., vol. 5, trans. James Strachey (London: Hogarth Press, 1964), p. 608.

72. Bolen, op. cit., p. 49.

73. Ibid., pp. 52–53.

74. Franz, *Projection and Re-Collection in Jungian Psychology*, p. 177.

75. Neumann, *Depth Psychology and a New Ethic*, pp. 30–31.

76. Eliade, op. cit., p. 508.

77. Jung, *Memories, Dreams, Reflections*, p. 175.

78. Ibid., pp. 175–76.

79. Ibid., p. 176.

80. Ibid.

81. In her biography of Jung, Hannah confirms the fact that Jung was in Scotland when the First World War began. The text reads: "One can imagine how little Jung had expected to be cut off in Scotland from his home by the outbreak of war. . . . One evening after supper in his Tower at Bollingen—he was well over eighty at the time—something must have reminded him of that adventurous journey home . . . [as] he described it in detail." Hannah, op. cit., p. 111.

82. In *Memories, Dreams, Reflections*, Jung cites August 1, 1914, as the start of the First World War (p. 176). The actual date was July 28, 1914. (C. L. Mowat, ed., *The New Cambridge Modern History*, vol. 12 [Cambridge: Cambridge University Press, 1968], p. 171.)

83. Jung, *Memories, Dreams, Reflections*, p. 176.

84. Franz, *C. G. Jung: His Myth in Our Time*, p. 106.

85. Ross Woodman, "Shaman, Poet, and Failed Initiate: Reflections on Romanticism and Jungian Psychology," *Studies in Romanticism* 19 (1980), p. 51.

86. Franz, *Number and Time*, p. 282.

87. Ibid., pp. 281–82.

88. Ibid., p. 283.

89. Ibid., p. 282.

90. Ibid., p. 283.

91. Ibid.

92. Ibid., n. 50, p. 283.

93. Adler and Jaffé, eds., *C. G. Jung Letters*, vol. 2, p. 595.

94. Hannah, op. cit., p. 128.

95. Franz, *C. G. Jung: His Myth in Our Time*, p. 263.

96. Jensen, op. cit., p. 109.

97. Olney, op. cit., p. 192.

98. Ibid., p. 193.

99. Jung, *Symbols of Transformation*, C.W., vol. 5, p. xxiv.

100. Edinger, op. cit., p. 149.

101. Jung, *Symbols of Transformation*, C.W., vol. 5, p. xxv.

102. Adler and Jaffé, eds., *C. G. Jung Letters*, vol. 2, p. 596.

103. Jaffé, ed., *C. G. Jung: Word and Image*, p. 155.

104. Jung, *Memories, Dreams, Reflections*, p. 252.

105. Ibid.

106. Ibid.

107. Ibid., p. 253.

108. Jung, "Synchronicity: An Acausal Connecting Principle," C.W., vol. 8, par. 966, p. 518.

109. Hannah, op. cit., p. 161.

110. Ibid., p. 128.

111. Adler and Jaffé, eds., *C. G. Jung Letters*, vol. 2, pp. 596–97.

112. Dourley, op. cit., p. 34.

Conclusion

1. Adler and Jaffé, eds., *C. G. Jung Letters*, vol. 1, p. 190.

2. Jung, "Synchronicity: An Acausal Connecting Principle," *C.W.*, vol. 8, par. 843, p. 438.

3. Jung, "On Synchronicity," *C.W.*, vol. 8, par. 983, p. 526.

4. Franz, *C. G. Jung: His Myth in Our Time*, p. 13.

Bibliography

Books and Articles by C. G. Jung

Jung, C. G. *Aion, Collected Works*, Vol. 9, pt. 2. Trans. R. F. C. Hull. Princeton: Princeton University Press, 1978.

———. "Answer to Job." In *Collected Works*, Vol. 11. Trans. R. F. C. Hull. Princeton: Princeton University Press, 1977.

———. *Dream Analysis: Notes of the Seminar Given in 1928–1930 by C. G. Jung*. Edited by William McGuire. London: Routledge & Kegan Paul, 1984.

———. Foreword to Suzuki's *Introduction to Zen Buddhism*. In *Collected Works*, Vol. 11.

———. Foreword to White's *God and the Unconscious*. In *Collected Works*, Vol. 11.

———. "Fundamental Questions of Psychotherapy." In *Collected Works*, Vol. 16. Trans. R. F. C. Hull. Princeton: Princeton University Press, 1977.

———. "General Aspects of Dream Psychology." In *Collected Works*, Vol. 8. Trans. R. F. C. Hull. Princeton: Princeton University Press, 1978.

———. "Instinct and the Unconscious." In *Collected Works*, Vol. 8.

———. Introduction to Wolff's *Studies in Jungian Psychology*. In *Collected Works*, Vol. 10. Trans. R. F. C. Hull. Princeton: Princeton University Press, 1978.

———. "Introduction to the Religious and Psychological Problems of Alchemy." In *Collected Works*, Vol. 12. Trans. R. F. C. Hull. Princeton: Princeton University Press, 1977.

——— . *Memories, Dreams, Reflections.* Recorded and edited by Aniela Jaffé. Trans. Richard and Clara Winston. New York: Vintage Books, 1965.

——— . *Mysterium Coniunctionis.* In *Collected Works,* Vol. 14. Trans. R. F. C. Hull. Princeton: Princeton University Press, 1976.

——— . "On Psychic Energy." In *Collected Works,* Vol. 8.

——— . "On Synchronicity." In *Collected Works,* Vol. 8.

——— . "On the Nature of Dreams." In *Collected Works,* Vol. 8.

——— . "On the Nature of the Psyche." In *Collected Works,* Vol. 8.

——— . "On the Psychology and Pathology of So-called Occult Phenomena." In *Collected Works,* Vol. 1. Trans. R. F. C. Hull. Princeton: Princeton University Press, 1978.

——— . "On the Psychology of the Trickster-Figure." In *Collected Works,* Vol. 9, pt. 1. Trans. R. F. C. Hull. Princeton: Princeton University Press, 1977.

——— . "On the Psychology of the Unconscious." In *Collected Works,* Vol. 7. Trans. R. F. C. Hull. Princeton: Princeton University Press, 1977.

——— . Prefaces to *Collected Papers on Analytical Psychology.* In *Collected Works,* Vol. 4. Trans. R. F. C. Hull. Princeton: Princeton University Press, 1979.

——— . "Problems of Modern Psychotherapy." In *Collected Works,* Vol. 16.

——— . "A Psychological Approach to the Dogma of the Trinity." In *Collected Works,* Vol. 11.

——— . "Psychological Aspects of the Mother Archetype." In *Collected Works,* Vol. 9, pt. 1.

——— . Psychological commentary on *The Tibetan Book of the Great Liberation.* In *Collected Works,* Vol. 11.

——— . "A Psychological View of Conscience." In *Collected Works,* Vol. 10.

——— . "Psychology and Religion." In *Collected Works,* Vol. 11.

—————. *Psychology and Religion.* New Haven: Yale University Press, 1978.

—————. "The Psychology of the Transference." In *Collected Works,* Vol. 16.

—————. "Psychotherapists or the Clergy." In *Collected Works,* Vol. 11.

—————. "The Relations between the Ego and the Unconscious." In *Collected Works,* Vol. 7.

—————. "Religion and Psychology: A Reply to Martin Buber." In *Collected Works,* Vol. 18. Trans. R. F. C. Hull. Princeton: Princeton University Press, 1976.

—————. "The Structure of the Psyche." In *Collected Works,* Vol. 8.

—————. "A Study in the Process of Individuation." In *Collected Works,* Vol. 9, pt. 1.

—————. "Symbols and the Interpretation of Dreams." In *Collected Works,* Vol. 18.

—————. *Symbols of Transformation.* In *Collected Works,* Vol. 5. Trans. R. F. C. Hull. Princeton: Princeton University Press, 1976.

—————. "Synchronicity: An Acausal Connecting Principle." In *Collected Works,* Vol. 8.

—————. "The Tavistock Lectures." In *Collected Works,* Vol. 18.

—————. "The Transcendent Function." In *Collected Works,* Vol. 8.

—————. "Transformation Symbolism in the Mass." In *Collected Works,* Vol. 11.

—————. "The Undiscovered Self (Present and Future)." In *Collected Works,* Vol. 10.

—————, ed. *Man and His Symbols.* Garden City, N.Y.: Doubleday, 1979.

Other Books

Adler, Gerhard. *Studies in Analytical Psychology.* London: Hodder and Stoughton, 1966.

Adler, Gerhard, and Aniela Jaffé, eds. *C. G. Jung Letters.* 2 vols. Trans. R. F. C. Hull. Princeton: Princeton University Press, 1975.

Blake, William. "To God," in Richard Wilbur, ed., *Blake.* New York: Dell, 1973.

Blofeld, John. *The Wheel of Life: The Autobiography of a Western Buddhist.* London: Rider and Company, 1972.

Bolen, Jean Shinoda. *The Tao of Psychology: Synchronicity and the Self.* San Francisco: Harper & Row, 1979.

Buber, Martin. *Eclipse of God: Studies in the Relation between Religion and Philosophy.* New York: Harper & Row, 1957.

Capps, Donald, Lewis Rambo, and Paul Ransohoff, eds. *Psychology of Religion: A Guide to Information Sources.* Detroit: Gale Research Company, 1976.

Capra, Fritjof. *The Tao of Physics.* London: Fontana, 1977.

Coward, Harold. *Jung and Eastern Thought.* Albany: State University of New York Press, 1985.

Dourley, John P. *C. G. Jung and Paul Tillich: The Psyche as Sacrament.* Toronto: Inner City Books, 1981.

Edinger, Edward F. *Ego and Archetype.* Baltimore, Md.: Penguin Books, 1974.

Eliade, Mircea. *Shamanism: Archaic Techniques of Ecstasy.* Trans. Willard R. Trask. Princeton: Princeton University Press, 1964.

Ellenberger, Henri F. *The Discovery of the Unconscious.* New York: Basic Books, 1970.

Fordham, Michael. *New Developments in Analytical Psychology.* London: Routledge & Kegan Paul, 1957.

Frankl, Viktor. E. *Man's Search for Meaning.* Trans. Ilse Lasch. New York: Pocket Books, 1974.

Franz, Marie-Louise von. *Alchemy: An Introduction to the Symbolism and the Psychology.* Toronto: Inner City Books, 1980.

———. *C. G. Jung: His Myth in Our Time.* Trans. William H. Kennedy. London: Hodder and Stoughton, 1975.

———. *Number and Time: Reflections Leading towards a Unification of Psychology and Physics.* Trans. Adrea Dykes. London: Rider & Company, 1974.

———. *On Divination and Synchronicity: The Psychology of Meaningful Chance.* Toronto: Inner City Books, 1980.

———. *Projection and Re-Collection in Jungian Psychology: Reflections of the Soul.* Trans. William H. Kennedy. Lasalle, Ill.: Open Court, 1980.

Freud, Ernst L., ed. *Letters of Sigmund Freud 1873–1939.* Trans. Tania and James Stern. London: Hogarth Press, 1961.

Freud, Sigmund. *The Future of an Illusion.* In *The International Psycho-Analytical Library,* No. 15. Trans. W. D. Robson-Scott. London: Hogarth Press, 1978.

———. *The Interpretation of Dreams (Second Part),* In *Standard Edition,* Vol. 5. Trans. James Strachey. London: Hogarth Press, 1964.

———. *Totem and Taboo.* In *Standard Edition,* Vol. 13. Trans. James Strachey. London: Hogarth Press, 1964.

Fung Yu-Lan. *A Short History of Chinese Philosophy.* Edited by Derk Bodde. New York: Free Press, 1966.

Goldbrunner, Josef. *Individuation: A Study of the Depth Psychology of Carl Gustav Jung.* Notre Dame: University of Notre Dame Press, 1966.

Hannah, Barbara. *Jung: His Life and Work.* London: Michael Joseph, 1977.

Harding, M. Esther. *The "I" and the "Not-I": A Study in the Development of Consciousness.* London: Conventure, 1977.

Heisig, James W. *Imago Dei: A Study of C. G. Jung's Psychology of Religion.* Lewisburg, Pa.: Bucknell University Press, 1979.

Heng Sure and Heng Ch'au. *News from True Cultivators: Letters to the Venerable Abbot Hua.* Vol. 1. San Francisco: Sino-American Buddhist Association, 1983.

Homans, Peter. *Jung in Context.* Chicago: The University of Chicago Press, 1979.

Hostie, Raymond. *Religion and the Psychology of Jung.* Trans. G. R. Lamb. London: Sheed and Ward, 1957.

The I Ching or Book of Changes. Trans. Richard Wilhelm; Trans. from the German by Cary F. Baynes. Foreword by C. G. Jung. Princeton: Princeton University Press, 1977.

Jaffé, Aniela. *Apparitions: An Archetypal Approach to Death, Dreams and Ghosts.* Irving, Tex.: Spring, 1978.

———. *From the Life and Work of C. G. Jung.* Trans. R. F. C. Hull. New York: Harper & Row, 1971.

———., ed. *C. G. Jung: Word and Image.* Trans. Krishna Winston. Princeton: Princeton University Press, 1979.

Jensen, Ferne., ed. *C. G. Jung, Emma Jung and Toni Wolff: A Collection of Remembrances.* San Francisco: The Analytical Psychology Club of San Francisco, 1982.

Jones, Ernest. *Sigmund Freud: Life and Work,* Vols. 2 & 3. London: Hogarth Press, 1967.

Koestler, Arthur. *The Roots of Coincidence.* London: Hutchinson & Co., 1972.

Kwok Man Ho, Martin Palmer, and Joanne O'Brien. *The Fortune-Teller's I Ching.* London: Guild Publishing, 1986.

Lu K'uan Yu [Charles Luk], ed., trans. *Ch'an and Zen Teaching.* Berkeley: Shambhala, 1970.

McGuire, William, ed. *The Freud/Jung Letters.* Trans. Ralph Manheim and R. F. C. Hull. London: Hogarth Press and Routledge & Kegan Paul, 1974.

McGuire, William, and R. F. C. Hull, eds. *C. G. Jung Speaking: Interviews and Encounters.* London: Pan Books, 1980.

Mowat, C. L., ed. *The New Cambridge Modern History.* Vol. 12. Cambridge: Cambridge University Press, 1968.

Needham, Joseph. *Science and Civilisation in China.* Vol. 2. Cambridge: Cambridge University Press, 1956.

Neumann, Erich. *Depth Psychology and a New Ethic.* Trans. Eugene Rolfe. Foreword by C. G. Jung. New York: G. P. Putnam's Sons, 1969.

Odajnyk, Volodymyr Walter. *Jung and Politics: The Political and Social Ideas of C. G. Jung.* New York: Harper & Row, 1976.

Olney, James. *The Rhizome and the Flower: The Perennial Philosophy—Yeats and Jung.* Berkeley: University of California Press, 1980.

Progoff, Ira. *Jung, Synchronicity, and Human Destiny.* New York: Dell, 1973.

Radhakrishnan, Sarvepalli, and Charles A. Moore, eds. *A Source Book in Indian Philosophy.* Princeton: Princeton University Press, 1973.

The Secret of the Golden Flower. Trans. Richard Wilhelm. Trans. from the German by Cary F. Baynes. Commentary by C. G. Jung. New York: Harcourt, Brace & World, 1962.

Sivin, Nathan. *Chinese Alchemy: Preliminary Studies.* Cambridge: Harvard University Press, 1968.

Smart, Ninian. *Concept and Empathy: Essays in the Study of Religion.* Edited by Donald Wiebe. London: Macmillan Press, 1986.

———. *The Religious Experience of Mankind.* New York: Scribner, 1969.

———. *Worldviews: Crosscultural Explorations of Human Beliefs.* New York: Charles Scribner's Sons, 1983.

Spinks, G. S. *Psychology and Religion: An Introduction to Contemporary Views.* London: Methuen, 1963.

Stevens, Anthony. *Archetype: A Natural History of the Self.* London: Routledge & Kegan Paul, 1982.

Suzuki, D. T. *Essays in Zen Buddhism.* First series. London: Rider & Company, 1949.

Welch, Holmes. *The Practice of Chinese Buddhism 1900–1950.* Cambridge: Harvard University Press, 1973.

White, Victor. *God and the Unconscious.* London: Harvill Press, 1953.

Wing-Tsit Chan, trans. and comp. *A Source Book in Chinese Philosophy.* Princeton: Princeton University Press, 1973.

With One Heart Bowing to the City of 10,000 Buddhas. Vols. 1–9. San Francisco: Sino-American Buddhist Association, 1977–83.

Woodman, Marion. *Addiction to Perfection: The Still Unravished Bride.* Toronto: Inner City Books, 1982.

Other Articles and Parts of Books

Bender, Hans. "Meaningful Coincidences in Light of the Jung-Pauli Theory of Synchronicity and Parapsychology." In Betty Shapin and Lisette Coly, eds., *The Philosophy of Parapsychology.* New York: Parapsychology Foundation, 1976.

Capps, Donald. "Contemporary Psychology of Religion: The Task of Theoretical Reconstruction." *Social Research* 41 (1974), pp. 362–83.

de Gruchy, John W. "Jung and Religion: A Theological Assessment." In Reno K. Papadopoulos and Graham S. Saayman, eds., *Jung in Modern Perspective.* Hounslow, Middlesex: Wildwood House, 1984.

Flew, Antony. "Coincidence and Synchronicity." *Journal of the Society for Psychical Research* 37, no. 677 (1953), pp. 198–201.

Fordham, Michael. "An Interpretation of Jung's Thesis about Synchronicity." *British Journal of Medical Psychology.* 35 (1962), pp. 205–10.

Franz, Marie-Louise von. "Meaning and Order: Concerning Meeting Points and Differences between Depth Psychology and Physics." In Renos K. Papadopoulos and Graham S. Saayman, eds., *Jung in Modern Perspective.* Hounslow, Middlesex: Wildwood House, 1984.

Frei, Gebhard. "Appendix: On Analytical Psychology— 'The Method and Teaching of C. G. Jung.' " In Victor White, *God and the Unconscious.* London: Harvill Press, 1953.

Freud, Sigmund. "Dreams and Occultism." In *Standard Edition*, Vol. 22. Trans. James Strachey. London: Hogarth Press, 1964.

———. "Dreams and Telepathy." In *Standard Edition*, Vol. 18. Trans. James Strachey. London: Hogarth Press, 1964.

———. "The Occult Significance of Dreams." In *Standard Edition*, Vol. 19. Trans. James Strachey. London: Hogarth Press, 1964.

———. "Psycho-analysis and Telepathy." In *Standard Edition*, Vol. 18.

Gammon, Mary R. " 'Window into Eternity': Archetype and Relativity." *Journal of Analytical Psychology* 18, no. 1 (1973), pp. 11–24.

Gatlin, Lila L. "Meaningful Information Creation: An Alternative Interpretation of Psi Phenomenon." *The Journal of the American Society for Psychical Research* 71, no. 1 (1977), pp. 1–17.

Henderson, Joseph L. "Ancient Myths and Modern Man." In C. G. Jung, ed., *Man and His Symbols.* Garden City, N.Y.: Doubleday, 1979.

Hillman, James. "Appendix: 'Psychology: Monotheistic or Polytheistic.' " In David L. Miller, *The New Polytheism: Rebirth of the Gods and Goddesses.* Dallas, Tex.: Spring, 1981.

――――. "Psychology: Monotheistic or Polytheistic." *Spring* (1971), pp. 193–208.

Jahoda, Gustav. "Jung's 'Meaningful Coincidences.' " *The Philosophical Journal* 4, no. 1 (1967), pp. 35–42.

Keutzer, Carolin S. "Archetypes, Synchronicity and the Theory of Formative Causation." *Journal of Analytical Psychology* 24 (1982), pp. 255–62.

――――. "The Power of Meaning: From Quantum Mechanics to Synchronicity." *Journal of Humanistic Psychology* 24, no. 1 (1984), pp. 80–94.

――――. "Synchronicity in Psychotherapy." *Journal of Analytical Psychology* 29 (1984), pp. 373–81.

McCully, Robert S. "The Rorschach, Synchronicity, and Relativity." In Robert William Davis, ed., *Toward a Discovery of the Person.* Burbank, Calif.: The Society for Personality Assessment, 1974.

Meier, C. A. "Psychosomatic Medicine from the Jungian Point of View." *Journal of Analytical Psychology* 8, no. 2 (1963), pp. 103–21.

Neumann, Erich. "The Psyche and the Transformation of the Reality Planes." Trans. Hildegard Nagel. *Spring* (1956), pp. 81–111.

Rao, K. Ramakrishna. "On the Nature of PSI: An Examination of Some Attempts to Explain ESP and PK." *Journal of Parapsychology* 41 (1977), pp. 294–351.

"Responses and Discussion" to James Hillman, "Psychology: Monotheistic or Polytheistic." *Spring* (1971), pp. 209–32.

Smart, Ninian. "The Scientific Study of Religion in Its Plurality." In Frank Whaling, ed., *Contemporary Approaches to the Study of Religion.* Vol. 1. Berlin: Mouton, 1983.

Stein, Murray. "The Significance of Jung's Father in His Destiny as a Therapist of Christianity." *Quadrant* 18, no. 1 (1985), pp. 23–33.

Whitmont, Edward. "The Magic Level of the Unconscious." *Spring* (1956), pp. 58–80.

Williams, Mary. "An Example of Synchronicity." *Journal of Analytical Psychology* 1 (1955–56), pp. 93–96.

Woodman, Ross. "Shaman, Poet, and Failed Initiate: Reflections on Romanticism and Jungian Psychology." *Studies in Romanticism* 19 (1980), pp. 51–82.

Wulff, David. "Psychological Approaches." In Frank Whaling, ed., *Contemporary Approaches to the Study of Religion*. Vol. 2. Berlin: Mouton, 1985.

Zavala, J. F. "Synchronicity and the Mexican Divinatory Calendar 'Tonalamatl.' " *Quadrant* 15, no. 1 (1982), pp. 55–70.

Zinkin, L. "The Hologram as a Model for Analytical Psychology." *Journal of Analytical Psychology* 32 (1987), pp. 1–21.

Index